# Mel Gibson

## and his movies

# Mel Gibson
## and his movies

BRIAN PENDREIGH

BLOOMSBURY

For Ewen and Catherine

First published in Great Britain 1997

Bloomsbury Publishing Plc
38 Soho Square, London W1V 5DF

PICTURE SOURCES

Avalon Flm Corporation: page 2 *top left & top right*
Branco Gaica: page 2 *bottom*
Kobal Collection: pages 3,4,5,6,7
Rex Features: page 8
St Leo's College, Sydney: page 1 *bottom*
State Library of New South Wales: page 1 *top*

Every reasonable effort has been made to ascertain and
acknowledge the ownership of copyrighted
photographs included in this volume. Any errors that have
inadvertently occurred, will be corrected in subsequent editions
provided notification is sent to the publisher

A CIP catalogue record for this book
is available from the British Library

ISBN 0 7475 3175 7 (hardback)
ISBN 0 7475 3664 3 (paperback)

10 9 8 7 6 5 4 3 2 1

Typeset by Hewer Text Composition Services, Edinburgh
Printed in Great Britain by Clays Ltd, St Ives plc

# CONTENTS

# ACKNOWLEDGEMENTS

First and foremost I must thank Jenny Pendreigh, my partner in both senses of the word, who helped with research and encouragement, and retyped the longest chapter in the book when I inadvertently replaced it on my computer disk with an *aide-mémoire* called 'Loose Ends'. Thanks also to Ewen McDonald for watching many of the films with me, reading every chapter as it was drafted, checking spelling and grammar and offering advice on sense, structure and content, and patiently explaining the finer points of *Hamlet* to my children.

I interviewed over one hundred people specifically for the book, from Zelma Ainslie, Mel Gibson's third-grade teacher in New York State, to Franco Zeffirelli, who directed him in *Hamlet*. Most are individually named in the text. My thanks to them all, particularly Monroe Reimers, Gibson's flatmate in Sydney and drama school contemporary; George Miller, director of the *Mad Max* films; Roger Ward, 'Fifi Macaffee' in *Mad Max*, who not only shared reminiscences but sent me material from his unpublished memoirs; Mark Lee, Gibson's co-star in *Gallipoli*; Michael Pate; Gillian Armstrong; and the many other actors, directors and technicians who have worked on Mel Gibson films from the early Australian period through to *Braveheart* and beyond.

I spoke to numerous individuals involved in *Braveheart*, but particular thanks go to actors Brian Cox and Peter Mullan for their frank recollections of the shoot in Scotland and Ireland.

This biography is not authorised by Mel Gibson, but I interviewed him in Scotland, in my capacity as cinema editor

of *The Scotsman*, when he was there for *Braveheart*; and again
in the United States after the Oscars. I have also drawn on other
interviews I conducted for *The Scotsman*, including one with
Patrick Stewart, who took a break from filming *Conspiracy
Theory* with Gibson to attend the British premiere of *Star Trek:
First Contact*; and another earlier session with Terry Gilliam,
in which he talked about his frustrating experience on *A Tale
of Two Cities*, the Mel Gibson epic that never was. Merely an
interesting aside at the time of the release of *12 Monkeys*, the
details constitute a brief but invaluable episode for this book.
Thanks to all those whom I have interviewed over the years
and whose comments now find their way into this volume.
And thanks, too, to all the other journalists on whose work
I have drawn for insight, understanding, facts, comments and
leads, even if some were hopelessly inaccurate; one previous
biography could be relied upon, whenever there were doubts,
to have got it wrong.

Researching Gibson's early years was a painstaking task
and my particular thanks are due to various individuals,
organisations and libraries: the National Library of Australia;
the State Library of New South Wales; the National Institute of
Dramatic Art in Sydney and its director John Clark; Gibson's
schools in New York State and Australia; and various churches
in Ireland, America and Australia.

An enormous debt of gratitude is due to the Australian Film
Institute, particularly research assistant Clare Stewart and Chris
Brophy, manager of AFI research and information. Thanks also
to Nancy Dick at the Dennis Wolanski Library of the Performing
Arts at Sydney Opera House for material on Gibson's stage
career; and to the National Library of Scotland and the library
of the British Film Institute.

Thanks to David Gow for helping complete my set of Mel
Gibson films; to journalist Siobhan Synnot for tapes of various
interviews; to those few who asked that their contribution should
be anonymous and to all the very many others who helped in
various different capacities along the road.

# 1

# FROM OZ TO OSCAR

'And the Oscar for best picture is presented to . . .' Magic words. There is silence as Sidney Poitier breaks the red seal on the last envelope of the night. Mel Gibson smiles, not a particularly happy smile, a tentative, nervous one, an attempt to hide the turmoil within. His brow is furrowed and there are lines around those famous azure blue eyes, reflecting the long, long hours and ceaseless worry of starring in, directing and producing one of the most ambitious historical epics that Hollywood has made since the days of Charlton Heston and Cecil B. DeMille. When the Oscar nominations were announced six weeks earlier *Braveheart* led the field with ten and was an early favourite to win best picture.

Mel Gibson had been one of the world's top film stars for a decade and a half, turning a low-budget Australian action movie called *Mad Max* into an internationally successful series, and following it up with the three *Lethal Weapon* films that grossed more than $350 million in North America alone and confirmed his place in the Hollywood stratosphere. Lethal and mad in the coolest sort of way, Gibson was the man millions of men fantasised about being. But his appeal extended beyond that of other action stars to women as well as men. *People* magazine had acclaimed him the sexiest man in the world, a title that would come to haunt him.

He wanted more than box-office success and popular adulation. He wanted to make serious films as well, films that had something to say, films that would challenge him as an actor and as a producer and director. He had won Australian film awards for a couple of his early roles, he impressed dubious critics with his performance as Hamlet and he had made the transition to directing with a small-scale drama about a disgraced teacher. Not only was he one of the most popular film stars in Hollywood, but he was also one of the most powerful. His commitment to a film could ensure it got made.

Gibson had never heard of William Wallace when he first read the script of *Braveheart*, but it seemed to offer him the chance to combine a great story about a national leader with action on a grand historical scale. He was never going to win an Oscar for *Lethal Weapon*, but get a few thousand others involved in the fight scenes and make one of the characters a real-life historical figure who dies for his beliefs and suddenly Gibson is in the running for Oscars for best picture and best director.

The Oscars are virtually unique in gambling terms, for unlike horse races you can go on betting after the race has been run – the voters have chosen the winner but no one can be absolutely certain which film it is until Sidney Poitier reads the name on the final card. Many of the Academy's five thousand voting members remain tight-lipped about their selections in the secret ballot. Nevertheless the pendulum seems to have swung against *Braveheart* in the days before the ceremony. The buzz is that *Apollo 13* will win. It is the only one of the five best picture nominees made in America, exactly the sort of situation guaranteed to rally nationalist sentiment among the predominantly American electorate.

The voters were faced with a choice between a hitherto obscure Scottish warrior called William Wallace, an Italian postman, a couple of effete middle-class English ladies, a talking Australian pig and a story of American ingenuity and fortitude in the face of adversity. *Apollo 13* seems tailor-made for the occasion and *Braveheart* has drifted in the betting from evens to 5–1 outsider. One fan, who has camped out on the sidewalk for four nights to see the stars, claims to have correctly predicted the best picture on each of her previous visits to the Oscars. This year she has a placard that declares '13 years + 13 winners = Apollo 13'.

On the night, *Braveheart* has failed to beat *Apollo 13* in any category before the final one. There is a hush of expectancy as the bejewelled celebrity audience in the Dorothy Chandler Pavilion waits for Sidney Poitier to confirm *Apollo 13* as the best picture of 1995 and bring proceedings to a close.

There are hundreds of film awards, but the Oscars are special. They date back to 1927 and the beginning of the talkies. They are Hollywood's own awards, giving big-name stars a chance to honour their peers. And yet the Oscars contrive to be much more democratic than other awards that are determined by select groups of journalists or committees of the great and the good. The Oscars are decided by the Academy of Motion Picture Arts and Sciences, whose membership includes actors, directors, writers, craftsmen and technicians. Membership is by invitation only. Potential candidates must have a solid body of work behind them. The Academy tends to be regarded as the Hollywood establishment, although there is a short cut to membership via an Oscar nomination, so it is possible to become an Academy member on the basis of a single film.

Members are divided into thirteen different branches representing the different branches of the industry, from acting to visual effects. Each branch decides the nominees in its particular specialism. For instance, the nominees for best director are determined solely by other directors. They vote and the top five become the nominees. Best picture nominees are determined by the entire membership, which helps explain why some films are nominated as best picture but the man or woman in creative control of the film is apparently snubbed. In the final round of voting everyone can vote in virtually all the categories.

An Oscar, or even a nomination, can substantially increase a film's performance at the box office. It has been calculated that the Oscar for best picture will boost a film's final takings by an average of $30 million. Studios spend millions on adverts in the trade press suggesting films 'for consideration' by voters and on videos, soundtracks and picture books that are delivered direct to voters' homes whether they be in Des Moines or Dorset. New films screened at cinemas in Los Angeles in the previous calendar year are eligible for the Oscars, but there is probably not a single voter who will have seen them all. If your film has been seen by only a handful of people, it is not going to win, no matter how good it is. Not every company can afford to send out thousands of videos, but the tactic ensured that voters all had the chance to see the Italian arthouse film *Il Postino*, which was distributed by Miramax and ultimately had the muscle of the Disney empire behind it, and it was rewarded with no less than five nominations.

Film studios actually discuss some films' Oscar chances before a single scene has been shot. They plan their release schedules carefully to open their main Oscar hopes at the end of the year, so that they will be fresh in voters' minds when they get their nomination ballots a few weeks later. *Sense and Sensibility*, *Nixon*, *Dead Man Walking*, *Richard III*, *Restoration* and *Mr Holland's Opus* all opened in the United States in December. *The American President*, *Casino*, *Get Shorty* and *Leaving Las Vegas* were all autumn or winter releases. *Braveheart* had opened way back in May.

Mel Gibson discussed his hopes for the film with me when it had its European premiere in Scotland in September. Ancient Stirling Castle, scene of William Wallace's greatest victory seven hundred years earlier, was taken over for a premiere party, and the Wallace Monument, a sandstone edifice that stands atop a nearby hill and looks like a medieval rocket, was lit up ready for blast-off. Mel Gibson attended in a kilt and was cheered by thousands of Scots, whom he had helped take pride in their own history. William Wallace had rallied the Scots against the English forces that occupied their land and, despite being heavily outnumbered, he defeated the English army at Stirling and drove them from the land. Although he was defeated in a subsequent battle, tortured and executed, his example inspired Robert the Bruce to another great victory which secured Scottish independence for four hundred years.

It is difficult for anyone outside Scotland to appreciate how much *Braveheart* meant to the Scots, just as it is difficult for any Scot to watch the film without a tear in his or her eye by the end. The film was debated by politicians and adopted as a source of inspiration by the nation's sportsmen. In its opening month, *Braveheart* was mentioned in no less than seventy-four articles in *The Scotsman*, Scotland's main quality national newspaper.

The English had driven Gibson's own ancestors out of Ireland, which provided some of the locations for the film. Although he had been born in the United States, he had spent much of his life in Australia and was more acutely aware of national differences than most Americans. After *The Man Without a Face*, he vowed he would never act and direct at the same time again. Now here he was starring in, directing and producing a three-hour $70 million epic with battle scenes that involved three thousand people at once. Gibson was justly proud of the film, but the word Oscar never dared cross our lips at that time.

*Braveheart* performed reasonably well but hardly spectacularly in North America. It was only No. 3 in the box-office chart in its first week, behind *Casper* and *Die Hard With a Vengeance*. Its opening weekend gross of $13 million compared unfavourably with $33 million for *Lethal Weapon 3* and $15 million for the lightweight comedy *Bird On a Wire*, in which Gibson had co-starred with Goldie Hawn. *Braveheart*'s American distributor Paramount felt it had not fulfilled its potential and re-released it in September. It re-entered the charts at No. 6, which the trade paper *Screen International* considered 'disappointing'. At the end of the year, however, there was no obvious candidate to dominate the Academy Awards as *Schindler's List* and *Forrest Gump* had done in the two previous years, and for the first time commentators were beginning to talk about *Braveheart* as an Oscar possibility.

Oscar voters select their choices for all sorts of reasons. They may be friends of the director, they may have worked on the film or may still be working for the film company behind it, or they may simply vote for the film and individuals they truly believe to be the best in each category – and it would be wrong to underestimate the importance of quality in voters' deliberations. History may quibble with their choices, but it is surprising how many do stand the test of time. Some voters, like voters in political elections, are influenced by the media and feel they should make sure they see the films that are picking up the critics' awards, many of which are announced long before the Oscar nominations are settled.

The New York and Los Angeles critics both went for *Leaving Las Vegas*, in which Nicolas Cage plays a man drinking himself to death and Elisabeth Shue is a prostitute. The Society of Texas

Critics made the complex and highly imaginative thriller *The Usual Suspects* their best picture and the National Society of Film Critics voted for *Babe*, the charming Australian comedy about a talking pig who thinks he is a sheepdog. The National Board of Review and the Boston critics backed *Sense and Sensibility*. Its director Ang Lee won best director accolades from the New York and Boston critics and the National Board of Review.

The February edition of *Empire* film magazine ran an item headed 'Oscar Race Is On' which did not even mention *Braveheart*, though just as it went to press the American Broadcast Film Critics Association voted *Sense and Sensibility* best film while making Mel Gibson best director. The Academy voters are not necessarily as adventurous in their selections as some of the critics' groups and, while *Sense and Sensibility* was looking a good bet for nominations, few commentators were taking seriously the idea that an Australian comedy about a talking pig would be an Oscar contender.

Over the years the Golden Globes have established themselves as probably the second most prestigious set of awards on the film calendar. While the Oscars are determined by five thousand leading actors, directors, writers and craftsmen, the Globes represent the views of fewer than a hundred members of the Hollywood Foreign Press Association. However, they seem to share the Academy's tastes and have an uncanny knack of picking the same winners. In 1995 Golden Globes went to *Forrest Gump*, director Robert Zemeckis and actors Tom Hanks, Jessica Lange, Martin Landau and Dianne Wiest, and in due course they all added an Oscar to their collections. Traditionally, as with the Oscar voters, the Hollywood Foreign Press Association give their best picture and best director awards to the same film, but in January 1996 they voted *Sense and Sensibility* best drama and Gibson best director, with *Babe* winning the award for best comedy.

'If Oscar's little cousin is sending a message to the Academy, it's only to declare March's upcoming race one of the most wide open for some time,' maintained *Empire* magazine. I had been preparing a lengthy article on *Braveheart* for *The Scotsman*'s *Weekend* magazine in anticipation of *Braveheart* winning at least a few Oscar nominations, but I was now sufficiently confident to gamble, run it ahead of the nominations and predict that the combination of commercial and critical respectability set the film up perfectly for the nominations a few days later. I also pointed out that the splitting of the Golden Globes for best drama and best director was not unprecedented, that it had happened three years earlier when *Scent of a Woman* was best film and *Unforgiven*'s Clint Eastwood was best director and that, come the Oscars, *Unforgiven* had won awards for both picture and director.

*Braveheart*'s ten Oscar nominations were spread across a wide range of categories, including best picture, director, original script, cinematography and music, though Gibson was not on the best actor short list, where there were several notable absentees. Ian McKellen had been thought a strong contender for *Richard III* and there had been considerable speculation about Tom Hanks making it three Oscars in a row for his performance in *Apollo 13*. *Apollo 13* received nine nominations, just one fewer than *Braveheart*. It was also nominated for best picture, but Hanks was not the only surprise omission from the *Apollo 13* roster. There was no nomination for director Ron Howard. *Sense and Sensibility* received seven nominations, including best picture, but again its director, Ang Lee, was missing from the directors list. The two directors who might have been regarded as Gibson's two main rivals for the director's Oscar had fallen at the first hurdle, though their films presented formidable opposition for best picture, a category which also included two surprise nominees, *Il Postino*, the first foreign-language film nominated for best picture for more than twenty years, and the Australian talking pig movie *Babe*.

Although Oscar nominations are not announced until mid-February, applications for press accreditation at the Oscars had to be submitted by the beginning of January. Reckoning that *Braveheart* could be in the frame, I applied for a place in the press room at the Dorothy Chandler Pavilion, where journalists can watch the ceremony on closed-circuit television and speak to winners in person almost immediately after they receive their awards. Flights, accommodation and car hire were arranged after the nominations were announced, without any definite confirmation of our place at the Oscars. Just two weeks before the ceremony, I finally received a fax from the Academy about my accreditation request: 'The 68th Annual Academy Awards Credentialing Committee regrets that the Academy is not able to accommodate your request.' I faxed the Academy, arguing that Scotland should be represented because of *Braveheart* and its importance to Scotland. A week later I phoned to say I had heard nothing about my appeal and was told that I would probably continue to hear nothing; the Academy could accommodate only three hundred print journalists and had five hundred others demanding to know why they were not among them.

Faced with the prospect of cancelling the trip or watching the Oscars on television in my hotel room, I spent an evening on the phone to the offices of Mel Gibson, writer Randall Wallace, producer Alan Ladd Junior and distributors Paramount and 20th Century Fox to see if they could use their influence. Most were supportive but said they could not interfere. At 1.30 in the morning I was woken by the telephone. It was 5.30 p.m. in LA on Friday, 15 March, just over a week before the Oscars. An Academy official explained places were now available for me not only in the press room but also in the arrivals area, which had not even been part of my original application. I never did find out how or why.

A week later two passes are duly handed over at the Hotel Intercontinental, in downtown LA, a green one for the arrivals line and a blue one for the press room. The press centre at the hotel is just a ten-minute walk from the Dorothy Chandler Pavilion of the Los Angeles Music Centre in a city so spread out that a short drive can mean half an hour. Some cities build upwards while others build outwards. LA covers a thousand square miles of dry desert basin between the San Gabriel Mountains and the Pacific Ocean, a loose federation of towns and neighbourhoods such as Hollywood and Beverly Hills, linked together by freeway. It is a young city – Hollywood was little more than an orange grove at the beginning of the twentieth century, connected to LA by rough country road – and it has all the vibrancy and brashness of youth. The downtown area is an island of skyscrapers on a plain of low-rise buildings, though the LA Music Centre is no skyscraper. The 3,000-seat Dorothy Chandler Pavilion, an elegant modern arts venue, opened in the late sixties and has been one of two regular Oscar venues since then. Uniformed Pinkertons men patrol the precincts.

With my blue pass clipped to my breast pocket I stroll past them into the auditorium, where lithe, leotarded figures loll around the white stage. Some seats are occupied by cardboard placards bearing pictures of the stars who will sit there on Monday night. Mel Gibson's placard occupies a seat at the end of a row, handy for nipping up to collect an Oscar or two. I park myself behind Kirk Douglas's placard and watch the dancers waltz with drapes and fly on wires to the music of *Pocahontas*, the Disney cartoon for which Gibson provided the voice of one of the principal characters.

Outside, the public are camped on the pavement in the hope of securing a seat in the temporary stands between the sidewalk and the entrance to the auditorium. They sleep out for up to four nights, cooking burgers, pancakes, bacon and eggs on little stoves, for the chance to see the celebrities arriving in all their finery. Movie people are America's royalty, the Oscars are the coronation ceremony and LA is in the grip of coronation fever.

Only the Super Bowl and a few other big football games get bigger television audiences. Flick through the stations and before long you will find some commentator predicting the Oscar winners or just predicting what the stars will wear. The big Oscar news story is Jesse Jackson's protest about the lack of African-Americans in the industry – only one of the 166 Oscar nominees is black – and Jackson is threatening a demonstration outside the ceremony. The newspapers and television are full of predictions and personal accolades, from sexiest scene – Bo Peep and Woody in *Toy Story* – to best friend of the tobacco lobby – John Travolta in *Get Shorty*. A nationwide poll of American movie-goers votes *Braveheart* best picture of the year, but most tipsters are backing *Apollo 13*.

The Directors Guild Award almost always goes to the eventual winner of the best director Oscar but this year it has gone to Ron Howard for *Apollo 13*, which has made a late showing in other awards too. It has been named best picture not only by the Chicago critics but also by the Screen Actors Guild – and actors represent a quarter of the Academy membership. It has been an unpredictable contest, but several commentators are suggesting that Howard's omission from the directors' short list may encourage voters to split their vote and back Gibson as best director and *Apollo 13* as best film. A few mavericks are predicting that the talking pig can go all the way, but on Oscar morning Duane Byrge of the *Hollywood Reporter* is about the only commentator predicting *Braveheart* for best picture, also tipping Gibson as best director and Randall Wallace to win the Oscar for original script. 'I'm putting my mouth (but certainly not my money) on *Braveheart*,' he writes. He reckons it could be very close between *Braveheart* and *Apollo 13*. The front-page headline is 'It's anybody's game tonight'.

Mel Gibson, who has a large seafront house in the surfing community of Malibu twenty-five miles away from downtown LA, is no longer following the expert analyses of who will win and why. His assistant called him to say he had been listening to it and it was making him very nervous. Gibson could do without the hassle. He had an appointment with his chiropractor instead. It was at his chiropractor a year or two back that he had met one of his great heroes, Kirk Douglas, who is receiving an honorary award tonight and whose film *Spartacus* was an inspiration to Gibson. They had bumped into each other in the elevator at the practice of Dr Hertz, who Gibson reflects was well-named. Gibson will not be wearing a kilt tonight, but a combination of Armani tuxedo and a waistcoat, or vest as the Americans call it, in the tartan of the Buchanans, which every Gibson is entitled to wear.

Five thousand miles away it is early evening when it is still morning in LA, and a wild-looking, long-haired, bearded man, a little older than Mel Gibson, arrives home at his tenement flat in the Pollokshields area of Glasgow. While Edinburgh is internationally known for its arts festival, Glasgow still brings to mind industry and shipbuilding, hard men and hard vowel sounds. He gets out the whisky and the Wallace liqueur, a honey poteen for which he and his friends have developed a taste. There will be a lot of them here tonight and a lot of drink consumed as they watch their absent friend on the television. This is Seoras Wallace, chief executive of the Wallace Clan Trust, consultant and fight arranger on *Braveheart*. It is not so long since Mel

Gibson sat on the floor of this flat and discussed his project with Seoras Wallace. He looks out the rudimentary tartan plaid he wore in the film and will wear again tonight.

At the Orchid Suites Hotel, behind the Chinese Theatre and the stars' hand prints, right in the heart of Hollywood, I check my passes for the umpteenth time and lay out my clothes on the bed. Rules issued to the media stipulate tuxedo or formal gown – 'any press representative not complying will be asked to leave'. I have already confirmed that an exception will be made. The MacDonald kilt, silver-buttoned black jacket, bow tie, hose and sealskin sporran have accompanied me from Edinburgh, so too has the leather belt with a buckle in the shape of a cross on a circle. The single word Braveheart is inscribed on it. But I have to improvise my necklace. Worried that I might lose my Oscar passes if I simply clip them to my pocket, I thread them through one of the laces from my training shoes, manoeuvring the dirtiest, blackest portions of the lace into a position where they will not be seen when I hang the passes round my neck.

The Oscar ceremony starts at 6 p.m., but LA traffic jams are notorious and limousines the length of buses reportedly bring the freeways to a standstill on Oscar day, so I leave the hotel at 1.30, make my way downtown using 'surface routes' and arrive at the Dorothy Chandler Pavilion at 2, with some four hours to spare. As I approach, a young woman comes towards me. '*Braveheart*,' she yells, 'yes.'

No one challenges me as I pass the crowds and approach the venue, nor does anyone direct me anywhere, so I climb over a small hedge and join the assembly of photographers and camera crews who have taken up position beside the red carpet that leads from sidewalk to auditorium. Press releases are distributed detailing the clothes and jewellery the stars are expected to wear, with Angela Bassett in a diamond and platinum bib necklace supposedly worth $8.5 million. Early arrivals smile hopefully at the cameras and are ignored. James Cromwell, *Babe*'s human co-star and a nominee for best supporting actor, arrives at about 3.40, with one wife, four children and no pigs. Two senior executives from the accounting firm of Price Waterhouse arrive with cases containing two identical sets of results. There is no sign of Jesse Jackson who has switched his protest to the

Hollywood studios of KABC-TV, which is broadcasting the Oscars.

Most of the stars arrive in the half-hour before the show, by which time there are at least seven helicopters overhead attempting to film the scene and avoid colliding and falling on our heads. 'Mr Howard, Mr Howard,' the photographers scream at the *Apollo 13* director and former *Happy Days* star. 'Let him finish his sentence,' snaps an aide. Howard finishes his sentence and turns to the press, but they have spotted Meryl Streep and are now shouting, 'Meryl, Meryl.' Howard will know in future not to finish his sentence. Some women are having difficulty keeping their breasts within their gowns. Nicole Kidman looks as if she is auditioning for *Sense and Sensibility II* in a lilac nightie. Several papers report next day that Sharon Stone 'joked' that her tight black turtleneck came from Gap and suggest it probably came from Valentino's. It subsequently turns out it did come from Gap, cost $22 and was so old you could not buy it any more.

Mel Gibson is among the last to arrive. He looks fit and healthy after a recent emergency operation to remove his appendix. It is only two weeks since he developed acute appendicitis on a flight from LA to New York and was rushed to hospital. He is accompanied by his wife Robyn in a white strapless gown, her dark hair piled on top of her head. Sticking even closer to Gibson is a burly bodyguard whose eyes continually scan the crowd, in search of assassins in the pay of the English court perhaps. Although his name remains unknown, his face is destined to appear in dozens, maybe hundreds, of newspapers around the world. Gibson has complemented his tartan waistcoat with a brooch in his lapel in the shape of a broadsword.

Backstage, or rather upstairs, three hundred overdressed journalists squeeze round tables in a grey-walled barn of a room, decorated with blue curtains bearing the Oscar logo and closed-circuit televisions which carry host Whoopi Goldberg's opening remarks. There is no sign of the mutli-coloured ribbon that Jesse Jackson had asked his supporters to wear. 'You don't tell a black woman to buy an expensive dress and then cover it with ribbons,' she quips. 'I had something I wanted to say to Jesse right here, but he's not watching, so why bother?'

She gets the show off to a flying start with her sassy barbed commentary.

By now it is two o'clock in the morning in Scotland, but the party is in full swing at Seoras Wallace's flat in Pollokshields. The flat is packed and the sound of excited chatter, guitar-playing and fiddle music fills the air and serves as a prelude to the main event of the evening.

In Los Angeles the first award of the night is for best costume. The costumes from the five nominated films are paraded by models as if this were a fashion show. The tartan looks excitingly different, but the award goes to James Acheson for *Restoration*, who strikes an immediate sour note in the press room by moaning about the models and the lack of consultation in the presentation. In this hi-tech age, in this hi-tech country, the results are still written up on a big blackboard by hand. And with the first result goes *Braveheart*'s chance of a sweep that would have equalled *West Side Story* as the film with the second most Oscars of all time – *Ben-Hur* won eleven.

Kevin Spacey wins the second Oscar of the night, best supporting actor for his performance in *The Usual Suspects*, an award many thought destined for *Apollo 13*'s Ed Harris. Journalists have to interview winners while keeping an eye on the show at the same time. And many are writing their copy on laptop computers and filing it over phone lines as they go. The major American papers have teams of three. *Braveheart* wins the Oscar for best make-up. The result means little in terms of the balance of power, for the only other nominees were *My Family, Mi Familia* and *Roommates*. *Restoration* beats *Apollo 13* for the Oscar for art direction, a category in which, surprisingly, *Braveheart* was not nominated. After four categories, *Braveheart, Apollo 13* and *Babe* have all had two nominations and *Braveheart* is the only one of the three to win an Oscar. It beats *Batman Forever* and *Crimson Tide* to win a second for sound effects.

But the big indicator for the main prizes could well be the next Oscar. The Academy Award for achievement in sound is hardly the most glamorous but it is a category in which *Apollo 13* and *Braveheart* come face to face. It signals the appearance of a kilt on stage, but it is the kilt of David MacMillan, one of the four-man team responsible for sound on *Apollo 13*. *Braveheart* wins the Oscar for best cinematography, but *Apollo 13* was not nominated. The next Oscar is for film editing. *Apollo 13*, *Babe* and *Braveheart* are all in the running. The last three winners of the Oscar for editing have been *Forrest Gump*, *Schindler's List* and *Unforgiven*; in other words, if you win best editing you win best picture. Mel Gibson offers an occasional word to Robyn, he looks intense, thoughtful, but he is not the sort of man to allow himself to be tortured by such analytical detail. The Oscar for best editing goes to *Apollo 13*.

Composer James Horner looks one of the best bets of the night, given that he is nominated for the music for both *Apollo 13* and *Braveheart*. The rules prevent that sort of thing happening in the acting categories, where, if an actor has two performances in the top five after the first round of voting, only the one with the most votes goes forward to the final ballot. Perhaps Horner's two nominations have split his vote, for the Oscar goes to Luis Enrique Bacalov for *Il Postino*.

Only one film can win best picture, but two films can win Oscars for best script, because there are separate awards for original stories and adaptations of books or plays. *Apollo 13*, *Babe*, *Il Postino* and *Sense and Sensibility* are all nominated as best adaptation, leaving *Braveheart* as the only best picture nominee up for best original screenplay. This should be a moment of triumph for Randall Wallace, who visited Edinburgh Castle as a tourist thirteen years earlier, saw a statue of a man with the same name as himself, researched the history of William Wallace and ended up with the script of *Braveheart*. Wallace is shattered to hear Susan Sarandon read the name of Christopher McQuarrie who wrote *The Usual Suspects*. A thinking man's thriller, it could have ended up a terrible mess in the wrong director's hands. Instead it collects a second Oscar and by now what looked like a certain best director Oscar for Gibson seems in serious doubt.

Smooth-cheeked, bespectacled Robert Zemeckis, who won the award last year for *Forrest Gump*, appears to present the award and reads the nominations with slow deliberation. Nothing seems certain. Englishman Mike Figgis has picked up a fair number of critics' awards for *Leaving Las Vegas*. Also in contention are Chris Noonan for *Babe*, the big feel-good movie of the year, and Scotsman Michael Radford who directed Massimo Troisi through one last great performance in the Italian-language film *Il Postino*, even though Troisi was dying as they worked. And there is Tim Robbins, a well-respected Hollywood figure who has made one of the most powerful films of the year, *Dead Man Walking*, a dramatised plea against capital punishment that avoids the easy route of sentimentalising its central character. Gibson, who supports capital punishment, shows no emotion as the envelope is opened. 'And the Oscar goes to . . .' says Zemeckis, for there are no winners and losers in these politically correct times, 'Mel Gibson.'

He raises his eyebrows as his name is read, nods and allows a suggestion of a smile. The feeling is more one of relief than triumph. He had, after all, been a very firm favourite in the absence of Ron Howard and Ang Lee. He rises to receive his Oscar without a glance at Robyn. He strides up, shakes Zemeckis's hand, takes the Oscar and looks it up and down, as if making up his mind whether to buy a curio in a junk shop. He seems to decide that he will take it after all. He lays it by the lectern and as the cheering subsides throws his arms wide. 'Oh, I don't write speeches,' he says, 'but I would like to thank a few people and I have it on a list.' He assures the audience that it is not a long list, despite visible evidence to the contrary. He begins by thanking the Academy, producer Alan Ladd Junior and writer Randall Wallace and runs through thirty-three other individuals and groups. Some of the names he rattles through but he pauses and looks up before stressing the name the Clan Wallace, provoking a whoop of delight five thousand miles away in Pollokshields where the fiddles and guitars have been laid aside and the whisky and Wallace liqueur taken up with great enthusiasm. Gibson concludes with thanks to his wife, his family, God and 'every director I've ever worked with', ending with possibly the three most important things in his life – his family, his religion and his work, with family first and films last. It is not a particularly emotional or inspired acceptance speech, retrieved at the end when he adds: 'Now that I'm a bona fide director with a golden boy, well, like most directors, I suppose, what I really want to do is act

. . . Thank you from the bottom of my heart. This is a truly wonderful evening for me.'

*Braveheart* has now won four Oscars and will finish with more than any other film tonight no matter what happens from here on. Journalists are hammering away at portable computers and issuing instructions over the phone, while keeping an eye on the acting honours which go as expected to Tim Robbins' partner Susan Sarandon for *Dead Man Walking* and Nicolas Cage for *Leaving Las Vegas*. All we need now is confirmation of *Apollo 13* as best picture.

Sidney Poitier, the first and only black man to win the best actor Oscar, steps forward to a standing ovation. 'Through pathways in the heart and across rivers of the mind, instincts guide us to a place somewhere in human consciousness that has no known address,' he begins. 'There we look inside ourselves, confront our demons and do battle with a mystery called the creative process.' Er, Mr Poitier, could you tell us who has won best picture please? 'Sometimes we win, sometimes not.' Sometimes we sit and wait. 'Such battles, such journeys, are the stuff of which movies are made and dreams are spun.' And which was the best dream? 'Among some of you here, who have been there, sit those of you who have brought us to this next moment.' A bottle of Wallace liqueur could not have improved on this performance. Finally he reads the names of the nominated films, along with the names of the producers, for the Oscar for best picture goes to the producers. *Apollo 13. Babe. Braveheart. Il Postino. Sense and Sensibility*. Ironically, *Babe* was made by Kennedy Miller Pictures, the same company that made the *Mad Max* films. One of the producers is George Miller, the Australian doctor turned film director who did as much as anyone to propel a young, unknown drama school graduate from Sydney to international stardom.

'And the Oscar for best picture is presented to . . .' There is a pause, but in our minds we can already hear the words *Apollo 13*, even as our hearts plead for *Braveheart*. Gibson waits silently, nervously, his mind cluttered with a thousand thoughts, none of them attaining any focus. Poitier's voice rings out through the hushed auditorium, sudden, rich, crisp, clear. '*Braveheart*.'

Mel Gibson looks slightly bewildered. The cry of 'Oh ya beauty' issues from a modest tenement flat in Pollokshields, Glasgow. There is some confusion in the press room as if Poitier has got his lines wrong. Gibson rises from his seat to the sound of James Horner's evocative score, which draws heavily on the bagpipe music of Scotland and the melody of the sad, old Scottish ballad 'Loch Lomond' about the spirit of an executed warrior returning to Scotland. At this moment the spirit of Scotland is with Mel Gibson. Meryl Streep looks totally amazed. Mel Gibson seems composed as he makes his way into film history, still clutching the Oscar he won minutes earlier as best director. He is joined on the stage by his co-producers Alan Ladd Junior, son of the tough-guy actor of the forties and fifties, and Bruce Davey, an Australian who started off as Gibson's accountant and jointly founded Icon Productions with him in 1988.

Gibson says: 'I've only got forty-five seconds and I don't want to hog the limelight from these two gentlemen who really deserve the statue. Thank you again, all those people I thanked before, and I owe a special debt of gratitude to Bruce here and Alan. Take it away, fellahs.' There is no sign of the financial crises and personality clashes behind the scenes: Randall Wallace had created the project, Ladd had championed it from early days and Gibson had shaped it and given it life. But Wallace is left Oscarless in the body of the hall while the third best picture Oscar is presented to Gibson's accountant.

Maybe Davey deserves an Oscar for best accountant, for the film-makers worked under tremendous financial pressures which have never been fully revealed. When the Hollywood money men did a detailed analysis of likely costs, they discovered that the provisional budget was out by a staggering $30 million; a major backer pulled out just weeks before filming was due to start; and when production did get under way the dollar plunged against the pound and the Irish punt and all sorts of cuts were implemented, ranging from the disbandment of the second unit – just as it would have come into its own in the battle sequences – through to measures to economise on toilet rolls.

It is to Gibson's credit that he overcame all such difficulties and produced such a magnificent film. Considering he has just emulated Clint Eastwood, Francis Ford Coppola and Frank

Capra with Oscars for best director and best picture, Mel Gibson is not exactly being self-indulgent. His acceptance speech for the Oscar for best picture is just twelve seconds long. He has much more to say in the press room, where I ask him what he was thinking and if he realised that *Braveheart* had not beaten *Apollo 13* in any category before best picture.

'I wasn't aware of that,' he says. 'There wasn't much going through my mind. I was just still up from getting the first one. It was real gravy. I kind of got more amped the second time, but I was mildly surprised. It was a crap shoot as far as I was concerned. There were so many good films. I can only presume that they [the Academy voters] saw in the story what I saw in it and that is it's one that sort of touched me in a deep spot and I also found it – the kind of story that it was – very compelling visually at the same time. I loved the material. I guess that they responded to it the same way that I did.'

But when does a film-maker know that he has a good film? Is it script stage, the beginning of filming, half-way through or at the end? 'You never know,' says Gibson. 'You're terrified while you're filming because you don't know. It may or may not work. You may be deluding yourself. You're kinda insane while directing a film . . . By doing the first one you prepare yourself for something a little bit bigger. You know you crawl before you can walk, walk before you can run.' He says he had to pace himself because *Braveheart* was such a huge film. Principal photography in Scotland and Ireland took no less than five months and for much of that time Gibson was working an eighteen- or even a twenty-hour day. 'There's just a lot of energy burnt up,' he says. 'I just put a lot of man-hours into the pre-production aspect, made sure I could take as many short cuts as possible.'

Pre-production had really begun thirty years earlier when Gibson was a child watching television in upstate New York and later in Sydney, Australia. 'I saw all the epics when I was a kid, growing up in the sixties and seventies, on television. And I always loved those films, the *Ben-Hurs* and the *Spartaci* . . .'

An American journalist points out that this is yet another film with British villains, ignoring the fact that it also has a British hero, that both sides are British. She is obviously using the word

British to mean English, which makes a change from people using the word England to cover the entire United Kingdom. 'In these epic films you know that there's somebody from every country who displays the same characteristics as those William Wallace displayed,' says Gibson. But his knowledge of national heroes has not been derived solely through Hollywood epics. 'Britain has its own heroes, you know, guys like King Caractacus and Alfred the Great.' Caractacus was a king in the west of England who resisted the Romans in the first century AD, though not as successfully as the people of Scotland did. 'Somebody has got to be the bad guy,' says Gibson. 'We probably made Edward I a bit more of a meanie than he actually was, but filmically it just makes it more compelling . . . I love the Brits. Hey, I'm an Anglophile.' 'He's a what?' one of the American journalists opposite me asks her neighbour. 'Anglophile, as in Anglo-Saxon,' says the more erudite of the two. Gibson's comment that he is an Anglophile may just make it into print, but the one about Caractacus is unlikely to see the light of day.

Of course the daftest, most obvious, question must be 'How does he feel?' 'Victorious,' he says. 'It feels great and it's wonderful to be recognised in a director category . . . It has to be fantastic.' He has an Oscar for each end of his mantelpiece and in due course, elsewhere, he will make them do a little dance together. 'It's like Oscar squared.' But how does he feel physically after his recent operation? 'I'm feeling great. I can't do a sit-up yet. But I have some very heavy people on the door just in case anybody here wants to burgle me. I miss my appendix, but I'm better off without it really.'

How does he feel about beating Australia's favourite pig and pipping his old buddy George Miller to the main prize? 'Hey, that film did all right at the box office. It brought home the bacon.' Mel Gibson is one of cinema's great jokers, with a ready quip or a gag to deflect any questions that might be getting a little too close to his real feelings about people he cares about. The press room explodes in laughter. That is one quote that will be in all the stories. An English journalist once told me that there were two kinds of Mel Gibson interviews: in one he says virtually nothing and you know you are in trouble right from the start; in the other he is extremely charming and very funny and only when you replay your tape do you realise he has said nothing. But there is a third type where he does offer up details of the man behind the façade of Hollywood stardom, if a question is framed the right way, if a subject surprises or truly engages him, or if he is in an exceptionally good mood. And tonight he is not going to hide his true feelings behind a joke. 'George I will always love,' he says. 'He's one of my mentors and when I was thanking all the directors I have worked with, he's one of the ones on the top of the pile there.' Of course honest sentiment can only go so far. 'It just feels good to win. I don't care about his pain.'

Winning a couple of Oscars is not going to stop Gibson doing more films like *Mad Max* and *Lethal Weapon*. 'I'll move along, wherever my nose takes me. I'm not quite sure where that will be at the moment. There's art to doing those films too, I think.' Asked what advice he would give young people who want to go into movies, he says: 'Just love them. That's it. It really is. If you follow what you love and put a lot of loving care into it, something is going to happen. Because what you're going to do is going to be for that reason and it's going to be good.'

Outside, the crowds have already dispersed and chauffeurs are waiting to take the stars round the big parties that have become as much a part of Oscar night as the gowns, the sentiment and the awards themselves. One of the biggest is the *Vanity Fair* party at Morton's, and *Braveheart*'s American distributor Paramount has taken over the famous Chasen's restaurant just round the corner, just round the corner from Morton's but ten miles from the Dorothy Chandler Pavilion on the outskirts of Beverly Hills, a fair drive along the still busy Hollywood Freeway and the Santa Monica Boulevard. No one should have difficulty finding it, however. Not only is it the best-known restaurant in Los Angeles, favourite of Frank Sinatra, Liz Taylor and Ronald Reagan, but searchlights rise from its grounds, cut the darkness of the night sky and guide guests to its doors.

This is a strictly private function, but Randall Wallace has secured me an invitation as a friend rather than a journalist. Uncomfortable with the pomp and ceremony of valet parking, I discreetly deposit my hire car in a side street and make my way down the red-carpeted sidewalk. Public and press are coralled behind crush barriers. Suddenly reporters and camera crews are screaming for interviews. I explain my non-involvement to one TV reporter, who asks for a few comments anyway, and I finish up giving another a detailed assessment of the impact of *Braveheart* and the Oscars on Scotland, a twirl of the kilt and some close-ups of my legs. At the door I suddenly wonder what I will do if my name is not on the guest list and picture an embarrassing journey down the red carpet in the wrong direction. 'Yes,' says the attendant, 'Brian Pendreigh and partner.' What I might have sold that partnership for!

Champagne is plentiful, but I have to limit myself to a single glass because I will be working right through the night. But that is one glass more than Mel Gibson will have. Having fought with the problems of too much drink for years, he no longer touches the stuff. Rather disappointingly, Chasen's speciality dish turns out to be nothing more exciting than chilli con carne. John Travolta, Kelsey Grammer and Billy Zane are supposedly among the two hundred guests but it is easy to miss people, for the restaurant is divided into several rooms, with an outside courtyard for those inclined to indulge the current fashion for huge stogies.

While helping myself to a second roast beef roll from one of the buffets, I literally bump into Randall Wallace. *Braveheart* has won five Oscars, equalling the achievement of *It Happened One Night*, *The Sound of Music*, *The Deer Hunter* and *The Silence of the Lambs*. But there was no Oscar for Wallace. He is devastated. How can *Braveheart* be best picture but not have the best script? There is no certain way of knowing why Wallace lost, though it seems fair to say the voters thought *Braveheart*'s greatest strengths lay not with the script while the success of *The Usual Suspects* was rooted firmly in McQuarrie's screenplay. But that is speculation. Nor does Wallace, or for that matter the makers of *Apollo 13*, know how close they came to victory. Voting figures are never released, but it could have been a single vote. There are always rumours after the event. What is not rumour is that debutante Barbra Streisand and veteran Katharine Hepburn got exactly the same number of votes in the 1968 Oscars and were jointly declared best actress. Wallace points out that those are his words up on the screens around the restaurant. Rather poignantly, *Braveheart* is showing without sound.

In several categories the Oscar has gone to specialist teams and each individual receives their own statuette. There seems to be one on every second table. One of the few other guests in a kilt is David MacMillan, part of *Apollo 13*'s winning sound team.

One of the very last Oscar-winners to arrive is the man himself, Mel Gibson, who has been heralded by a piper hired by his *Maverick* co-star, close friend and partner in mischief Jodie Foster. He appears with his Oscars and his surly, burly one-man secret service. Even in the confines of a private party he plays parrot to Mel Gibson's Long John Silver. He is wearing a hearing aid as if in continual contact with some unseen command centre. It may be for effect. Alternatively he may just be deaf. Gibson props himself up on the back of a seat in one of the booths and holds court for A-list fans who want to congratulate him. Even here some ask for autographs. 'I'm talked out,' he tells me. 'I've been talking since I got out the place. I'm just very proud and happy to have won.'

It is past midnight. The streets are quiet now, but the night air remains warm. It takes only minutes to drive back to the Orchid Suites Hotel in Hollywood where I work through the dawn, writing and filing copy from my laptop computer, across the telephone lines, through the ether and onto the page. By the time I am finished, the *Los Angeles Times* and the *Daily News* are on the newsstands. 'A Night to Kilt For', puns the *Times*, badly. Bob Strauss of the *Daily News* has written: 'The biggest surprise winner of the 68th annual Academy Awards was saved until the very end . . . For all its pretensions to historical import, *Braveheart* works best as a ripping action attraction, and it was surely the film's superb, bone-crunching battle scenes that lingered in most voters' minds.' And above the story is a simple two-word headline for the man of the moment: 'Great Scot'.

# 2

# NATIVE NEW YORKER

By 1983 Mel Gibson was on the point of establishing himself as Australia's biggest star since Errol Flynn. To the *Los Angeles Times* he was 'Mel Gibson, the very hot Australian actor'. Then came the news that turned the world upside down. Gibson was not Australian at all, he was a native New Yorker. For decades Australian cinema had been the poor relation of Hollywood. It was finally making films that overseas audiences wanted to see. And it turned out that its one genuine international star was American. Even now papers and magazines frequently refer to Gibson as Australian, but he was born in the United States, spent the first twelve years of his life in the United States and is, and always was, a US citizen.

He was born on 3 January 1956 in Peekskill Hospital, in the town of Peekskill, on the Hudson River about forty miles north of New York. He was the middle child of eleven. The family lived in the tiny Irish-Italian fishing community of Verplanck, just outside Peekskill, in a house on Seventh Street. It had been little more than a wooden shell, without electricity, plumbing or even glass in the windows, when the Gibsons took it over. Hutton Gibson was a railroad worker and did not have much money. But he rebuilt, renovated and extended that house to make it fit for a family. He was a strict father and a strict Roman Catholic. He had trained for the priesthood but would eventually quit the Roman Catholic Church because it was too liberal. He was to become the guiding light in Mel Gibson's life, the man who shaped his religious and social views and whom Mel Gibson would cite as his hero.

On 14 January in St Patrick's Catholic Church on a hill overlooking the Hudson, the new addition to the family was baptised Mel Colmcille Gerard Gibson. The Mel in comedian Mel Smith's name is short for Melvin. Mel Brooks is a Melvin too. But Gibson's name is Mel, pure and simple. He was named after a fifth-century Irish bishop, a nephew of St Patrick, patron saint of Ireland. Gibson's mother, Anna Reilly, was born in a rural part of County Longford in Ireland. The local cathedral was St Mel's in the town of Longford and the local parish church was St Colmcille's in the village of Aughnacliffe. Colm is an Irish form of Columba, another ancient Celtic saint, and Colmcille means Columba of the Church. More often than not, showbiz and cinema writers have spelt it 'Columcille'; the name can be spelt with a 'U', but St Patrick's Church's baptismal register records Gibson's name without it.

Anna Reilly was born in 1923, a time of particular strife in Ireland. The southern part, including County Longford, had won its independence from England, but only at the cost of partition. The north-eastern counties were to remain part of the United Kingdom. Civil war raged through 1922 and 1923. Even after the civil war, Ireland was plagued by political division, internecine feuding and continuing poverty. When she was still a little girl, Anna set sail with her parents for a new life on the other side of the Atlantic.

Mel Gibson's family is Irish on both sides. His father's grandfather, Patrick Mylott, shipped out from County Mayo to New South Wales in the middle of the last century when famine, chronic poverty, disease and English oppression prompted mass emigration and the creation of the great Irish diaspora. Mylott acquired land at Tuross, about 160 miles south of Sydney, and prospered as a farmer. He also had a wine merchant's business in Sydney itself. He had seven daughters and one of them, Mel Gibson's grandmother, became a professional concert singer and protégée of Australia's nineteenth-century showbiz superstar Nellie Melba.

Eva Mylott was the family's first international celebrity. Fans may wonder whether she passed on some of her talent to her descendants. Mylott's cousin Marie Narelle was also a singer. Hutton Gibson was a noted chorister, one of Mel Gibson's sisters has sung professionally and, although Mel Gibson's fame is not attributable to his singing, he did sing in one big hit musical film – Walt Disney's *Pocahontas*, for which he provided both the talking and the singing voice of John Smith.

Eva Mylott won a singing competition at the age of seven, and Nellie Melba subsequently heard her and arranged her training. In 1902 a farewell concert at Sydney Town Hall realised a sum of £335, before she sailed for Europe. She lived in London for five years, toured with Melba and sang to royalty. The success of a North American tour prompted her to settle in New York. Eva Mylott was the first of three generations of the family to undergo a mid-life move between Australia and the United States. In due course her son Hutton would emigrate to Australia with his wife and ten children – the eleventh was adopted in Australia. And Mel Gibson's main home is now in California.

An American correspondent wrote of Eva Mylott in the Sydney *Bulletin*: 'New York is a cold and critical town and about as impressionable as flint . . . But she had a voice, a personality, a capacity for hard work, and she was a good looker.' The *Bulletin* described her as 'titian-haired' and 'Junoesque'. It seems it is not just talent that she had in common with her grandson. 'The whole family runs to chubbiness a bit,' he says, 'so I've got to watch what I eat.' Eva was greeted by hundreds of fans and given a civic reception on a return visit to Sydney in 1912. Back in the United States she met Hutton Gibson, a wealthy businessman and a partner in the Gibson Brothers brass foundry of Chicago. He was based on the east coast and they settled in the town of Montclair in New Jersey. But sadly they had only a few years together. Eva died of cancer in 1920.

Hutton Gibson Junior was born in 1918, Eva died shortly after the birth of a second son and the Gibson family were hard hit by the Great Depression of the 1930s. There never seemed much chance that Hutton Gibson would follow his father into business. He was a serious youth who spent much of his time immersed in books on religion. He entered a seminary with the intention of becoming a priest. If he had done so, there would have been no Mel Gibson. Many find the discipline and denials of seminary life and priesthood difficult, if not impossible. But Hutton Gibson was the opposite. He was dismayed by talk of reforms within the Church. After the US entry into the Second World War, he exchanged one strict male-only institution for another and joined the army.

Although he never returned to the seminary, he remained a strict Roman Catholic. Mel Gibson grew up in a house full of statues and pictures of Jesus and the Virgin Mary, a house in which the music on the record player was not the exciting pop sounds of the Beatles but rather the steady monotony of Gregorian chant. But these were mere tokens of a much deeper faith. 'The greatest benefit anyone can have is to be a Catholic,' Hutton Gibson told one interviewer. 'You have the life-long satisfaction of being right.' It was a satisfaction the Pope had no right to feel, according to Hutton Gibson, who believed the replacement of the old Latin Mass was nothing less than heresy.

Hutton Gibson wrote a book called *Is the Pope Catholic?* And in another, *Paul VI's Legacy: Catholicism?* he said: 'Have you had to make excuses lately for your bishops and priests? Are you quite happy with the twists and turns Catholicism has taken? A religion is either true or false. God's revealed religion was, necessarily, true and complete. Change is incompatible with revealed truth. False religion cannot benefit anyone, least of all Catholics. Are such matters to be left entirely to theologians? But theologians were responsible for most heresies and schisms ... Is the Pope really a Catholic? Are you going to bet your one and only soul on it, blindly?'

He served as secretary of the Latin Mass Society before condemning them as 'nostalgia seekers', orchestrating his very own schism and forming the Australian Alliance for Catholic Tradition. In one of their newsletters he argued that the Catholic Church had been infiltrated by Jews. He believed the Pope's occasional use of Jewish priestly ceremonial garments was evidence. In an interview with the *Sydney Morning Herald* in 1979, before his son became a star, he said: 'If the Catholic Church has been correct through the ages then I am correct. I have changed nothing. To remain correct I need only adhere strictly to what the Catholic Church taught me.' His philosophy boiled down to two basic tenets: 'There's right and wrong,' he once said, 'and that's all there is.' He stopped going to church, but prayed at home and prepared religions tapes for his children. He brought them up to adhere to his deeply conservative.

Despite the fights and drinking of his wilder days and the relationships he had with other women before he met his wife, Mel Gibson today remains a chip off the old block. He describes his youth and early adulthood in biblical terms as his 'wilderness' years. He was an altar boy and, like his father, considered taking holy orders. 'But I don't like taking orders at the best of times,' he quips. Mel Gibson frequently follows a serious point with a joke, as if he is embarrassed by or uncertain of displays of emotion, feeling and spirituality. He loves puns and says, not that he was an altar boy, but that he was a 'falter boy'. The puns are often not very funny.

'Dad taught us all the Ten Commandments. He just laid them on us and said remember them. He was strict. But he didn't do what most parents do, and say "Be a dentist". Even when you came home with a bad report card, he'd say "I know you're smart." He never dictated to any of us what to become. He only told us how to become . . . Follow the Ten Commandments. Very simple.'

There seems little real chance that Gibson would have taken holy orders. 'You entertain these thoughts, a priest or brother. But I knew I couldn't cut it. I probably would have been banished. For not going along.' He wholeheartedly agrees with his father's criticism of the path the Roman Catholic Church has followed in recent times. 'When they changed the language they changed the intent, the meaning and the form so that it isn't really the same thing,' says Gibson Junior. 'I had Irish ancestors who died for their religion. You can't forget that. They croaked for it.' *Braveheart* hinges on the concept of martyrdom.

Mel Gibson's views on contraception and his apparent distaste for homosexuals should come as no surprise. In a controversial interview with a Spanish magazine in the early nineties he said he became an actor despite worries that people might take his choice of career to mean he was homosexual. 'But with this look, who's going to think I'm gay?' he reportedly said. 'It would be hard to take me for someone like that.' On contraception, he said: 'God is the only one who knows how many children we should have, and we should be ready to accept them.' Such views may not be typical of Hollywood but they are entirely consistent with the views of a father who claimed to be a stricter Catholic than the Pope.

Hutton Gibson first visited Australia during the Second World War. He was wounded at the Pacific island of Guadalcanal, scene of intense fighting between American and Japanese troops in 1943. The following year he married Anna Reilly in Brooklyn, New York, where she had grown up after moving from Ireland. She was a warm and friendly, if rather plain, young woman. At least initially, her family and friends found Hutton Gibson austere and distant, though they were impressed by his obvious intellect and self-reliance. He had been the son of a rich industrialist but he was not proud and took a job with the New York Central Railroad. It provided him with the money to support his new wife and begin a family. He worked up to sixteen hours a day as a brakeman. Nevertheless, he found the time and energy to father four children in six years, and Anna was still in her mid-twenties.

Hutton Gibson needed a new house for his growing family and Verplanck was convenient for his work on the railroad. It is a little old village in an area unusually rich in history because of the importance of the Hudson River, on whose eastern bank Verplanck is situated. On the other side of the river is West Point Military Academy and Newburgh, where George Washington based himself for part of the War of Independence. South of Verplanck is Sing Sing Prison and Tarrytown, setting for Washington Irving's stories of Rip Van Winkle and Sleepy Hollow. Further north are the Roosevelt homes and the Vanderbilt Mansion. But it was no stately home to which the Gibsons were moving.

'I remember the first day they ever came,' recalls Ed Stinson, who was to become a close friend of the family and godfather to one of their children. 'The real estate man brought the man in and I said "Jeez, I can't believe anybody would want to buy that house." But, sure as heck, they bought it. He bought himself a heck of a lot of work at the same time. The man just started from scratch and he put all the utilities into it and rebuilt the whole house, with four or five kids running under his feet.'

Stinson worked just over the fence at the Sun Oil depot. 'He stuck with it, he stuck with it until he had remodelled it all and the part that shocked me was, after he remodelled everything, it seemed like the day everything was finished, they sold the house and moved away.' The work on the house took years and Stinson saw the family grow and multiply during that time. He remembers Anna Gibson carrying Mel home from Peekskill Hospital and the christening at St Patrick's.

Mel Gibson's godparents were Helen Broadley, a childhood friend of Anna, and her husband Frank. The christening was the only time Helen Broadley ever saw her godson, because the Gibson family moved further upstate and subsequently emigrated. But she continued to correspond with her friend, until Anna's death in 1990, and received regular updates on her godchild and his career as an actor. More than forty years after undertaking the role of godmother to Mel Gibson, Helen Broadley was still living in New York, in the borough of Queens, and taking enormous pride in her godson's achievements.

'His mother and I, we grew up together and were friends practically all our lives,' she tells me. 'Mel's mother's name was Anna Reilly, but everybody called her Anne. I knew her mother and I also knew her old grandmother, who smoked a corncob pipe. This is back in Brooklyn when we lived next door. They got married and moved to Washington Heights and then they went to Croton-on-Hudson and then they went to Peekskill. We used to go up on Sunday on the New York Central train. Red worked on the New York Central Railroad – we always called him Red. [Hutton Gibson was nicknamed Red because of his red hair, not his political views.] I didn't know him. He was always busy working and taking care of the kids. They were very, very religious, very respectful, very helpful. I remember the little girl coming and taking our coats. They were very well-mannered because Red was a good disciplinarian.'

She remembers well the day of Mel Gibson's christening because her youngest daughter, who is a few years older than Gibson, locked herself in the bathroom of the rebuilt Gibson home. 'Red had to put a ladder to the side of the house to get her out.' She looked forward to letters from Anna about her godson and photographs of him. 'He was always making a funny face and at one time in a letter – he doesn't know because I've never spoken to him – in the letter she called him "your godson, the actor". And it was funny, years later he became an actor ... We carried him to church and I've never seen him. I did ask Anna to ask him to send us a picture and she sent me a lovely eight by ten picture autographed by him. And it says "To Helen and Frank. Love Mel". My nieces and my daughters loved him, they all wanted a picture, but I couldn't write for any more pictures.

'I've seen him many times on television, and I've told many people and it's funny, you know, the reaction when you say you're his godmother. They think you know him. I say he wouldn't know me if he fell over me. But I see him all the time and I've been keeping track of him. He really wanted to be a news reporter or something. I think he's too modest and humble for all this celebrity status.'

She missed some of his more recent films, including *Braveheart*, because she was into her seventies by the time of its release and it was difficult for her to get out to the cinema. 'This is not such a good neighbourhood,' she says. 'You've just got to be careful and not go out at night.' She watched her godson's Oscar triumph on television. But the great irony is that Gibson flew to Los Angeles for the ceremony from New York, where he had been filming the tough thriller *Ransom* in Queens itself. While shooting one scene, a real police chase drove right through the set. The great family man never knew that his godmother was living just a few minutes' drive away.

Ed Stinson recalls the Gibsons as a wonderful big family. 'I used to see them every day of the week except Saturdays and Sundays. It was like calling roll every day. They would come out and they knew I was working there. They got to know my name and I would have to answer every one of them every day of the week to let them know that I recognised them, because they would just keep yelling at me until I did recognise them, no matter what I was doing. Mel stayed out more than the rest. He had bright eyes and always had a smile on his face, I wouldn't say a hell-raiser, but he held his own, put it that way.

'The family was their own recreation. I never knew them to have a toy as kids have toys today or bicycles. They seemed always to make their own fun. They ate very well. The father was insistent on vitamins and in all the years I knew them there I never saw a doctor at their door one time. They seemed to be very healthy children. The whole family just meshed together as far as getting along with one another was concerned. Hutton would dust them off every once in a while, there's no doubt about that, if they stepped out of line.'

Gibson admits he hits his own children, going so far as to claim that it is impossible to 'raise a decent human being' without a modicum of violence. 'I just give them a crack that will sting and bite,' he says. 'Provided you have warned them at least three times and as long as when it's all finished you are back to square one again, it's OK. I believe in strict discipline.' He goes on to add: 'But I haven't got the heart to go through with it most of the time.' It is an indication of the human side of Gibson that softens his strict religious and social views. He is not like other progressive-thinking, liberal Hollywood stars. What he is like is millions of blue-collar fathers in that huge unsophisticated expanse of America that lies between Hollywood and New York, millions of fathers in Australia, in England, Ireland and Scotland and, indeed, all over the world.

By the time Mel Gibson had reached school age he had another four brothers and sisters and Hutton Gibson found a larger house, with a few acres attached, one hundred miles away, amid mountains and lakes, in the farming community of Mount Vision. Hutton Gibson acquired a few animals and had thoughts of living off the land. Mel Gibson had twin brothers who were just a year younger than he was and another brother who was a year younger than that. They constituted their own happy, rough-and-tumble little gang.

'There were rock fights, injuries, fist fights,' he says nostalgically. 'There was spending the days in the top of an apple tree, just eating the fruit and dreaming . . . Falling leaves. Climbing trees. Lump-jumping – a thing we used to do out in the back paddocks, a kind of lowland which had these big hillocks, and in between it was just wet muck. It smelled and was full of frogs. I was real good jumping on the lumps. You'd be going a hundred miles an hour, so you wouldn't hit the wet.' It might have seemed a potentially idyllic life, but in the meantime Gibson's father was still working on the railroad down near Verplanck, staying with Anna's sister in New York or sleeping in his car, using the Sun Oil depot in Verplanck to clean up and going home to his family at weekends.

The children attended Laurens Central School, a small pre-war school a few miles from their home. Mel Gibson was there for three years. Zelma Ainslie, his third-grade teacher, recalls him as 'a cute little boy, who just loved to play little jokes and have fun', a description not entirely dissimilar to that provided by those who have worked with him much more recently. 'It's been a long, long time, but I look at him and I still see the same looks,' she tells me.

In an interview with Australia's *Cinema Papers* magazine in 1983, Gibson said: 'I have been doing that since I was little, standing up and telling jokes. You know how little kids do it. They love the attention – especially if they come from a big family, and I have ten brothers and sisters. I used to get a kick out of affecting people, no matter what sort of effect. That is what drives you on.'

Dreams of life on the farm were shattered when Hutton Gibson had a terrible accident at work on the railway. He fell from a train and sustained back injuries which necessitated a series of operations. Not only was he incapacitated, his employers denied responsibility and refused to pay compensation. These were extremely difficult times for the Gibson family, who moved back downstate to a cheap property near Salisbury Mills, on the opposite side of the Hudson from Verplanck. Hutton Gibson did not sit around feeling sorry for himself. Just when their fortunes seemed at their lowest, he managed to bring some money into the household by winning several thousand dollars on the *Jeopardy* television quiz show. It was one of a number of quiz successes in the United States and Australia.

He retrained in the comparatively new field of computer programming and sued the railroad. The case dragged on for months, and months became years, but in 1968 Hutton Gibson ended up with a settlement of $150,000, which was worth a lot more then than it is now. It was certainly enough to give him and his family a new start. It would finance an extended European holiday, at a time when holidays abroad were the preserve of the rich, and it would set the family up on the other side of the world. This was the swinging sixties, free love, long hair and LSD, but Hutton Gibson was no swinger. He preferred the prospect of living in Australia which, due to international time differences, was still in the fifties. Despite his conservative views on many issues, one subject on which he did agree with the American hippies was the Vietnam war. One of the reasons for the move was his opposition to the war and his wish for his children to avoid being drafted.

In an interview in 1996 Gibson said it was untrue that his father moved to Australia so his sons would not have to go to Vietnam. 'To him it was a whole new frontier,' he said. 'And at the time it really was. Back then, Australia had tremendous opportunities, and we had relatives there. He wanted to check it out.' Gibson criticised journalists for getting their facts wrong, but over the years he has repeatedly been quoted as saying that Vietnam was one of the reasons the family moved to Australia. Ten years earlier he said it was ironic that he was playing a Vietnam veteran in *Lethal Weapon* 'because when I was 12 my father . . . moved the whole Gibson family from America to Australia to avoid his sons having to serve in Vietnam'. There are bound to be inconsistencies, in facts and opinions, cropping up over the years, whenever the media focuses on an individual as intently as it had done on Mel Gibson.

The Gibsons took a few months to finalise their affairs in America and say goodbye to friends and family. They left New York State in July 1968 and did not arrive in Australia until October, after touring Scotland, England, Italy, Switzerland and the ancestral homeland of Ireland. They were happy days for Mel Gibson and his family. He paid his first visit to the Highlands of Scotland, which he would later revisit for *Braveheart*. 'I found it to be quite magical, beautiful,' he says. 'When I worked with Franco [Franco Zeffirelli, director of *Hamlet*] we worked on the east coast, up near Aberdeen, and that was nice, but I sort of wanted to get back to that mountainous kind of stuff. We spent three or four months in the British Isles just travelling around.'

There was also a pilgrimage across the Emerald Isle. His mother was born in Ireland, his father could trace his roots to Ireland, he was named after a couple of Irish churches and he was born into an Irish-American community. He has spoken of the martyrdom of Irish ancestors. Writing in London's *Time Out* magazine in 1985, Joan Goodman observed that 'his Irishness has almost a mystic hold on him'. He told her he empathised with the Irish-Australian background of his character in *Gallipoli*. 'I have a similarity with his Irishness,' he said. 'His Irish feelings come through . . . Sometimes I feel I've caught something from him, some disease from that character.' He played Irish-American in *Mrs Soffel* and said: 'He's a caveman, a very literate caveman. I can see something of myself in him. At 19 I was a lunatic too. He's Irish and so am I. I understand it and I want to communicate Irishness – the madness of it. I was told by a woman that if you're Irish the world sooner or later is going to break your heart.'

Journalists seem to have had recurring problems not only with Gibson's nationality but also with that of his parents, commonly confusing his mother with his grandmother, and saying he is the son of an Australian opera singer. It is an important point: his immediate forebears – his parents – are not American and Australian-born, but American and Irish. When we discussed his nationality, he summed it up thus: 'My mother's from Ireland, my grandmother's Australian – my dad's mother – and he was born in America. So a bit of a mix.' But it is essential to sort out this mix to understand where Gibson comes from. The bottom line, in his own words, is: 'It all goes back to Ireland.'

Nevertheless he was quite prosaic about Ireland and the Irish leg of his childhood world tour when we discussed it in 1995, a decade after the *Time Out* interview. 'I went to see the place where my mother used to live and it was just a pile of rocks and stuff like that,' he said. Gibson is a very unpretentious individual. Other Hollywood stars have waxed lyrical about the significance of their ancestry, particularly any trace of Native American blood, which will have endowed them with a special spirituality, though Celtic is fashionable too. Gibson, however, told Michael Dwyer of the *Irish Times* when he went to Ireland to film *Braveheart* that he did not feel any spiritual connection with Ireland. 'I like it here for sure . . . Everyone seems friendly.' Of course it would have made a better line if

Gibson had called Ireland his spiritual home, but he was not going to do that.

His roots are Irish and Gibson has called himself Irish, but the most immediate national influences on Gibson were the two countries in which he grew up. He spoke to me about having a dual perception of the world, a perception that had been shaped by spending his first twelve years in New York State and the remainder of his childhood and his youth in another country. While it may have shared the same language, the people used and pronounced it differently. In the eighties the world may have thought that new screen sensation Mel Gibson was an Australian, born and bred. But in 1968 he was very obviously an American, a stranger in a strange and sometimes threatening land, a land with a different climate and different attitudes, a part of the British Commonwealth, with the Queen of England as head of state. The Gibson family had said goodbye to the United States, possibly for ever. For them Australia was the new world. For Mel Gibson, in particular, difficult and unhappy years lay ahead.

# 3

## LIFE DOWN UNDER

At school in Australia other boys picked on Mel Gibson because of his American accent. The youngster, who would one day play Mad Max, Martin Riggs and William Wallace, was bullied by his peers and was desperately unhappy. To try to win their approval, he played the fool and was ritually and repeatedly beaten by the Christian Brothers who ran the school. He dropped out, unsure of what he wanted to do with his life. He already had the beginnings of a drink problem when somehow he managed to land a prized place on the acting course at NIDA, the National Institute of Dramatic Art, the Australian equivalent of England's RADA and New York's High School for the Performing Arts. And, of course, Mel Gibson took to it like a duck to water and went straight from NIDA into *Mad Max* and the role that made him an international star. Except that is not the way it happened.

Few people know how close Gibson came to being thrown out of NIDA. Some of his teachers believed he would simply never make the grade as an actor. It was only by the skin of his teeth that he avoided being expelled, an impoverished foreigner in a foreign land, with a drink problem, an attitude problem and, if he managed to sort those out, a possible future selling insurance or working in some other humdrum job or simply languishing on the scrapheap of life.

Gibson has become increasingly articulate and dispassionate about the upheaval in his life at the age of twelve when he was uprooted from New York, deposited on the other side of the world and forced to adjust to a new society. 'I'm an American citizen by birth,' he tells me. 'If you're born and raised in America you are really very proud and rightly so: it's a great nation. It's very interesting to go somewhere else and observe the place from a distance. It gives you a real objectivity, I think, which is important for an actor. You can go into a place like Australia from the United States, and although the cultures are very similar, it's different enough so that you have to examine where you came from; who you are in relationship to these people. And then in adopting the things you like about that culture, you give away some of the things that you had. You focus on their culture and your culture and you're always looking and making observations about things. It's a healthy thing.'

His tone was slightly less positive, and there were hints of his difficulties in adjusting from one society to another, when he spoke to Margaret Smith of *Cinema Papers* in 1983: 'I was brought up in one environment until about the age of 12 and understood it. Then I was suddenly shifted to another. I could immediately sense the difference in, for instance, the extent to which people expressed themselves. Americans, you know, are very expressive, which I think is better than the up-tight reserve Australians have. It is a sort of hang-up from the English. But, as with everything, it has its good and bad sides.'

Mel Gibson was in the news when he first arrived in Australia in 1968. 'So you think YOU have trouble keeping your children within spanking distance,' said the Melbourne *Herald*, reporting that the family was travelling with ten children, one trunk, twenty cases and twelve bags. Anna Gibson, who was now styling herself Anne, was quoted as saying: 'It was a little trying and hard to keep things organised. But we made it. I got a bit of a shock at Rome Airport, though. I counted one . . . two . . . three . . . and there were only nine. We finally found Mel in the bathroom.' The article finished with another quote saying that she was really looking forward to getting back to work in the kitchen.

The Gibsons moved into a house in the Mount Kuring-gai area on the northern outskirts of Sydney. Mel Gibson enrolled in St Leo's Christian Brothers School, a relatively new school, built in 1956, the year of the Melbourne Olympics, run by an Irish religious order, with an emphasis on religion, sport and discipline. Gibson had to wear a uniform, including a straw boater. He hated the school. 'I had a fairly rough time of it,' he says. 'The kids made fun of me and called me Yank.' He managed to be the class clown, a rebel and a loner. 'I used to misbehave a lot . . . I couldn't hack hanging out with a group that did a certain thing. I just couldn't swallow it. I used to think sometimes that these people had something that I didn't: they had an identity.' Instead of adopting an Australian accent, he began talking in a Scottish one. Ultimately, Gibson became so bitter and twisted by his treatment that he devised a perverse game in which he would deliberately try to provoke the teachers into beating him. A former classmate once recalled a competition which Gibson won by being strapped twenty-seven times in a single day.

Gibson says some of the teachers were 'regular sons of bitches'. He told the American *Interview* magazine: 'They had hard-line discipline, which ain't all bad. When I was there I really rebelled against it, but you've got to toe the line sometime.' Despite the clowning and apparent exhibitionism, he found it difficult to stand up in class and talk as himself. 'It was awful. I had the worst fear. I think the reason I was so petrified was because I wanted to, and I was afraid that I would be tongue-tied and not able to talk.' It was as if he had confidence to talk in the character of someone else, but not as Mel Gibson.

At home he enjoyed big action films on television, thrillers in which the tough guy hero was really just a softie at heart, and comedies, particularly the Three Stooges. At St Leo's he developed his own talents for slapstick and for mimicry, using his teachers as subjects and audience, even if they were less appreciative than future audiences would be. He appeared in one school drama production, in which he played a traditional villain in a black cape.

He transferred to Asquith Boys High School after his father fell out with St Leo's on some religious point, by which time he had a reputation as a troublemaker. He later admitted he had been a 'wild teenager', drinking to excess and driving dangerously. The story about how he drifted into acting when his sister filled up a drama school application form has come up time and again. Gibson himself has often been quoted on it. He supposedly went along to NIDA auditions with a fairly cavalier attitude. This may all be true, but Gibson has been known to elaborate on stories during interviews, crack the odd joke that ends up being taken seriously and even spin the odd yarn, in the great tradition of earlier film stars such as David Niven, who produced several volumes of best-selling but unreliable memoirs. Gibson probably does it as much to amuse himself as anything else.

Gibson attended Asquith as a day pupil for only a short time and completed his Higher School Certificate by attending evening classes at Asquith and at Hornsby Technical College. He made some money by selling insurance, but not much. Tom Eakin taught him biology at evening classes at Asquith, in a class that included men as old as forty or fifty. 'He was a very quiet kid and he would sit at the front of the class in the science laboratory as if he was day-dreaming, deep in thought, and I would ask him what he thought he would do when he left school. And he would say, quite strongly: "I'm going to NIDA." I would say: "Oh yes, you'll never make it." But he did.

'I often talk to our boys in the school at the present time and relate Mel's story to them, because some of them aren't very interested. I have some of the classes who are a little bit lower. And I tell them just the story about Mel: "He didn't appear to be interested in school." And they would say: "Oh, yes." And I would say: "But, listen, listen, what he did, while he may have been day-dreaming like you boys are, he was setting a goal; he knew exactly what he wanted to do and he went out and got it." So I still use Mel today as a teaching tool. And they sit and think about that.

'He didn't fit in at school too well. He was a bit wild. But I had no trouble with him. He was the most well-mannered kid I've ever met. He just didn't fit in with the system, as some boys don't.'

Back in the eighties, after Gibson had established himself as a major star, he told interviewers how he ended up in acting. 'I went to university to do an arts degree. I went to a newspaper to try to be a journalist cadet. And I went to the National Institute of Dramatic Art to audition ... I didn't choose it; that is the weird point. It was set up for me by a member of my family who did all the applying, sending my request form into a place which handled auditions. When she told me that she had done it, I didn't really go for it much, but then I sat down and said: "Well, why not? Why not two days out of my life?" But I felt I was going to make a jerk of myself in front of a lot of people.'

It may seem odd, but it is clear from Gibson's own comments and from the comments of those around him, as a child, as a student and as a superstar, that Gibson is, and always has been, an essentially shy, retiring person. The bravado masks a deep uncertainty about himself. He is never quite sure how far he can go, whether it be in class with the Christian Brothers, in interviews with the sharp minds and pencils of the press, or in drama school, where two thousand applicants chase twenty-five places on the acting course. 'They made me do all these silly things – improvise, sing, dance – and I got in. I guess they saw something in me. The guy asked me why I wanted to be an actor, and I said: "I've been goofing around all my life. I thought I might as well get paid for that."' The class of '77 was, in due course, to establish itself as the most distinguished ever to graduate from NIDA.

But of course no one, teacher or student, knew that in 1975, at the outset of a three-year course of voice work and Shakespeare, music and movement, dialect and dance. John Clark, director of NIDA in 1975 and still director more than twenty years later, auditioned Gibson, not that he remembers anything about it. The audition he does clearly recall is that of another applicant, with a more forthright approach to her craft, a girl by the name of Judy Davis, who went on to star in *My Brilliant Career*, *A Passage To India* and *Husbands and Wives*.

Her contemporary Mel Gibson was soon prompting excited discussion among the staff too. NIDA is understandably proud of both Davis and Gibson now, but back in the mid-seventies staff were at a loss to know what they could 'do' about Gibson except throw him out. And he certainly would not have been the only one not to make it to the end of his course, for in those days NIDA functioned a little like the Open golf tournament – after first year, half the students simply did not make the cut and were eliminated. And a few more were likely to join them before graduation day. 'That was a system I did away with as soon as possible. It was just appalling,' says George Whaley, who became head of acting at NIDA at the beginning of Gibson's second year. He championed Gibson's cause against hostile colleagues and was rewarded for his faith when Gibson's company, Icon, helped finance his film *Dad and Dave: On Our Selection*, with Gibson himself returning to Sydney to introduce it at its premiere in 1995.

NIDA is Australia's national theatre school, set up in 1958 under the auspices of the Australian Broadcasting Corporation and the University of New South Wales, which has provided space for it on its campus in Kensington, a posh suburb of Sydney. There are about 150 full-time students each year, studying acting, directing and various other theatre-related disciplines. NIDA is now housed in a purpose-built complex that includes teaching studios and theatres, but when Gibson and Davis were students it occupied modest buildings that had previously been part of the Kensington racecourse, including the jockeys' changing rooms. They were used by the military during the First World War and soldiers trained there before going off to be slaughtered at Gallipoli. Gibson would pay homage to the complex's earlier occupants in the film *Gallipoli* a few years later. Clark describes the previous buildings as 'pretty slummy and rather dilapidated and awful'.

It was to these huts that Gibson came to learn about acting in 1975. 'He was a big sort of gawky kid, you know,' says Monroe Reimers, one of Gibson's contemporaries. 'He had long hair. He actually looked like a lion, because he had hair down to the middle of his back, like really long hair.' Reimers, who is now a television actor and writer, became particularly friendly with Gibson and they shared a flat, along with another student, Steve Bisley, who co-starred in Gibson's first two films, *Summer City* and *Mad Max*. 'We used to call it Cockroach Castle – great parties though.'

Gibson was brought up a strict Catholic and he continues to take his Catholicism seriously, but Monroe Reimers says it never seemed to impinge on his lifestyle as a student. 'It wasn't like he was a goody-goody boy. He was just like one of the guys, like all of us heathens.' Religion never inhibited him when it came to girls. 'It didn't really stop him, but I'm sure he must have felt pretty guilty for it afterwards . . . He thinks it's pretty important. He's been told that it's pretty important, but it's worth nothing really, because all it does really is it stifles him inside, makes him unhappy . . . His father is a fanatic . . . and Mel is in awe of him, which I think is the worst thing.'

George Whaley believes Gibson's religion has not only shaped him as a man and an actor but may have been a factor in his decision to go into acting in the first place. Whaley points out that a disproportionately high number of Australians in the performing arts come from Catholic backgrounds. 'It comes out of the music, the ritual and the colour and movement,' he says.

Even by student standards Gibson was poor. Whaley paid him to do some work on his house. What little money he had was spent on beer, rather than food. Gibson and his pals were not above ordering a hamburger and running off without paying for it.

'He was very, very funny, a great sense of humour,' says Reimers. 'He used to like all those old Jerry Lewis movies and Bud Abbott and Lou Costello. He liked the gag culture.' Gibson relished the more physical side of the course. 'One of the exercises was that we had to create an affliction for ourselves, like a broken hand or some sort of thing, and live with that affliction for twenty-four hours,' says Reimers. 'And Mel and I were catching this bus home and he decided to just have one arm, so he stuck his hand inside his shirt and let his sleeve just dangle and pretend that he had no arm. And the bus going home was stopping and starting again and jerking and he was standing up and he was such a ham and he was trying to hold on to his feet and hold on to his books and everyone thought poor sucker and obviously felt so sorry for him. They must have been thinking God, you know, such a good-looking guy, such a well-built guy, and he's only got one arm.

'A lot of that stuff he did in *Lethal Weapon* he used to do at NIDA. That mad guy that hits his head was created at NIDA.' But Gibson was proving less adept at the internal aspects of acting and was coming under a lot of pressure from staff at NIDA to get to grips with it. 'He's very good at emotions of anger and pain,' says Reimers. 'He's not very good at the joy and the happy side of life . . . Those have to be internal, because if you externalise them, no matter how good you are, they look false.'

Gibson was also having trouble with dance and movement. 'It took me a while to manage that,' he later admitted. 'There were four of us more beefy ones. I always had two left feet and was always half a beat behind everyone else.'

Reimers says: 'If you didn't turn in a reasonable performance or if you did really, really badly at NIDA, what they used to do is they would summon you into the White House – this building that was called the White House – and they would tear strips off you, and they would do it in front of everyone else. It was like the most humiliating thing . . . At any minute you could be turfed out . . . That always hovered over you. After first year we had a holiday and then there was the big thing – who is going to stay in and who is going to be thrown out. When we left that building no one knew who was going to be coming back. And then when I got my letter saying that I had to come back I rang Mel immediately and his mother picked up the phone – his mother was just this gorgeous woman – and she said, "Ah yes, he's in for another year," and then she got me to him.'

There are plenty of people who are happy to say they saw Gibson's potential from the start, fewer to claim that they always knew he was crap. John Clark is cautious about what he says about official NIDA attitudes. His assessment of the young Judy Davis is 'superb'. His comment on Gibson is: 'We're a little bit particular about what we say about people when they were students, because I think it [NIDA] is an opportunity to muck up . . . I remember in that first year it wasn't by any means obvious to a lot of people that they were going to make it, but then suddenly they blossomed when they matured a bit and got a bit more sense of what they were doing. I think that happened with Mel and happened with a lot of people. Mel blossomed when he got courage. I think it was also courage that led to *Braveheart*.'

Gibson survived the end-of-first-year 'cut', but he was still not exactly blossoming when George Whaley arrived at NIDA at the beginning of his second year. 'How to put this in a polite

way? When I would call my staff together for assessments and
we would discuss progress, there was always worry about Mel,
and I couldn't understand this because I thought he was splendid.
Now some of the worry was a hangover from first year, which
obviously was not a very distinguished year for him, but I think
the other and more important aspect of that worry was that Mel
was different. He was shy, he was retiring, he was not up-front
and in your face. He was the sort of person who never stood
out in a crowd, who only stood out when he was working. He
was an incredibly gifted actor, but there was a constant chorus
of "What can we do about Mel?"'

Gibson once recalled that he was so nervous in a NIDA
production that his knees buckled under him. 'I just rattled
off my lines and went off,' he said. Whaley helped him develop
the confidence to exploit his natural presence by trying different
approaches to even quite simple roles. Reimers remembers being
with Gibson in a bar one night, Gibson was having terrible
difficulties over his interpretation of a particular part, and he
'drifted away' into a 'dream-like state'. Reimers' comments
about Gibson shutting himself off from the surrounding world to
concentrate are reminiscent of reports from the set of *Braveheart*,
except in the first instance he was an unknown drama student
and in the second a world-famous actor directing a multi-
million-dollar movie.

Reimers recalls the outcome: 'He said: "I will show them. I
will show them. I've got it. I've got it. I will show them." He
turned in this performance which was just like "Wow". You
never saw anything like it. He kind of gave the character a lisp
and it was then that he kind of understood what it took to be
an actor . . . He wasn't a bookish student. He doesn't appear
to be a person who sits and analyses things, but actually he is.
He thinks very deeply about what he does.'

He played Romeo opposite Judy Davis's Juliet, a production
staged before a handful of onlookers in the hall that served as
NIDA's theatre. It had previously been the racecourse's tote
building, the nerve centre for betting on the horses. Actors
often found themselves shouting lines so they would be heard
over the noise of rain drumming on the metal roof. Gibson
was extremely nervous about the prospect of playing Romeo,

feeling more suited to comedy and character parts, and had to be coerced into playing it. Monroe Reimers says the director really pushed Gibson to bring out the vulnerability within the character and he rates Gibson's performance as the best he has ever delivered. 'That was a really fantastic performance, but I've never seen it in his professional life.'

By the end of second year, Gibson had improved to the point where he was offered his first film role. He subsequently dismissed *Summer City* as a 'cheap, nasty flick', renamed it *Summer Shitty* and has even omitted it from official biographical details in recent years. There is no denying its cheapness – the budget was cited at the time as A$200,000 and cast and crew had to sleep on the floor of a local hall. Writer/producer/co-star Phil Avalon now admits the true cost was about A$60,000. At the time, the Australian dollar was worth slightly more than its American counterpart, though by the early eighties the position was reversed. On the basis of Avalon's figure, Mel Gibson's first feature film cost only about £45,000 to make.

*Summer City* was never intended for general cinema release, but for the 'surf circuit' – cinemas and halls in New South Wales's seaside resorts, where the audience would be composed mainly of surfers. *Summer City* was not only shown in ordinary cinemas, but broke house records in some. In October 1978, ten months after its release, the Sydney *Sun* described it as a 'youth cult movie' and reported that it was about to open in thirteen countries overseas. Gibson's dismissal does *Summer City*, and his fans, something of a disservice – though viewers familiar with the Gibson of *Braveheart* and *Lethal Weapon* may be surprised at the sight of a rather chubby young actor sharing his first screen kiss with another man and sporting a hairstyle that is somewhere between blond and orange and looks to have been inspired by a soldier's bearskin hat.

Australia had had a successful film industry of its own before the Second World War, but hardly any locally-produced feature films were made between the mid-fifties and the early seventies. Australian star Chips Rafferty and director Lee Robinson set up a company in the late fifties, financed by public subscription, but it folded after making three films. Later features, such as *The Sundowners* (1960) and *On the Beach* (1960), were either American or British productions, made on location in Australia.

The renaissance in Australian film did not happen simply by chance. In 1971 the government started making money available to support production. The bawdy comedies *The Adventures of Barry McKenzie* (1972) and *Alvin Purple* (1973), the latter starring Barry Humphries, were popular with local and international audiences. Tim Burstall, director of *Alvin Purple*, had worked mainly in documentaries and children's films in the sixties, while Bruce Beresford, director of *Barry McKenzie*, had been employed by the Nigerian government film unit and the British Film Institute. Australian cinema found international critical success with two 1975 films, *Sunday Too Far Away*, which attempted to do for sheep-shearers what the Western had done for cowboys, and *Picnic At Hanging Rock*, Peter Weir's eerie yet elegant mystery about the disappearance of a small party of schoolgirls in the Victorian countryside on St Valentine's Day 1900. It was against this background of booming film production and growing confidence in the local product that Mel Gibson worked his way through NIDA.

Phil Avalon was an actor and model, with a CV that included the children's television series *Skippy* and the centrefold of *Playgirl*. He also helped finance *Summer City* by buying and selling second-hand cars. He intended the film as an Australian version of *American Graffiti* and spiced up his own experience to produce a storyline about four friends who set off for a weekend of sunshine, surfing and sex in the early sixties. There was to be lots of music and a violent climax. What Avalon lacked in financial resources, he made up for in enthusiasm. He would play one of the four, Robbie. And he recruited John Jarratt, a NIDA graduate who had appeared in *Picnic At Hanging Rock*, to play Sandy, who is about to settle down and get married. He needed to find two more actors who would work for next to nothing in the other two main roles – Boo, the loud-mouthed exhibitionist, whose single-minded pursuit of sex ultimately leads to tragedy, and his quiet sidekick Scollop, whose life revolves around surfing.

It was Jarratt who suggested Avalon consider Mel Gibson and Steve Bisley. An informal audition was arranged at Avalon's house and he was knocked out by what he saw – from Bisley. He immediately cast him in the main role of Boo. Gibson came across as being very shy and unassuming, which Avalon reckoned would be fine for Scollop.

Gibson and Bisley wanted to go a week early to the main location at Catherine Hill Bay, a small mining town on the coast of New South Wales between Sydney and Newcastle. They had no money and suggested they drive up in the old Chevrolet that the characters use in the film and sleep in the hall the production was going to use as a base. Avalon takes up the story: 'I said: "Yeah, you can take the car and use the hall up there. I don't have any money for the fuel or anything like that, but there's a car across the street that's just been rolled over the cliff there: you can climb down there and milk the petrol out of the tank if you wish." And next minute I saw them scurrying down the cliff with this jerrycan and hose. And that's how they got up to the location.'

The local ex-servicemen's hall served as production head-quarters, hotel and cinema. Avalon hired a projector so cast and crew could watch the rushes of the film as soon as it had been developed. He remembers their first footage: 'The character that I played had to go round to Mel Gibson's house and pick him up, and the fellow who played his father was a non-actor we just found somewhere around the place and we were all laughing about him. The whole place went up because of the old man, because he was a real find . . . and then Mel pops out and he comes across to the car with me. And I thought "My God! This guy's got a really good screen presence."'

Avalon entrusted the job of directing the film to Christopher Fraser, though his own duties did not stop at writing, producing and acting. He also served as caterer for a cast and crew of twenty-five and juggled shooting schedules to ensure he was always free to prepare the food ahead of meal breaks. 'Quite often they wouldn't be too impressed when yesterday's leftovers became today's stew,' says Avalon. 'I would just do the best I could.'

As well as having to work under severe financial constraints, the production also had to contend with numerous other problems. There was a petrol strike and they had to store exposed film in the fridge at the local pub until they could get enough petrol to take it to the laboratory in Sydney. Serious injury was only narrowly avoided when a car crashed and was written off. The town was threatened by a bushfire and production was suspended for four days while cast and crew worked with local residents in trying to bring it under control. When filming the dance in the local hall, the cameraman needed to persuade local residents to allow him to plug leads into their electricity supplies to enable him to rig up sufficient lighting. Because of the sudden surge in usage the town was blacked out for an hour.

There was friction between the visitors and the local population after the cast and crew were temporarily evicted from their hall for a wedding. In a real-life scene that presages *Braveheart*, Gibson and Bisley dropped their trousers and flashed their naked bottoms at wedding guests, according to Avalon's well-practised recollections. The males in the party were neither amused nor intimidated. 'About fifty of them came tearing out looking for the culprits . . . They were so wild-eyed with rage they would have just about killed Mel and Steve if they'd got to them. It was a desperate situation and I suddenly remembered there was a .303 army rifle in the back of my car that was a prop for the film. I grabbed the rifle and threatened to shoot the first one that made a move.'

There was friction, too, between Avalon and his cast when he ran out of money and could not even pay them the low wages they had been promised. The whole project looked in jeopardy, but Avalon managed to come up with extra cash from various sources, including an $18,000 loan from the father of the film's production co-ordinator Lionel Slutzkin.

*Summer City* is not *Braveheart*. It is not even *Mad Max*. But compared to other micro-budget genre movies, it is not at all bad. And certainly nowhere near as embarrassing as the soft-porn early films of various other Hollywood stars. It shows a certain ambition, or pretension, by beginning with monochrome television news and pop footage that establishes the period, and a pre-title scene of a graveyard and what sounds like a judicial voice pontificating on the events we are about to see, making the whole body of the film a flashback. Having said that, the body of the film is fairly mindless late-night fare about young men in pursuit of fun.

Boo is first seen necking in a car with a girl, when his mate Scollop arrives. This is Gibson's first screen scene, apart from a glimpse of him in the graveyard. He is wearing an orange sweater that does not quite reach the top of his jeans. 'Hey, Boo . . . I thought you were going bowling tonight,' giggles a leering Scollop. I am not sure what the words in the middle of the sentence are. Much of the dialogue is difficult to make out, partly because of the strong accents and partly because it has not been very well recorded, though that never prevents the viewer getting the drift of what is happening. Despite occasionally jerky camerawork, the film is quite artfully shot, with an early scene of a surfboard placed carefully on the roof of a car as the sun rises in the background. And it is skilfully edited, with dialogue scenes alternating with music.

The four young men set off on a journey in which they chat up a shop assistant and almost get into a fight with another motorist, but he has forgotten to put the hand brake on and his car rolls away. Gibson and Bisley are seen topless, drinking beer, in the back of the Chevrolet, at which point Gibson has his first kiss. The second half of the film concerns their stay at the beach. Gibson is given a brief opportunity for physical acting when his character pretends to be blind, although his surfing scenes were done by a stand-in. It is in the nature of the part that he has little to say, but he does explain to Sandy that surfing for him is 'a way of life'. The short speech gives him the chance to demonstrate the physical restlessness – the shrugging of shoulders, rubbing of chin and raising of eyebrows – that will become familiar features of his acting.

The film comes to a climax after Boo seduces a local girl, Caroline (Debbie Foreman), and her father comes looking for him. Coincidentally, Sandy overhears Boo telling Scollop that the girl in the car at the beginning of the film was Sandy's fiancée. Suddenly Boo is under threat on all sides in a very moralistic ending. Although it is Bisley who seduces Foreman in the film, it was Gibson and Foreman who became a couple off-screen, a relationship which also ended badly, with a terrible row and Foreman slashing her wrists.

Foreman dropped out of films. When Avalon last saw her, she had been extremely upset by an exposé of the details of her relationship with Gibson. Avalon became a full-time producer and his films include *Fatal Bond*, with Linda Blair and Mel Gibson's brother Donal. Avalon and Mel Gibson do not keep in touch. Avalon saw him at the premiere of Whaley's *Dad and Dave: On Our Selection* and caught his eye. 'As I was trying to squeeze my way through the crowd, he got surrounded by about twenty other people and I didn't have a hope of getting anywhere near him to shake hands. It was very disappointing.'

Both Jarratt and Bisley went on to develop successful careers as actors in Australia. In the mid-nineties Jarratt hosted Channel 7's *Better Homes and Gardens* programme. Bisley was very much the star of *Summer City*; he had the big showy part. He teamed up with Gibson again in *Mad Max*, this time in the buddy role, but he had the misfortune that his character was killed and therefore had no prospect of going on to bigger things in the sequels, as Gibson did. Nevertheless Bisley became one of the foremost figures in Australian theatre, film and television. His credits include *The Sullivans* and *GP*, which was inspired by the American series *ER*. Bisley fell out with Mel Gibson in the early nineties after Gibson accused the local actors' union of harming the film industry with its restrictions on foreign actors. Bisley now refuses to talk about Gibson.

Monroe Reimers also fell out with Gibson, supposedly over the treatment of a mutual friend by Gibson and Gibson's wife Robyn, who allegedly complained about her phone bill after the friend had looked after the Gibson farm in Victoria for them while they were away. Reimers was also reluctant to talk about his ex-flatmate at first. Does Reimers keep in touch with Gibson? 'He doesn't keep in touch with me. He obviously has got a whole bunch of lackeys now and is surrounded by sycophants . . . I think he was a lot sweeter at NIDA and a lot nicer. He's very cocksure and confident now.' But Reimers believes the cocksure image is just a front. 'It's always a front,' he says.

That is probably true. It was not just the prospect of goofing around that attracted Gibson to acting. 'My crutch is hiding in someone else's personality,' he once said. 'That's an excuse –

trying to be someone else – it's a whole different set of ground rules.' And on another occasion he said: 'When you have a mask on, you can do almost anything – pull down your pants in public, whatever, it doesn't matter.' Writing in the *National Times* of Australia in 1984, Kristin Williamson observed: 'He's honest, funny and very shy, unless he's acting. So he ACTS being interviewed.'

Contemporaries remember *Romeo and Juliet* for the remarkable coupling with Judy Davis, but the other play that many recall enthusiastically is Brendan Behan's *The Hostage*, which was staged before public audiences in Gibson's final year at NIDA. Bisley and Davis were top of the cast list, Gibson was bottom. 'He played the IRA guard,' says Whaley, who directed it. 'I don't think he had any words. He (the character) wasn't very intelligent. His job is to guard the hostage. And you couldn't take your eyes off him, because what Mel managed to do, in a role that wasn't spectacular, was extraordinary. And it was all totally appropriate. The decisions he made about the character and the physicalisation of the character, the decisions he made about how that character moved, how that character handled his rifle were hilarious but still absolutely correct, not just burlesque for the sake of burlesque.'

Gibson was well on his way to becoming a very fine, physically expressive actor by the time he left NIDA. 'When I auditioned for NIDA I'd had no training,' he says. 'But I learnt the short cuts at NIDA, how to transmit clearly to others – not just with words.' He was in the right place at the right time. But then so were many others. And it was Mel Gibson who became the international superstar, while the others were left behind. He put up money for a scholarship at NIDA but did not even respond to an invitation from St Leo's in 1996 to revisit the school he attended for five years. It is now co-educational and is no longer run by the Christian Brothers.

# 4

## MAX AND TIM

Mel Gibson was still at drama school when he secured the
lead role in his second film, though it hardly seemed any more
promising than *Summer City*. The budget for this second film
was higher, but not much. Cast and crew were still going to have
to sleep on mattresses on the floor, though this time it would
be in a private house. The film was going to cost well under
half a million dollars, at a time when the average Hollywood
film was costing more than ten times as much. And it was to
be an extremely ambitious action movie, full of spectacular car
chases. Many in Australia believed that even an experienced
director would be unable to pull it off, not that it had an
experienced director. It is as if the film had been organised
by someone dyslexic. They did not have a director in charge,
but a doctor, albeit one who was a great film fan and wanted
to be in movies. It looked like a recipe for disaster, but *Mad
Max* duly went into *The Guinness Book of Movie Facts and
Feats* for grossing more money, relative to cost, than any other
film in history.

It duly noted: 'The record budget/box office ratio was 1:285
in the case of the $350,000 Australian production *Mad Max*,
which grossed $100 million in its first two years of distribution.'
Mad Max became a cult hero for our times. Dr George Miller
fulfilled his dream and became a leading international film
director and producer. Gibson became a star, but he needed
to return to the role of Max to break the American market,
where the first film did less well than in other countries.
And Gibson needed Max's help on a third occasion to

boost his career after his first Hollywood films flopped at the box office.

George Miller studied medicine at the University of New South Wales, along with his twin brother John. They also made a short amateur film together. It was extremely short, it lasted only a minute. But it won a competition in 1971 for which the prize was a course at the Melbourne Film Workshop. It was there George Miller met Byron Kennedy, with whom he was to develop a partnership that lasted until Kennedy's death in a helicopter crash in 1983. *Violence In the Cinema Part 1*, a satire that ran to all of fourteen minutes, won two Australian Film Institute Awards and was shown at the Moscow Film Festival. Miller took up a residency at Sydney's St Vincent's Hospital, but spent his free time making short films and began developing an idea for something much bigger. The new wave of Australian films had been dominated by low-brow comedies and small-scale up-market dramas. But Miller wanted to take on Hollywood in the arena of mainstream action film, with goodies and baddies, car chases, crashes and explosions. He envisaged a feature film that would take elements of Westerns and Japanese samurai films and biker movies and relocate them in Australia in the near future, where a few young policemen are fighting a losing battle to maintain law and order.

Miller and Kennedy faced considerable scepticism, but came up with a scheme which would provide them with research opportunities and preliminary funding at the same time. Kennedy told the Australian publication *Cinema Papers*: 'George and I funded it by doing three months of very intensive emergency radio locum work: I drove the car while he did the doctoring. We got a lot of anecdotes and stories for the film by visiting road accident victims who had come through traumatic experiences. In that short period we were able to earn a fair bit of money too to enable us to finance the writing, the presentation and the development, which took about 14 months of intensive work.'

They got their meagre budget together from private sources and set about assembling cast and crew. Mel Gibson and NIDA classmates Steve Bisley and Judy Davis all tried out for the film. How Gibson was beaten up shortly before his screen test, and how his bruised and battered appearance helped him get the lead role and launch him on the path to stardom is one of the great stories of cinema. Back in 1979, when the film came out, Gibson discussed his audition with John Hanrahan of the Sydney *Sun* and recalled that Miller asked him to begin by telling a joke. 'I can't remember what I told him, but I had a really positive feeling when I left.' A few days later he heard he had the central role of Max Rockatansky.

It was only in later interviews Gibson started talking about having been beaten up so badly that his nose was broken and one eye was completely closed on the day of the casting session. 'It was at a party and three guys really worked me over,' he told one reporter. 'A couple of days later I went with a friend to a casting agent who was auditioning for *Mad Max*. I looked a mess. I had cuts, bandages, bruises . . . But the agent asked to take some pictures of me. They were looking for rough guys.' Great story. Years later, however, casting director Mitch Matthews disputed this rather juicier version and maintained there were no cuts, no bandages and no bruises.

The video test apparently no longer exists. The one man who can provide a definitive version of events is the man who had to sit down and assess Gibson's potential on the basis of that test – director George Miller. I asked him if he remembered the casting session and whether the legend was true or false. 'I remember it very well,' he tells me. 'When he came in he wasn't beaten up. How he got the role was he did an extraordinarily good screen text. And even though I'd virtually never been on a film set before I was able to recognise something exceptional in him as I watched him through the video camera. He just engaged me right at the beginning of that test. I didn't know much about him, except that he was at the national drama school, NIDA, and I think he was doing, at the time, *Romeo and Juliet* with Judy Davis. He just brought the video screen alive in this very crude little video test we were doing.

'He did show me a little later some photographs of his face after he did take a beating . . . He was completely unrecognisable in the photographs . . . But by the time I saw him it was all but healed . . . He wasn't beaten up . . . I wasn't looking for someone with a beaten-up face, I was looking for someone – even though I didn't know it, I couldn't articulate it, at the time – that really engaged me on the screen.' The legend diminishes Gibson's own inherent qualities. It was natural screen presence that won him the part, though Gibson subsequently impressed Miller with his dedication to the craft of acting.

Bisley landed the role of Max's partner Jim Goose but Judy Davis was considered too strong for the female roles. As in *Summer City*, Bisley was playing the more extrovert character and Gibson the quieter one, but this time the focus was on the quiet man.

Miller and Kennedy did not want any recognisable faces in the film; they could not afford recognisable faces anyway, for they were paying standard minimum fees. One exception was Roger Ward, a well-established Australian actor, whom Miller wanted as Max's boss, the police chief. Ward recalls the bespectacled young man turning up on his doorstep in a crumpled suit, with a script in his hand. Ward was immediately impressed by what he read, a story of cops and bikers waging war on the highways, but Miller wanted him to shave his head and to work for the same minimum wage as everyone else. Ward was keen to play the role, and even agreed to shave his head, but would not work for less than $1,000 a week. He remembers Miller scribbling down a series of figures on the back of the script and then proclaiming: 'I can do it!' Miller then added: 'I'll condense all of your work into the one week.'

These days Gibson's image as a major star precedes him wherever he goes and no one ever meets him without having formulated some preconceived idea of what he will be like. But in the late seventies many of those with whom he worked were surprised that this unassuming young man was so compelling on screen, and the flip side of the coin was that many were disappointed and even dismayed that the fledgling star seemed so ordinary in real life. After a disastrous interview at the outset of his career, the interviewer branded Gibson 'dreary and inarticulate'. Gibson says: 'There were some questions that I simply couldn't answer, so I was just sitting there open-mouthed and the interviewer was getting really snotty.' Unfortunately open-mouthed silence does not go over well on radio. Off screen, Gibson was neither intellectually nor even physically impressive.

Ward was surprised at the 'small, spindly youngster' Miller had hired as Mad Max. Ward recalls Gibson was very quiet and at the same time annoyingly confident. Gibson has said he was extremely nervous. 'He's a very shy sort of guy and hides his emotions, so he may have been nervous, but he certainly didn't show it.' Gibson subsequently won Ward's respect with the way he tackled the part, not even flinching when Ward stood on his toes during an important speech.

Actors had to pay their own way to Melbourne, where a large house served as both production headquarters and hostel accommodation. 'It was incredibly low-budget,' says Miller, 'to the extent that I would Gestetner and collate the pages with Byron Kennedy. And, not only that, I'd get on my motorbike and deliver it to people. Byron Kennedy and I were not only producers, director and writer, we were sort of runners as well.'

Gibson joined the production straight after finishing at NIDA. When he arrived at the house, the door was answered by a man swathed in bandages. He was stunt co-ordinator Grant Page. This was clearly not going to be an easy shoot, and more than once Miller's skills as a doctor would be required. Already Page had been involved in a motorbike accident, in which the actress who was to have played Max's wife was also badly injured, necessitating the late recruitment of Joanne Samuel as substitute. Miller had been impressed with her at the original auditions but her appearances in Australian soap operas, particularly *The Young Doctors*, counted against her in his quest for unknown faces.

There were not many lines for Gibson to learn. Max was clearly hewn out of the same rock as Clint Eastwood's Man With No Name in the *Dollar* Westerns and his later Dirty Harry character – the strong silent type. Ward's character Fifi Macaffee has the best line in the film when he says: 'People don't believe in heroes any more. Well, damn them, you and me, Max, we're going to give them back their heroes.' The emphasis was on the action and everyone worked very long hours in the countryside around Melbourne, tailoring carnage and mayhem to Miller's particular artistic vision, and working miracles on a minuscule budget. Ward says: 'At one stage there were so many actors sleeping on the floor that we had to do it in shifts. The motorcycle gang, who worked nights, slept in the day, while the cops, of whom I was a member, came back at dusk to crash in the beds that the others had just left.' The bikers scrawled messages on the walls threatening to kill the cops. Some of the bikers were genuine wild men, more or less playing themselves, and the actors playing the cops were never entirely sure whether they could treat the messages simply as a joke.

Joanne Samuel recalls it was 'a really radical set'. She says some of the actors who were playing 'bikies' adopted a Method approach to their parts, rode from Sydney to Melbourne in a pack and were living out their roles off camera. Gibson, on the other hand, she recalls as an easy-going, fun-loving young man, with a great sense of humour, though she did sense his nervousness in some of their scenes together. 'I always remember him being able to tell a great yarn, tell a story and have you hanging, listening to his story, and I think that came across in *Braveheart*.' Despite the cast's youth and inexperience and the tiny budget, Samuel felt *Mad Max* was special. 'I didn't know how financially successful it was going to be, but I knew it was different.'

'Ah, *Mad Max*. So many moons ago,' says Hugh Keays-Byrne, who played the Toecutter, leader of the biker gang. 'The wages were low, the commitment was high, much promise in all directions. Three to a room in Melbourne; hot bike rides on cold early mornings. It was dubbed in the USA without our permission. We took action to gain payment for video sales. I was billed for a back bike tyre worn out doing donuts in my own time, so it goes. Mel was, in those days, a quick sort of chap fresh onto the scene. Him and Bisley "the Goose" felt like movers, made me feel like an old theatrical. Me and the other bad guys, Tim Burns, David Bracks et al, had little to do with them, save leaving stage blood notes in their flat to set the pace for the work ahead.'

*Mad Max* opened in Australia to generally good reviews, though there was concern about the violence and moral tone of the film. Beverly Tivey of the Sydney *Sunday Telegraph* called it 'one of the finest achievements of the Australian film industry'. She felt the stunt work and special effects stood comparison with the best Hollywood could produce. Another review compared Gibson to a young Marlon Brando. In *The Bulletin*, Phillip Adams remarked on Miller's 'sheer brilliance' as a film-maker while lamenting the 'dangerous pornography of death'. In a rather sniffy review in Britain's *Monthly Film Bulletin*, Tim Pulleine complained about 'a gloatingly unambiguous endorsement of sadistic rough justice'. Max is a policeman and the film ends with him effectively executing one of the bikers, Johnny the Boy, by handcuffing his ankle to a crashed truck, starting a fire and suggesting the villain might just have time to saw through his ankle before the truck explodes. His behaviour may be explained, though not justified, by the bikers' murder of his baby son. Any moral justification must lie in the context of a society in which law and order has apparently broken down.

The fact that the film is set in a fictional future society is vital, not simply for the film's moral justification but for its entire concept. For Miller is dealing in myth, indeed creating myth and quite deliberately creating an icon and a post-modern hero in the character of Max Rockatansky. This is a world turned upside down. The skinhead and the slob at the beginning of the film are cops. They argue over who is going to drive before joining the high-speed pursuit of a psychopath called the Nightrider. Meanwhile Max takes his time putting on his leather jacket, his gun and his sunglasses. Miller treats him as if he were one of those mystery celebrities on *A Question of Sport*, where the panellists have to guess the identity of a person from a few teasing glimpses. Only after the Nightrider has ploughed his car into an overturned tanker do we see Max properly for the first time, tough, perhaps, in his black leather uniform, with its suggestion of bondage and S&M, but also very young, innocent, pretty, even angelic.

We cut to a picture of domestic bliss where Max relaxes with his wife and child. Meanwhile, in a scene that begins as a reworking of *The Wild One* and then echoes *High Noon* and *Once Upon a Time In the West*, the Nightrider's gang go to meet him at a station in a small town in the middle of nowhere. 'Nothing came in on the train except a couple of crates and a . . . coffin,' says the stationmaster. The gang roars along the highway with the Toecutter sitting in the back of a truck cradling the box. Johnny the Boy is arrested at the scene of a gang rape, but later released because no one will testify. Goose attacks him and the bikers subsequently ambush Goose and leave him for dead. This is a perversely complicated procedure: they sabotage his bike, and lie in wait for the recovery vehicle sent to pick him up.

Max and his family go on leave, and by chance bump into the bikers again. One of the most impressive aspects of the film is Miller's pacing, slowing the film down during a couple of the domestic scenes in order to crank up the tension, creating a mood of incipient menace in the woods with music and camerawork. The worst of the violence is suggested: the viewers do not see Goose on a life-support system, just Max's reaction; nor do they see Max's wife and child run down by the bikers, just a child's shoe flying through the air and a ball rolling slowly down the road in the wake of the disappearing bikers. The child, Sprog, is DOA, the wife has multiple traumas.

Max is not only a post-modern hero but also a hero in the great tradition of Byron, a hero motivated by loss. The film becomes a classic revenge Western, in which the hero tracks down the villains on a lawless frontier. A man's gotta do what a man's gotta do. And an audience has got to empathise. The film is not without a certain surreal black humour. Johnny the Boy pleads with Max that he is not bad, he just has a personality disorder. The moment is straight out of *West Side Story* when the hoodlums burst into song to explain their condition to Officer Krupke. No one sings here. Max shows no emotion as he drives away and an explosion rises behind him, signalling the completion of his task. The final shot is an open road, an uncertain future, ahead of him.

Miller was not entirely happy with the film, feeling that the financial constraints seriously compromised his intentions. However, the public loved it. 'When *Mad Max* had been out for a while I thought I'd better go along and see what it was like,' said Gibson. 'I sat in the middle of about eight hundred bikies . . . I must admit I didn't like what it seemed to do to the crowd. A lot of them seemed to take it a little too seriously. But

I suppose there'll always be those sort of people. I'm just glad a couple of those blokes didn't bother to look at who was sitting next to them.' Gibson has been ambivalent about the violence in the *Mad Max* films over the years. Later he described *Mad Max* as a comic-book story. 'Everyone is ready to laugh at it,' he said. He has contended that violence in the movies only inspires violence in those who are already sick.

He has also been slightly ambivalent about *Mad Max* itself. Comments in 1984 prompted the headline in Sydney's *Sunday Telegraph*: '*Mad Max* was just a load of rubbish, says Aussie star'. He did describe it as rubbish, but went on to elaborate: 'Basically we were working in that B-road film, schlock, trash genre.' He felt Max was 'a cardboard guy', which is not entirely true; ultimately he is a man with all feeling drained out of him. Gibson's face is a blank canvas in that final scene. He looks entirely comfortable in the role, never showing off or over-elaborating. Roger Ward remembers Gibson wanted to improvise and develop scenes. 'The director told him "No, I want you to read your lines as if you are reading the grocery list, with no emotion whatsoever." In his later films, particularly the *Lethal Weapon* films, he's over the top with his hand movements and his wacky wackiness. That's because he can do what he likes and the directors let him. But I don't like that. I think the directors should pull him back a bit.'

Though there are a few moments when Max's emotions do explode, and there is scope for Gibson's talent for mime when Max is shot in the leg near the end of the film, one of the major requirements for the success of the character is restraint. In the final sequence Gibson is required to rid himself of all sign of emotion. When he has done that, all that is left is charisma.

*Mad Max* was phenomenally successful not only in Australia but also in Europe and particularly in Japan, where it was one of the highest-grossing films of 1980. Gibson said: 'I think it has got more universal appeal than *Picnic At Hanging Rock*. Japanese just seem to like it. It's something they identify with because, I think, it is a tale of a traditional warrior.' Yoshio Sakai, editor of Japan's *Cinema* magazine, said at the time that it appealed to young men who would not normally go to the cinema. The Japanese of course have regularly embraced ultra-violent entertainments and yet have an extremely low crime rate. In another variation on a theme, Gibson said: 'There is something to be said for seeing violence on the screen. I enjoy it myself and I am a non-violent person. I think it is something of a release.'

In the *New York Times*, Tom Buckley wrote: '*Mad Max* is ugly and incoherent, and aimed, probably accurately, at the most uncritical of moviegoers.' The aim seemed less accurate in North America than elsewhere. The distributors objected to the Australian accents and Gibson, a native American, suffered the indignity of having his dialogue dubbed by someone else. The film did only modest business on its initial American release, though it subsequently acquired a cult following.

Such was the success of Roger Ward's character in the film that he was regularly asked to shave his head for other roles. Miller wanted him to appear in the second *Max* film as the masked villain Humungus, but they fell out over money and over Miller's insistence that although he did not want Ward to audition, Ward must prove his suitability for the role by telling Miller a joke. Ward told him: 'A joke! George, you came to my home and almost pleaded with me to play Feef. Now, two years down the track, you're asking me to beg. The character hardly grunts, for Christ's sake.'

Many years later Ward attended the Australian premiere of *Braveheart*, where there was an unexpected break in the screening – as was the case at the European premiere too. He nipped out to the toilets to be told by a bouncer on the door: 'You can't go in. Mr Gibson's in there.' Ward replied: 'So what? Is he so well hung he's using the entire God-damned urinal?' Ward, who is a considerably more formidable figure than the average bouncer, brushed past. 'During *Max 1* we not only shared the shit-house but the floor we slept on, the odd slut who happened to drop around, and star billing after the film was released.' Gibson seemed smaller than Ward remembered. 'But thankfully none of his humility was abandoned. He was the same 21-year-old kid to whom I had taught everything he knows.'

After NIDA and *Mad Max*, Mel Gibson and Judy Davis both accepted contracts to work for the South Australian

Theatre Company in Adelaide and Gibson appeared in four of their plays during 1978. It is a period he regards with mixed feelings. He went from playing *Mad Max* – which of course was still many months away from being unleashed on the public – to playing chorus in *Oedipus*. Gibson was by no means determined to pursue film stardom to the exclusion of stage work. He has often spoken of his love of the immediacy of theatre and readily accepted the need to serve his time learning the ropes. 'I was doing my apprenticeship as a spear-carrier for $150 a week . . . It was refreshing to take it easy for a while.'

But his friend, teacher and sometime director George Whaley says that privately Gibson disliked the company and thought he was getting very little out of the experience. Not only were his roles small, they were also boring and gave him little in the way of a challenge. 'It was one of those Australian theatre companies with lavish production values, lots of sets and lots of costumes,' says Whaley, 'but fairly conventional productions of the standard repertoire.' In Shakespeare's *Henry IV*, Gibson played Gadshill, Vernon, Mouldy *and* Mortimer.

On the positive side, Gibson met his future wife, nurse Robyn Moore, a dark-haired woman, attractive rather than beautiful, much the same age as Gibson. 'Robyn and I were actually sharing a house. It was just an arrangement, purely platonic. I had to have a place to live and it was cheap lodging at $15 a week. We didn't get married until 1980.' Robyn was to remain in the background, providing support, encouragement, stability and censure for her husband, never apparently overawed or even overimpressed by his rise to fame and fortune.

Gibson was rescued from bit parts in Adelaide by Michael Pate, a swarthy Australian actor who had had a successful career in Hollywood in the fifties and sixties, particularly in Westerns. He appeared in *Hondo* and *McLintock!* with John Wayne, Sam Peckinpah's *Major Dundee* and such television classics as *Gunsmoke*, *Rawhide*, *Maverick* and *The Virginian*. He was now back in his native country, had just produced the period drama *The Mango Tree*, and was about to produce and direct a film of Colleen McCullough's first novel, *Tim*, a portrait of a relationship between a middle-aged businesswoman and a slightly retarded young man she employs in her garden.

Pate wrote the script himself, secured backing from several organisations, including the Australian Film Commission and Kerry Packer, and recruited the American actress Julie Harris, who had played opposite James Dean in *East of Eden* twenty years earlier. His son Christopher Pate, who had played Jesus in the Australian stage production of *Godspell* and starred in *The Mango Tree*, was front runner for the title role. A few weeks before the filming was due to begin, Harris's own son fell ill and she dropped out, which in turn inhibited a final decision on the role of Tim.

Keeping his eye firmly on the American market, Pate recruited Piper Laurie, though she was younger than Harris, and, as an actress, more glamorous and less intellectual. Pate had met her when he first went to Hollywood. 'Piper Laurie was renowned at Universal in those days, in 1950, as the "Dandelion Girl",' he says. 'She used to be given dandelions to chew or hold in her teeth or whatever.' She appeared in a string of forgettable costume dramas before winning an Oscar nomination for *The Hustler* in 1962. More recently she had been Sissy Spacek's religiously fanatical mother in *Carrie*, playing against type. In her mid-forties she was still a very attractive woman and more than a decade later she was to play the role of the adulterous sawmill manager in David Lynch's cult serial *Twin Peaks*.

Her arrival prompted Pate to amend his script, making it less of a serious drama and more of a romantic fairytale. 'It was a sleeping princess that's woken up,' says Pate. The character of Tim was to be the catalyst. Pate decided to go back to square one in his search for a male lead, and it was his son Christopher who suggested a young actor he knew through NIDA circles called Mel Gibson. Pate saw the screen test Gibson had made for *Mad Max*. He does not remember Gibson being all cuts and bruises, only that he was not impressed. 'It was just like – sit there, stand there, say the words that we've given you on this page and thank you very much, that's very nice, we'll get back to you, don't ring us. It was a very ordinary and poor little test. You wouldn't cast anybody on it.'

Pate went to Adelaide to meet Gibson. And was still not impressed. 'We had a bit of a chat and he was extremely nervous. He smoked about a packet of Marlboro while we had a couple of cups of coffee and I thought, well, this is no good. I wanted to get him in another atmosphere, so I suggested that we drive up to the north of Adelaide for lunch . . . We went up in his car, in which there seemed to be a tremendous amount of underwear and clothing, as if he were sleeping in it at the time.' Pate told me that after a drink or two Gibson finally began to relax. 'He sort of went around saying hello to people and being a little bit of a clown, but he was so sweet and so nice and so lovely that I made up my mind right then that he would be wonderful in the part.' Pate, who had not even had the chance to see him on stage, had no difficulty in persuading the South Australian Theatre Company to release him.

Pat Evison, who plays Tim's mother, had preconceptions of Tim, based on McCullough's description of him as looking like a Greek god. 'When I first saw Mel I was a little disappointed because he's not tall, as I thought Tim needed to be . . . Mel was quite a shy person really I suppose, because he was a lot younger than the other people in the cast. Piper Laurie already had a world reputation and both Alwyn [Alwyn Kurts who plays Tim's father] and I were pretty well known in Australia by that stage . . . But on the other hand he was quite delightful and had a good sense of humour. At lunch and in conversation he would have quite a witty quip.'

Gibson admits he found the prospect of the film daunting. He had a lot more dialogue than in his previous films and the character was obviously much more challenging. Pate did not want a drooling moron but a slightly simple young man who had to be convincing not only in terms of the drama but also in terms of the unlikely romance that develops between the two principal characters. Gibson visited a centre for retarded people, studied them and talked to a specialist, but decided on a different approach. 'I felt Tim was a child-like behaviour thing I had to study, more than an abnormal pattern,' he says. 'I began to really study my little nephews, their normal speech patterns, how they reacted to statements. A small child takes everything literally.'

Pate says: 'One of the best ways of getting something out of Mel was explaining the scene to him and then letting him go. For instance, early on in the film, when he's crossing the street to come to the pub, I said, "Mel, there's A and B; I want you to go from A to B, right?" At the beginning of the film Gibson is dressed in singlet and short shorts, which make him look like an overgrown schoolboy. He bounces along the pavement, steps onto the road, swinging his arm, waves to a motorist and breaks into a loping run. Pate continues: 'And when he was going up the beach with her, I said to him, "Look, you're a little puppy dog wanting attention from her, and you're beginning to get some and you want more."' Gibson not only runs alongside Laurie, but playfully skips round her, as if he might snap at her heels at any moment. 'I didn't even want a second take,' says Pate.

At almost A$600,000, it was Gibson's most expensive film yet, but it was still very cheap by American standards. Gibson's novel approach to the role works – he has all the enthusiasm, insecurity and openness of a child, even if he is in danger of overdoing it just very occasionally. It is easier for the audience to empathise with a child than an idiot and the film succeeds as melodrama, romance and double-thickness weepie. It is very much a woman's picture, balancing the machismo of *Mad Max*. 'Mel was like a glass that you could completely see through,' says Pate. 'He was very transparent and I think that was one of the lovely things about his performance, that he kept that wonderful openness and naivety.'

Pate and Laurie manage to negotiate the pitfalls of taste and decency that surround her character's sexual awakening by a man who is young enough to be her son and who has all the sophistication of a child. Nevertheless the film has its shortcomings. The music is overblown, the editing clumsy at times and in a hospital scene where Tim's father tells Tim that his mother has 'gone', the audience might be tempted to wonder if the lighting cameraman has gone with her. Laurie delivers a fine performance, though the baggy shapeless gowns that her repressed Miss Horton is forced to wear not only desex the character but make her look like a glove puppet on the loose.

In Perth's *Sunday Times*, Leslie Anderson wrote: '*Tim*, which has not been received favourably by all critics, would have been an unmitigated disaster without Mel Gibson.' Not only did Gibson win the Australian Film Institute award for best actor, but Evison and Kurts won the awards for best supporting actress and actor.

Four years after making *Tim*, Gibson said: 'At the time, it wasn't obvious to me, but looking at it again recently I realised that things like the music were quite bad.' Gibson had previously praised Pate as 'an actor's director' and Pate, believing that he was dealing with a major new talent, wanted to draw up a contract for two more films but could not get his backers to commit to the plan.

Pate and Gibson did not keep in touch, though Pate contacted Gibson in 1995 about the possibility of Gibson's film production company Icon investing in a project Pate had developed. 'He got back to me twice on the phone and was very enthused about it . . . I was asked would I accept some notes from a consultant to do a rewrite and add some scenes, which I did . . .' But phone calls and fax messages and even a visit to America failed to elicit any further communication from Gibson, even to say he was not interested. After trying throughout virtually the whole of 1996, Pate gave up. He says: 'There would be no point in me commenting on Mel's lack of professional manners – they're well known in Australia and worldwide . . . There's probably a couple of dozen, three dozen, who knows, a hundred projects waiting for Mel to take a decision.'

After the completion of *Tim*, Gibson returned to the stage. His opportunities with the South Australian Theatre Company may have been limited and uninspiring, but 1979 presented him with starring roles in three plays representing three very different aspects of mainstream theatre. First he reprised his role of Romeo in Shakespeare's *Romeo and Juliet*; then he appeared in the light, folksy Australian comedy *On Our Selection*, Whaley's adaptation of the classic misadventures of the Rudd family; and finally he played Estragon in Beckett's *Waiting For Godot*, one of the greatest works of twentieth-century drama.

*Romeo and Juliet* was staged in Perth in February, before transferring to Sydney – and before the public had had a chance to assess either *Mad Max* or *Tim*. Director John Bell was looking for a lusty, energetic interpretation from a young cast. 'Romeo is a young guy who is just dying to be loved,' said Gibson. 'In fact he does die for it.' The production was so physical, with so much running and jumping and fencing, that the actors were picking up injuries like footballers in a derby game. Gibson dislocated his thumbs and nursed a leg injury that meant he had to put his entire weight on the other limb. Juliet was played by Angela Punch, who had recently won awards for her performances in the Australian films *Newsfront* and *The Chant of Jimmie Blacksmith*. But it was Gibson who came out best in the reviews for *Romeo and Juliet*.

The most remarkable review was that of Barry Lowe in the *Newcastle Morning Herald*. Under the headline 'A moribund version of Shakespeare's classic', he criticised the production as plodding and moribund, suggesting there were so many things wrong with it that he did not know where to begin. He complained about Mercutio's thick Scottish accent and considered Punch's Juliet lacklustre. He continues: 'This is particularly true when she is in juxtaposition to Mel Gibson's superlative performance as Romeo. If ever there was a star in the making this is it. Gibson has all the prerequsites for superstardom. His speaking voice is distinctive and his acting superb. His Romeo is a knock-out. His fiery spirit as the young lover who will not be separated from his true love, his impetuosity, his unthinking temper, his moonsick adolescent love, are all so convincing that he almost carries the show alone.' It is not only the sort of review that an actor might wish to carry around in his wallet, but, with all that has come to pass, the sort of review that Mr Lowe might like to carry around himself, introducing it in moments of self-congratulation at dinner parties and including it with any job application as evidence of remarkably sound judgement.

*On Our Selection* was a hugely popular comedy about a rural Australian family, first staged before the First World War, having been adapted from earlier stories. It toured regularly for two decades, there was a silent film and another version in 1932 was the highest-grossing film of its time in Australia, prompting several sequels. The original play was radically rewritten by Gibson's mentor from NIDA, George Whaley, and he directed it himself at Sydney's little Jane Street Theatre, with Gibson playing the boyfriend of the daughter of the family. It received excellent reviews. More than a decade later it was turned into a feature film by Whaley, with the support of Gibson's production company Icon, though Gibson declined the chance to appear in it. The film version had the rather cumbersome title *Dad and Dave: On Our Selection*, and although the cast included Leo McKern and Noah Taylor, it flopped at the Australian box office.

Gibson and Whaley went straight from *On Our Selection* into *Waiting For Godot*, Samuel Beckett's brilliant tragi-comedy, ostensibly the story or non-story of two tramps waiting for someone who never comes, but really a study of the human condition. Again Gibson and Whaley got excellent reviews. Michael le Moignan in the *National Times* wrote: 'Mel Gibson as Estragon gives the best performance I have seen from him, agile and expressive, punch-drunk from life's battles, but still standing, still breathing, and asking no more.'

Opposite Gibson in the role of Vladimir was an actor who was to remain virtually unknown outside Australia, while Gibson became a Hollywood superstar, until suddenly seventeen years later his performance as pianist David Helfgott in the film *Shine* brought Geoffrey Rush enormous international acclaim and a best actor Oscar. Gibson and Rush shared a spartan apartment while working together. 'We were both after the same girl at one point,' recalls Rush. 'And I got her. I still enjoy dining out on that one.' Rush had also appeared with Gibson in *On Our Selection* and reprised his role as Dave in the film version.

Gibson again exploited his capacity for physical theatre in *Waiting For Godot*. He had to stand on one leg, with the other outstretched for several minutes, and he commented that the part demanded more physical strength and discipline than anything else he had played. Liz Porter, who interviewed him for *Cleo* magazine, noted: 'His face in repose is absolutely ideal for serious dramatic acting roles. But when he talks and jokes he's all teeth, flashing eyes and eyebrows shooting up and down. Many of the comic expressions he used . . . are in fact his own, just exaggerated.' Porter also noted he was smoking a lot of cigarettes and had lengthy coughing fits which would leave him gasping and his eyes streaming. He was to make numerous attempts over the years to quit. The astute Mr Lowe suggested Gibson had the flair for the pathetic comedy of Bert Lahr and Buster Keaton.

*Waiting For Godot* and *Mad Max* both opened in Sydney in July 1979 and *Tim* premiered in Melbourne just a couple of weeks later. These were good times for Gibson. He had now proved he could act on screen and on stage, that he was an actor who could rise above mediocre productions and who, with the right material and the right support, would positively excel.

Later that year there was something of a *Mad Max* reunion when Gibson made another film with Steve Bisley, Hugh Keays-Byrne, Roger Ward and George Miller, though you will not find it listed on any official Gibson filmography. *The Chain Reaction* is a thriller about an accident at a nuclear power plant, written and directed by Ian Barry. Bisley was the lead, Miller was associate producer and directed chase scenes, while a bearded Gibson made only a fleeting appearance as a mechanic.

Of the four films Gibson had now made, three had been with Bisley. And in two out of the three Bisley was the principal star. Roger Ward maintains Mel Gibson and Steve Bisley were both exceptionally talented young actors, but that Gibson was the one whose talent was complemented by looks and charisma in a combination that would propel him to superstardom. Few remember *Summer City* and *The Chain Reaction*, while *Mad Max* has become cinema history.

# 5

# TWO WORLD WARS

Mel Gibson paid tribute to the fortitude and bravery of the Australian fighting man in two consecutive films dealing with the two world wars. One was an international co-production inspired by the daring exploits of Australia's elite special forces, with an imported Hollywood star in the lead role. The other was a strictly Australian affair about the common man going off to the slaughter of trench warfare. It was the latter, *Gallipoli*, that was to win Gibson a second Australian best actor award and international acclaim, while the earlier *Attack Force Z* is now all but forgotten, a good subject for a quiz question but unlikely to figure in any season of Gibson's work. It was one of his unhappiest shoots.

Long after the film had been completed, Gibson described it as 'a terrible film, a vulgar attempt at a war action movie, with Aussie WASPs shooting Chinese dressed up as Japanese. You do that kind of film because you're starving to death.' Gibson was not the superstar he is today, nor was he starving to death, however. In the two years since graduating from NIDA he had had a string of starring roles on stage and screen, the likes of which most actors only dream about. What is true is that *Attack Force Z* turned out very differently from the way Gibson might have thought it would under director Phil Noyce, one of the new wave of Australian film-makers. But it had been conceived with commercial considerations very much to the fore.

It was an Australian-Taiwanese co-production, designed to further the international ambitions of the resurgent Australian film industry and backed by the Australian Film Commission.

However, there was friction within the Australian contingent at the last-minute replacement of Noyce and at the star treatment given to American John Phillip Law who took top billing over Gibson and Sam Neill. There were also serious cultural difficulties. Not only had a kung fu sequence to be worked into the film for the Asian market, but many of the cast and crew could not speak English. But Gibson did get the chance to eat dog. 'It was delicious,' he recalled, 'tasted like rabbit.' That was about the only part of his time on the film that he enjoyed.

Z Special Force was an elite fighting unit that undertook operations behind enemy lines in the Pacific in the Second World War, the Australian equivalent of Britain's SAS. In 1943 a handful of Z men managed to canoe into Singapore harbour, blow up or incapacitate seven Japanese ships and make their escape. In another raid, all twenty-three Z men were either killed in action or executed. Australia was to provide the basis of the story and Taiwan would provide the locations. Both countries would provide actors. Z Special Force drew men from the Australian army and navy and from other Allied forces. The film-makers could hardly have been any more prescient in giving the two Australian parts to Mel Gibson and Sam Neill, the New Zealander who had just made *My Brilliant Career*, with Judy Davis, and went on to star in *Jurassic Park* and other big Hollywood movies.

Executive producer John McCallum first saw Gibson during the shooting of *Tim*, when McCallum lent his house to his old friend director Michael Pate to use as Piper Laurie's seaside retreat. McCallum reckoned Gibson had tremendous star potential. Nevertheless, Gibson and Neill had to surrender top billing in *Attack Force Z* to John Phillip Law who had played the title role in *The Red Baron* and appeared in numerous other films. He remains best known for his performance as the angel in *Barbarella* with Jane Fonda. He had recently completed another film for *Attack Force Z*'s Taiwanese backers and was considered a good investment for the Asian market. Although he was the star of *Attack Force Z* and almost twenty years older than Gibson, the audience was to be asked to believe Gibson was the senior officer, a captain in the Australian army to Law's lieutenant in the army of the Dutch East Indies.

The producers also showed an eye for talent when they hired Phil Noyce who had just made *Newsfront*, a portrait of newsreel film-makers which incorporated genuine newsreel footage, and who later directed *Patriot Games* and the film of *The Saint*. But it was to be an unhappy and abortive appointment. Noyce developed the script, he rehearsed the cast and then he was replaced by Tim Burstall, another Australian, who had more experience and a good commercial record, having directed the comedies *Stork* and *Alvin Purple*. 'Phil had a connection with the Z men because his father had been a Z man and Phil went up there and worked with a couple of writers and wanted to swing it in directions that Lee Robinson [the producer] and John McCallum didn't really want,' says Burstall. 'They felt he was taking it away from a straight adventure thing. Anyway, they fell out . . . I was then rung up at a certain point and asked would I take it over, starting shooting immediately.'

McCallum describes the production as 'fraught'. He found his Taiwanese partners very difficult, and his differences with Noyce came to a head over Noyce's refusal to accept the actor who had been contracted for a tiny role of a farmer near the beginning of the film. According to McCallum, it developed into a situation where either the actor or the director had to go, and although the actor had only one brief line of dialogue, McCallum was not prepared to sack him and thereby further alienate the Taiwanese, so he sacked Noyce and brought in Burstall.

Law was happy with the change, but Gibson and Neill felt their allegiance was to Noyce. Burstall says: 'Mel is a terrific actor and so is Sam, but there were a lot of problems . . . They were consulting their agents and so forth about whether they could pull out or not, so it wasn't pleasant.' Gibson and Neill both stayed, but the atmosphere was extremely strained and Gibson and Burstall had several rows on set. Gibson was particularly unhappy at the idea that his character, who is supposedly a crack commando, would get himself into a situation where his gun has jammed and he is virtually helpless, just so the Asian star Koo Chuan-Hsiung could show off his kung fu and save the day. Like most of the other Asians in the cast and crew, Koo did not speak English. 'A lot of the direction was done through the interpreter,' says Burstall.

Koo was a major star in Asia with his own entourage and an annoying tendency to underline his status by turning up late. Cast and crew were accommodated in different hotels, depending on their nationality and importance, and there was little sense of unity on the film. John Phillip Law told me Koo did attempt to break the ice in his own memorable way. 'He took us all together over to some club for dinner. And it turned out to be a big brothel . . . It was a big compliment to us all, Tim and the principals. It was a night out with the boys.'

But Law was never one of the boys as far as Gibson and Neill were concerned. 'John Phillip Law was at that stage a bigger name than either Sam or Mel,' says Burstall. 'I've forgotten what we were paying them, but it was something like a thousand a week and I think John Phillip Law was on about fifty for the picture or something of that order. I suppose there was some feeling about that. His conditions of course were different. He had cars picking him up and that sort of thing. So there was a bit of a feeling from the Australian cast.'

John Phillip Law was certainly a bigger star than Gibson in literal terms. At 6 foot 5 inches, Law was eight or nine inches taller and in their scenes together Law would often be crouching or kneeling. Law reckons his height has cost him film roles and envies Gibson and other shorter stars. 'A smaller man always seems bigger on film,' he says. 'They can be more expansive. I mean look at the Jimmy Cagneys and the Edward G. Robinsons and all these guys. They were all little guys. They could put their arm out and it wouldn't go out of frame. There's a tendency for small guys to be a little bolder anyway, and that I think is something that comes over on film.'

Gibson plays Captain Kelly, commander of a five-man squad who land in enemy territory under cover of darkness to fulfil a secret mission, the details of which are known only to Kelly. Their arrival was shot in Australia because the film-makers could not get the use of a submarine in Taiwan, but the picture is so black they could have filmed in Taiwan without a sub for all that you see of it. The cinematography is very dark throughout. The squad encounter early resistance and one of their number is shot in the leg. The Z men's ruthlessness is quickly established when Neill's character shoots dead the injured man. By chance they happen upon the local resistance leader (Koo) and a relationship develops between his daughter (Sylvia Chang) and Law's character, Lieutenant Veitch. His character is the only one whose background and motivation are fleshed out. Kelly supposedly comes from the landed gentry, but that does not come across either from the story or Gibson's characterisation.

The resistance leader helps Kelly and his men locate the wreckage of an aircraft and its VIP passenger, a Japanese war ministry representative who now wants to defect. Kelly's orders are to rescue him or make sure he is dead. His men want to kill him, but Kelly is determined they should get him out alive and there ensues a pitched battle which leaves Japanese and Chinese bodies strewn across the landscape two or three deep. For the most part the film seems like a deeply old-fashioned, mindless, even anachronistic *Boy's Own* war entertainment, and yet the final scenes are not so much ridiculous as surreal. It is after all an inherently absurd situation in which Z men and Chinese are dying to save one of their enemy's leaders, one of the men behind the war.

All the Z men, except Kelly, are killed. 'I think we made it,' he says when he and the Japanese defector reach the fishing boat that will take them to their submarine. He looks over at the other man and realises for the first time that he has been shot through the chest and he, too, is dead. Kelly looks away and then holds his head in despair. This is a potentially great scene, crying out for a close-up it never gets. The surrealism and pathos come as a surprise at the end of an otherwise routine war film. Gibson has very little in terms of character with which to work. It is not entirely clear whether he is giving a very impassive performance or simply cannot be bothered. Either way, he just about gets away with it.

Although shot at the end of 1979, *Attack Force Z* did not open in Australia until 1982, after *Gallipoli* and *Mad Max 2*. The Melbourne *Sun* called it 'a flat-footed attempt at an action-adventure movie' and gave it one star, though not all the critics thought it bad. When it was shown in Cannes the previous year, *Variety* said: 'As a good example of a well-paced, finely-acted film, it is not much short of super.' And when it was shown on television in 1984 the *Sydney Morning Herald* even compared it to *Gallipoli*. 'In many ways *Attack Force Z* is a WW2 version of *Gallipoli*,' wrote Geraldine Walsh. 'We love failures.' It is a curious film, certainly more interesting than Gibson made out. It may just be possible that the true source of his embarrassment was his behaviour during filming and the resultant performance.

*Attack Force Z* had been such a difficult and unpleasant shoot that McCallum cancelled plans for a second Taiwanese co-production, though he would have been happy to work with Gibson again. 'I phoned Bill [Gibson's agent Bill Shanahan] about a year later and said, "We've got another script for Mel; what's his starting price?" He said, "A million and a half US." So I put the phone down quickly.'

Between *Attack Force Z* and *Gallipoli*, Gibson returned to the stage in a play called *No Names . . . No Packdrill*, which was also set during the Second World War and opened in Sydney Opera House's drama theatre in April 1980. This time Gibson played an American deserter from Guadalcanal, where Gibson's own father had been wounded. Gibson's character, Rebel, is on the run in Australia and falls in love with a young widow. She and a criminal friend engineer Rebel's escape. Lucy Wagner said in *Theatre Australia*: 'The triteness of their drama is given depth only by the skill and sincerity of its players: Noni Hazlehurst, Mel Gibson and Brandon Bourke are all at the top of a new generation of Australian actors.' The production was directed by George Ogilvie, who would direct Gibson again in *Mad Max Beyond Thunderdome*. The play was later filmed as *Rebel* with Matt Dillon in Gibson's role.

Gibson's girlfriend, Robyn Moore, was pregnant and there was never any question of an abortion in the mind of the deeply religious young actor. 'It's inhuman because it destroys life,' he later said in an interview with *Cosmopolitan*. 'Who presumes to know where life starts? I'll tell you one thing – the foetus grows, its heart beats.' Gibson once told a German journalist that the notion of birth control was unnatural. 'You're not

meant to do that kind of stuff,' he said. 'It's weird.' Irked at
being lectured, she suggested he was the one who was weird.
'But I'm only weird now,' he insisted. 'I wouldn't have been so
weird in 1920.'

Gibson and Moore had now known each for a couple of
years. Gibson had concluded she was the sort of stable, sensible
girl he would like as his wife; and a stark contrast to women
in his own line of work, about whom he made his views clear
when he said: 'Some of them are nice but they can be difficult.
I think it's better to marry outside the profession.'

Gibson has old-fashioned views on women. Asked if he would
describe himself as a feminist, he once said: 'I think that word
feminist is bull. Feminist – it's a term invented by some woman
who got jilted.' On another occasion, before his big Hollywood
breakthrough, he said he liked living in Australia because, unlike
the United States, it was 'a nice, comfortable, male-dominated
society'. You can never be quite sure whether Gibson is serious.
He told one journalist that women were 'all right as long as you
keep them barefoot and pregnant'. Gibson says it was a joke,
though the journalist took him seriously and printed it. But as
the old saying goes, many a true word is spoken in jest.

Moore seems to have had no expectations that she was
marrying a future superstar. Gibson says: 'She didn't have
much faith in my acting but she thought as long as she could
work we'd be all right.' They married quietly, without press
coverage, on 7 June 1980 in Sydney. Their first child, Hannah,
was born in November, with Gibson disappointed to be unable
to attend, but nevertheless listening, in tears, at the other end of
a telephone. It must have cost a small fortune, for at the time
he was in Egypt, finishing his next film, *Gallipoli*.

It is difficult to represent the importance of the Gallipoli
campaign to the Australian consciousness in terms of American
or British equivalents. Battles such as Agincourt, Bannockburn
and Trafalgar might come to mind, but they are much more
distant in time. And they are commemorated by the English,
the Scots, the British as victories, whereas Gallipoli was one
of the biggest military disasters of all time, with more than
thirty thousand Allied soldiers killed in nine months, a quarter
of them from Australia and New Zealand. The anniversary

of the invasion of Turkey, on 25 April 1915, is still an important national holiday in Australia. It commemorates not a victory but a spirit of sacrifice and a sense of duty to something greater than the individual. The nature of that something – exactly what the men were fighting for – is a moot point.

Many Australians still make their own personal pilgrimage to the Gallipoli peninsula, and more specifically to the place now known as ANZAC Cove, after the men of the Australian and New Zealand Army Corps, whose graves stand in line after line of painful, silent witness. Director Peter Weir visited the battlefield after attending the London premiere of his film *Picnic At Hanging Rock*, which was proving such a critical and commercial success. 'I saw no one in two days of climbing up and down the slopes and wandering through the trenches, finding all sorts of scrap left by the army – buttons and bits of old leather, belts, bones of donkeys and unbroken fruit-salts bottles. I felt somehow I was really touching history . . . It totally altered my perception of Gallipoli.' These were not the buttons of nameless statistics in history books, but of real men like Weir himself. The big difference was that they would not be going home to Australia again.

He worked with playwright David Williamson on the script. But like many others before and since, they found it very difficult to turn history into a human story that would engage the audience. 'We put the legend to one side,' says Weir, 'and simply made up a story about two young men, really got to know them, where they came from, what happened to them along the way, spent more time getting to the battle and less time on the battlefield.' The central characters are Archy Hamilton and Frank Dunne who start the film not as soldiers but as a farm boy and a railway worker, and as sprinters. Archy runs for honour and love of running. Frank runs for money, though it is Archy who wins when they come up against each other at an athletics meeting in Western Australia. The country has been fired by news of the invasion of Turkey. The army is recruiting at the race meeting and the band plays 'It's a Long Way to Tipperary'. Archy, who has grown up on stories of Kipling and empire, is determined to enlist. Frank, who is of Irish descent and whose grandfather was killed by the British, is adamant he is not going.

The two principal actors were both involved long before production began. Gibson had been approached to play one of the leads at an early stage. He was excited by the subject matter and the prospect of working with Peter Weir – just as he had been excited by the prospect of working with Phil Noyce. Mark Lee's initial involvement took a very different form. Lee had been acting since he was a child but had no previous starring roles in major films. 'There was a photo shoot about a year before they got the money and I was involved in that, just as an extra,' says Lee. 'They just got a group of actors dressed up on some sandhills and took some photographs. They were doing a brochure to sell the idea of the film. And then the situation changed and they actually got the money through other sources anyway.'

Although modestly budgeted by Hollywood standards, at under $3 million, *Gallipoli* was the most expensive Australian film ever made. Weir got backing from two major Australian figures in the worlds of media and entertainment – record producer Robert Stigwood and newspaper publisher Rupert Murdoch, whose father had covered the Gallipoli campaign as a reporter. They formed R&R Films, announced ambitious plans and, after filming on *Gallipoli* concluded, signed Gibson up for further projects. Although R&R Films never fulfilled its plans, Murdoch got involved in a rather larger film company in 1985 when he took over 20th Century Fox.

Gibson was already cast as Frank when auditions were arranged for Archy. The part of Archy is just as important, and actually slightly bigger than that of Frank. The film opens and closes with shots of Archy. The film-makers needed a young actor who could hold his own against Gibson, who personally took a hand in assessment of candidates. Lee was blond, blue-eyed, youthful and seemed a good contrast, though his nervousness and inexperience were to become a source of some concern when filming began. Having worked with Roger Ward, Piper Laurie and John Phillip Law on previous films, Gibson found himself in the role of the more experienced, established star for the first time.

In a relationship that mirrored that of Frank and Archy,

Gibson and Lee were to become close personal friends during pre-production and production of the film. They hung out together and shared a series of intense personal experiences, including the births of their respective daughters, Gibson's while they were in Egypt, Lee's a few weeks earlier while they were shooting at Port Lincoln in South Australia. They experienced the birth of a new generation while making a film about the death of an earlier one. *Gallipoli* was the story of the death of a generation, though of course there had been survivors and indeed many veterans were still alive in 1980.

Gibson and Lee read extensively on the subject and together visited old men who could tell them exactly what Gallipoli was like, the physical conditions and the mental anguish of not knowing whether you would be alive at the end of the day. It was perhaps the Turkish commander Mustafa Kemal who summed up best what was expected from the men on both sides when he said: 'I don't order you to attack; I order you to die.' And yet many cheated death. Some lived, some died. It seemed so arbitrary.

'I think the major thing that came to the fore,' says Lee, 'was the fact that we realised that none of them were regular soldiers. They were basically men from the city or the country who just went. And what became very clear to us was they were pretty much like we were, nineteen or twenty years old, who knew nothing about it, just went because it was something different . . . We met quite a few, but there was one New Zealander who had not been back to New Zealand since the end of the war. And we asked him why he hadn't. And he just said, "Oh, you might say I was a bit of a lad," and refused to elaborate. He was kind of funny, very alert and much younger than his years. And when I saw the film there were elements of him there, in Mel's character.' Gibson says: 'All of them, when I asked if they'd do it again, said no. They said they wouldn't join again of their own free will to fight somebody else's war.'

There was tremendous anticipation around the film. It seemed to have everything to consolidate Australian cinema's growing reputation – Gibson, Weir, Stigwood, Murdoch, a healthy budget and a subject that still stirred tremendous national feeling. Most of the filming was done in South Australia,

initially in the Lake Torrens area where cast and crew slept
in caravans and halls and worked long hours in very hot and
dusty conditions. The location where Frank and Archy set off on
a trek across the desert was reportedly infested with funnel-web
spiders. 'They're the most vicious spiders in the world,' Gibson
has been quoted as saying. 'If they bite you, you're a goner.
Deadliest things around – big, black, hairy and very aggressive.'
Lee told me he never saw any funnel-web spiders and never
heard them mentioned.

As well as reading extensively about Gallipoli and speaking to
survivors, Gibson and Lee prepared for the other aspect of their
parts – as runners – by training with one of Australia's Olympic
coaches. Although Archy beats Frank in the film, there was never
any question about who would have won a race between Gibson
and Lee. 'I would have lost,' says Lee. 'Mel was actually very,
very good. He was a really fine runner.' Gibson had been a
keen sportsman at school.

The film is in three parts, Australia, Egypt and Turkey, and
the Australian episodes initially revolve as much around running
as war. Coincidentally, *Chariots of Fire*, another period film
about running, was being made at much the same time. After
the race meeting and the failure of Archy's first attempt to join
up because he is too young, Archy and Frank hop on a train,
which Frank says will take them to Perth. Instead they find
themselves stranded in the desert and set off on foot. Gibson
and Lee would get up at three in the morning to fly to remote,
virgin territory on which to film as day broke. In one of the film's
defining scenes, Frank and Archy meet a man with a camel in the
middle of nowhere. He has not heard about the war. 'How did
it start?' he asks. 'I don't know exactly, but it was the Germans'
fault,' says Archy, explaining that he is off to fight in Turkey.
'If we don't stop them there, they could end up here.' The old
man looks around and says: 'And they're welcome to it.'

Frank and Archy are given hospitality by an outback family
who one after another raise their glasses to the Light Horse
Regiment. The scene ends delightfully with Frank raising his
eyebrows in response, but he is beginning to waver and declares
there is no way he would join the infantry. He tells his father he
is not going to fight for the British Empire, just 'learn a trick or

two and come back an officer'. Archy joins the Light Horse, but Frank does end up in the infantry because he cannot ride. Neither could Gibson at the time. Tim McKenzie, who plays Barney, one of Frank's mates from the railroad, recalls Gibson was scared of horses. 'I remember during that scene, even though he was scared of the horse, quite literally scared of it off screen, when he walked up to the horse and started talking to it, saying to it "I'm your old Uncle Frank, tough but fair", he didn't show any visible fear at all.'

As troops embark at the docks, those on the quayside sing 'Australia will be there' and in Egypt the locals greet soldiers with the words 'Hello Australia'. A disagreement in a shop ends with the proclamation 'You're dealing with Australians'. The Egyptian interlude provides the opportunity for humour and not only expressions of national identity but inter-state rivalry. Frank and Archy are reunited in an exercise that ends with everyone pretending to be wounded so they will be carried off the field. The soldiers are pestered the whole time by locals trying to sell them everything from fake antiquities to oranges. 'We're dead, mate. Piss off,' says Frank. On the basis that Frank would be useful as a runner and the Light Horse are not taking their horses, Frank manages to get a transfer into Archy's regiment. Egypt was the last stop for the production and spirits were high, even though most of the cast and crew, including Gibson, were ill there.

Everyone was determined to battle on, do their bit and help each other out. It was perhaps a reflection of the spirit of Gallipoli and certainly a stark contrast to the atmosphere on *Attack Force Z*. 'I remember one early morning,' says Mark Lee, 'we were setting up to shoot on top of one of the pyramids, and there's your director, your producer, your main cameraman and your two main actors lugging gear up the side of a pyramid. That sort of typified the feeling on the film, that we were wanting to make it work.' He remembers another scene in which Frank and Archy race to one of the pyramids, bobbing around various obstacles, with Lee's character actually dipping between a camel's legs at one point. At the end the two actors spontaneously burst out laughing. Lee says it was entirely unplanned, but Weir kept it in the film. However uncomfortable the Egyptian shoot may have been for cast and crew, that moment seems to symbolise the adventure holiday that Egypt represented for the young men of 1915.

The mood changes dramatically as the film enters its final section, lurching from the colour and gaiety of a ball in Cairo to the dark sobriety of the men in their boats arriving in Turkey to the sound of Tomaso Albinoni's Adagio in G Minor for Strings and Organ, which creates a similar sombre mood to Oliver Stone's later use of Samuel Barber's Adagio for Strings in *Platoon*. Music is enormously important in *Gallipoli*. The troops' arrival in Turkey is also an excellent example of how to shoot an atmospheric night scene without losing your cast in the darkness, as happened in *Attack Force Z*.

The coast around the South Australian fishing town of Port Lincoln served as Gallipoli and local tuna fishermen were enlisted as extras. It was out of season, and Egyptian interiors were shot in empty tuna factory premises. The fishermen watched the rushes with cast and crew. They would bring beer, and evenings would often end with a party. It occurred to Gibson at the time that these were exactly the sort of men who would have been at Gallipoli sixty-five years earlier. The extras sat for hours in open boats on cold nights but never complained. 'I watched these guys who were tough on the exterior but soft underneath,' says Gibson. 'They were so much like the real guys . . . Every extra regarded his little role as very important, as the Anzacs regarded their roles, in a way.' One of the extras remarked to Gibson that the difference was that they had a warm bed to which to go home at the end of the night. Gibson would climb the cliff above the beach and would think about the film and the battle. 'I would sit up there, often by myself, sometimes with Mark, and look down on it . . . It was a work of art, that main set where we shot the landing and the stuff in the trenches. I had huge goose-pimples the day they did the master shot of the landing, those little boats going ashore, the Anzacs in the water . . . I had this feeling about what it would be like to have been there . . . Gallipoli was our Alamo.'

The Anzac troops, of which Frank and Archy were a part, were to be used for a diversionary charge on Turkish lines while another wave of British soldiers landed far to the north at Suvla Bay. The Anzac charge was to be preceded by an artillery barrage on the Turkish positions. Watches are not properly synchronised and the barrage seems to finish seven minutes early. The Australians stay put, while the Turks resume their positions. When the Australians do go over the top they are mown down and pile up around the trenches. A colonel called Robinson orders another attack. On close examination of the film it is clear he is meant to be Australian and not British as has been suggested elsewhere.

Frank is sent to speak to a more senior officer in an attempt to overrule the order, while his colleagues prepare for the possibility of staging a further attack, knowing it is pointless. With quiet dignity, they prepare to die. Frank dashes back towards his position with instructions that the attack is postponed, but in the meantime Colonel Robinson insists they go again. Final letters are written, cigarettes smoked, prayers said. Soldiers embrace and say goodbye to each other. Archy should have been the runner for the day but persuaded his officer to use Frank instead. He digs his bayonet into the trench wall and hangs from it his watch and his running medal. He repeats the mantra that began the film, urging himself to run like a leopard.

The officer does not talk of democracy, nationhood or freedom, he simply tells his men to remember who they are – men from Western Australia. While running through the network of trenches towards them, Frank hears the whistle blow to signal the attack and realises he is too late. Archy dashes as fast as he can towards the enemy lines, bodies falling all around. The frame freezes when a bullet at last halts his progress. And the awful truth dawns. He had not even taken his rifle.

The film was well received in Australia and America, though there were a few reservations in Britain. John Pym in *Monthly Film Bulletin* wrote: 'Weir states the case for innocence, but leaves matters there; his film strenuously avoids argument in favour of the creation of mood.' There was some concern in Australia that, despite the title, less than half of the film took place in Gallipoli and there was little explanation of the aims of the campaign, which was devised by Winston Churchill, initially

as a naval action, to knock Turkey out of the war and open the
sea route to Russia.

Military historian Kenneth T. Jackson later wrote: 'In the
main, *Gallipoli* stays faithful to the historic record, but there
are some glaring omissions . . . The film fails to explain the
purpose of the attack . . . Nor does the viewer learn that the
entire invasion force was withdrawn in December 1915, its
mission a total failure. The film, however, does accurately
depict the competition to enlist, the camaraderie in the ranks,
and the soldiers' quiet courage in the face of death. It is superb
in conveying the tragic futility of the Great War and thus ranks
with *All Quiet On the Western Front* and *Paths of Glory* as
one of the greatest anti-war movies of all time.'

Gibson says: 'Some people obviously want to see the whole
campaign. They are interested in something closer to documentary style, which *Gallipoli* isn't. *Gallipoli* is about the First Great
War, which changed the world and people's ways of thinking
for ever. It was the death of innocence.' Gibson sees his own
character as the more complex of the two, the survivor, 'the
person you see around today'. While most people refuse to
mourn the passing of a world order in which thousands
went unquestioningly to their deaths for something they did
not understand, Gibson seems strangely ambivalent. He views
Archy and his generation romantically, as the last of the knights
in shining armour, 'uncomplicated and pure'. He says: 'People
today are too complex.' *Gallipoli* was the first film about which
Gibson was unreservedly enthusiastic.

The politics of and reasons for the First World War and the
aims of the Gallipoli campaign are largely irrelevant to Weir's
film, which is about the ordinary man in warfare in 1915. The
vision has to be that of 1915 man, not 1980 man. For Archy
the war has nothing to do with the death of some archduke
in Bosnia or the class struggle; his country is at war and it is
someone else's fault, uncomplicated and pure. Frank ultimately
goes to war because his mates all go to war. *Gallipoli* is perhaps
more a portrait of men going to war than a story; slow, moody
and actually quite small-scale in terms of its ambitions. It is the
portrait of two ordinary men.

Both Gibson and Lee were nominated for best actor in the

Australian film awards. Gibson won. Lee subsequently appeared mainly in Australian television and theatre and has seen very little of his former co-star. 'It's now worlds apart,' he says. 'It's the malady of the industry – you develop very strong friendships but for brief periods of time.' He paints a familiar picture of a co-star who was witty with his fellow workers and shy and awkward with the press. But Lee noted another quality – Gibson's determination to exert complete control over his performance – 'He moves it like a machine' – and understand how it fitted into the bigger picture. 'I was always kind of just feeling my way, and still am. But he had that sort of drive.'

Co-star Tim McKenzie says Gibson was always bright and cheery, with none of the tantrums associated with stardom or the intensity of Method acting, though he adds that Gibson remained very focused on his character between takes, 'thinking about it or concentrating'. He also noted at the time that as filming progressed Gibson seemed to grow in confidence. McKenzie was only twenty when he made *Gallipoli*. He still acts occasionally but he has a 'day job' too, and not the traditional one of waiting tables. He is a barrister in Sydney. As day jobs go, it is one of the better ones.

*Gallipoli* did reasonably well in the United States, but in retrospect the producers felt they should have changed the title because, while the name Gallipoli carried enormous emotional charge in Australia, it meant little to Americans, with their notorious ignorance of geography and world history. In Britain the film was sold on video with the marketing line 'From a place you may never have heard of . . . a story you'll never forget.' Which is outrageous. William Sorlie was a lance corporal in the Royal Scots. He was twenty-two when he was killed at Gallipoli on 28 June 1915. He was my grandmother's brother. Families throughout Britain as well as Australia have their own William Sorlies. The vast majority of Allied casualties were British. Of a thousand men from the Lancashire town of Bury who landed in Gallipoli in April 1915, only forty-three remained on active service at the end of the war. What Mel Gibson and Mark Lee did was to suggest faces for names in family histories; lend life, however brief, to men in uniforms in sepia photographs from long ago.

# 6

# LIVING DANGEROUSLY

*Mad Max 2* completed the job the original *Mad Max* had begun. A budget ten times that of the first film enabled director George Miller to stage stunts and sequences that were previously beyond his resources and create a much more stylised, more obviously futuristic action film. Both the film and the international marketing were carefully planned. It opened neither in Australia nor the United States, but in Japan, where *Mad Max* had been such a phenomenon and the sequel seemed certain to get off to a good start. Miller and Warner Brothers, who were backing *Mad Max 2* from the outset, had high hopes that it would break the all-important American market. It was decided not to call it *Mad Max 2* in the United States because the original had been less successful there than elsewhere and it seemed a tricky proposition to sell a sequel to a film that most people had never heard of. So it was *The Road Warrior* that finally acquainted most Americans with Mad Max and with Mel Gibson.

Gibson was shocked at the adulation and hysteria during a lengthy promotional visit to Japan. He claimed his hand was swollen from signing autographs and that fans woke him up at night. 'I let this one girl in,' he said. 'I thought she was room service, and she was really emotional, couldn't speak a word of English, but she was weeping and wailing and shaking and touching me the whole time.' New York seemed like a return to normality. He was walking along the street when he heard a voice shout to him, 'Hey, Mel, how ya doin'?' He turned, saw it was a construction worker and wondered momentarily where they had met. And then he realised they had never met, and that the man 'knew' him from the cinema screen. Nothing would ever be the same again. Gibson had achieved worldwide stardom and in the process had lost the right to walk down a street as an anonymous individual.

*Mad Max 2* completed the job of turning Gibson into a major star and of turning Max into an icon. It opens with a dark, solitary figure, standing slightly awkwardly, silhouetted against a purple and orange sky. An elderly, hesitant voice speaks. 'My life fades,' it says. 'The vision dims. All that remains are memories. I remember a time of chaos, ruined dreams, this wasted land.' It pauses. 'But most of all I remember the road warrior, the man we called Max.' Miller skilfully intercuts news footage of violence, war, riots and disorder with black and white excerpts from *Mad Max*. The narrator speaks in the terminology of myth about 'two mighty warrior tribes' and a war that engulfed the planet, and he recalls that in the roar of an engine Max lost everything and became a shell of a man, haunted by his past. At the end of *Max 1*, it seemed Mrs Max might survive being run down by bikers. The beginning of *Max 2* makes it clear that she did not.

*Max 2* was made three years after the first one but it is unclear how long has elapsed in terms of Max's story. Certainly the A$4 million budget enabled Miller to create a world for him that bore much less resemblance to the world in which his public lived. In the first film characters still had jobs and trains ran, vehicles were flashy rather than futuristic, the bikers seemed little different from the bikers in *The Wild One* and the locations were just a short drive from the film's Melbourne base. In the sequel, Miller gave the villains shaved heads and Mohawk hairstyles, black leather gladiator costumes and an array of weird custom-built cars that seemed influenced both by science fiction and the chariots of ancient times. In contrast he dressed the good guys in white, with the exception of Max who was also in black. This time Miller could afford to choose exactly where he wanted to shoot and opted for the area around Broken Hill, in the Far West region of New South Wales, the state's empty quarter, the outback. The locations lend the film a barren, post-apocalyptic ambience; an atmosphere of life on the edge of existence.

Broken Hill is the one sizeable community in a vast expanse of nothingness. It was founded in the late nineteenth century after the discovery of silver. Irish, German, Italian and Maltese immigrants poured into the area, hundreds of miners died in the dangerous conditions and the town became the scene of violent labour disputes. Broken Hill is still the richest silver, lead and zinc deposit in the world and it remains a hard-drinking industrial town, despite the development of a significant artistic community, attracted by the proximity of nature at its most basic.

'There were some very tough lads there,' says Gibson, 'but we got along very well. I used to have a pair of pinkish bedroom slippers and I wore them everywhere. They thought it was a great joke, Mad Max wearing pink bedroom slippers. One night I went into the local pub and one of the boys showed me that on the roof of the pub he had written "Mad Max drives a Mini and wears pink bedroom slippers". Well, I got on his shoulders and crossed out the word "pink" and wrote in "red". That could have been a situation that got out of hand, but it turned out to be good fun.' This easy-going, jokey relationship with tough locals stands in marked contrast to Gibson's experience on the third *Mad Max* film. While Max drives what looks like a variation on the Batmobile, Gibson did indeed drive a Mini, though it belonged to his wife; his own car was an old Ford. It is difficult to appreciate just how quickly life changed for Gibson after *Mad Max 2*.

He had reservations about making the second *Mad Max* film. He worried about the violence and he admitted his character was limited, which prompted one Australian journalist to ask him if he did it only for the money. He had actually managed to get himself an unprecedented percentage deal, which tied his pay to the film's performance. Gibson said: 'The money was of course a consideration. I've just bought a six-bedroom house in Sydney and have to be able to pay for it. But the money wasn't the major consideration. I knew I would enjoy making the film.' He had concluded in his own mind that the violence was merely 'fun and games'. 'The fantasy is the thing that saves it,' he said. 'When you look at it in that light, the harshness of the violence isn't there.'

Gibson and Miller both preferred *Mad Max 2* to its pre-decessor and Gibson found it interesting to contrast Miller's approach to that of Peter Weir, director of *Gallipoli* and his next film *The Year of Living Dangerously*, who he feels is a more instinctive director. 'There's an exactness about George,' he says. 'For each character he's got a different coloured line: blue for Max, green for Pappagallo . . . and these lines reflect the characters' highs and lows, what they're doing, where they are going during different parts of the script.' Gibson said Miller approached his work like a mathematician, and indeed Miller, who had given himself just two out of ten for *Mad Max*, awarded himself six for *Mad Max 2*.

Gibson also called Miller 'a formula man' and there are several formulae and equations within *Mad Max 2*. Max himself is introduced as the icon. He travels alone, but for a dog. It is a violent world, in which petrol is like gold. At the scene of a crashed tanker, he clashes with a couple of tough, homosexual, punk bikers, part of a vicious gang who will reappear shortly. Max subsequently gets involved in a confrontation with the owner of a gyrocopter. The Gyro Captain (Bruce Spence) is not so much a villain as a comic balance to Max's solemnity, the other side of the human equation, comedy to tragedy. Max is the strong, silent type – Gibson reckoned he had only fourteen lines in the whole film. The Gyro Captain may be a wily, potentially dangerous individual but, superficially at least, he is also a figure of fun – in longjohns, an overcoat and a ridiculous cap, forever rabbiting on about his memories of lingerie or some other inconsequential nonsense. Max's personality is grounded in his V8 Interceptor, while the Gyro Captain's flits around in his gyrocopter.

The Gyro Captain leads Max to a small refinery which is besieged by the gang to which the bikers belong. The basic plot device of the peaceful community, the thugs who terrorise it and the taciturn mysterious stranger who wanders into the conflict has been used, with variations, in dozens of films, particularly Westerns, including *Shane* and *Pale Rider*. Max is prepared to help Pappagallo's little community, not because he feels it is the right thing to do but because they impound his vehicle. Max's roots as a hero, supposedly motivated only by self-interest, can be traced back through the Man With No Name to Rick in *Casablanca*. But Max cannot remain untouched by Pappagallo's community, which includes a boy, seemingly an orphan, who has grown up wild. Max of course had lost his baby as well as his wife. When it comes to the crunch, like Rick in *Casablanca*, Max is prepared to risk his own life for the greater good. It is ultimately revealed that the narrator is the boy as an old man, and that Max was left behind in the wasteland when they moved on.

*Mad Max 2* was a major international box-office hit and was well received by the critics, most of whom agreed it was better than *Mad Max*. Gibson's own characterisation seems tougher, deeper. Vincent Canby of the *New York Times* said: 'Mr Gibson recalls the young Steve McQueen. It has something to do with his looks . . . and also with the kind of cool, infinitely pragmatic manner with which he deals with his existential situation . . . I can't define "star quality", but whatever it is Mr Gibson has it.' There is no doubt it is a much slicker film than *Mad Max*, but the first film's rawness was part of its appeal, along with the freshness of the concept of a futuristic Australian action movie. The stunts and final chase sequence are exceptionally well handled but chase sequences, no matter how well they are done, are one of the most overrated elements of the action film, and the intricacy of some of the action in *Mad Max 2* clutters, and perhaps paradoxically slows down, a simple story, which is essentially The Good, The Bad and The Road Warrior. But for audiences around the globe, it worked. And no one seemed bothered by the fact that, in a world where people kill for petrol, the villains never seem to run short for their vast fleet of vehicles.

Gibson was surprised by the scale and speed of his success. He said he was maintaining a normal lifestyle in case it all suddenly collapsed again. Robyn Gibson was obviously not overwhelmed by her husband's celebrity nor inclined to incur unnecessary expenditure. For her husband's twenty-sixth birthday she gave him an electric sander and he set to work on his next project, turning the former boarding house they had bought in the Sydney seaside area of Coogee into a family home. By the time of *Mad Max 2*'s release, Robyn Gibson was pregnant again with twins.

Gibson's film income enabled him to return to the stage without any immediate financial worries. He appeared in a series of short plays before audiences of 120 in Sydney for less than $200 a week. 'I was desperate to get back on stage,' he said in *Theatre Australia* magazine in December 1981, the month *Mad Max 2* opened. 'It's very important for me to keep up stage technique.' Among the plays he did around this time was one about sexual fantasies called *Porn No Rape Trigger*, a curious choice for a man who would shortly be complaining about sex scenes in movies.

*Mad Max 2* was not the only new Mel Gibson project on Australian screens in December 1981. Gibson was also starring in *Punishment*, the culmination of a short and inglorious television career. Just as his healthy bank balance enabled him to indulge his love of theatre, it also enabled him to turn his back on TV. One of his first professional acting experiences had been as a naval officer on the soap opera *The Sullivans*. 'It was a shocking experience,' said Gibson, 'terrible scripts, no rehearsals, just knock it over in a day. I did two weeks' work and I was on screen every night for three weeks. I played a naval officer – I inspected navels.' He also appeared in several other series – *Cop Shop*, *The Oracle*, *Tickled Pink* and *The Hero* – before graduating to guest star in *Punishment*. A series set in a prison, Gibson co-starred with Mike Preston, who played Pappagallo in *Mad Max 2*. Gibson complained to *Theatre Australia* that miserable scripts, directors who did not give a damn and lack of time to develop characters were normal in Australian television. 'So I think why push shit up a hill?'

He also dismissed suggestions of a third *Mad Max* film. 'I think George Miller will call it quits. He's got other interesting projects. And I don't think I want to do another one either. There's always a danger of being typecast. Maybe in four years' time I'll feel different. Maybe I won't be able to pay the rent.'

Early in 1982 Mel Gibson reunited with Peter Weir, director of *Gallipoli*, to make *The Year of Living Dangerously*, an adventure romance, adapted from a novel by C. J. Koch by Weir, Koch and *Gallipoli*'s scriptwriter David Williamson. With a budget of A$6 million, it continued Gibson's progress on to bigger and bigger films. Although it was an Australian production, the money came from America, courtesy of MGM. It had a largely American cast, including Sigourney Weaver, star of *Alien*, and exotic Asian locations. The story takes place against a background of violent political unrest in Indonesia in 1965. Gibson plays an Australian journalist and Weaver a British diplomat with whom he becomes romantically involved. The mixture of romance, adventure and a volatile foreign setting bore some resemblance to *Casablanca*.

The Indonesian dictator Achmad Sukarno had alienated the West and built up relations with China. He predicted 1965 would be a 'year of living dangerously'. He was right. Tens of thousands of Indonesians were killed after the failure of an attempted coup. Despite the scale of the violence, this episode was, by 1982, more obscure to Westerners than *Gallipoli*. Nevertheless the maelstrom of Islam, communism and military force that lay behind it remained extremely potent in south-east Asia. Weir opted to shoot in the comparatively friendly setting of the Philippines under President Marcos. But it was to prove a time of living dangerously for everyone involved with the film. Gibson ended up living out his role in the film – risking his life every minute he remained in the country and finally making a dash for the airport to get out before it was too late.

He plays Guy Hamilton, a radio journalist with the Australian Broadcasting Service, in Jakarta on his first foreign assignment. He encounters cynicism from other Western correspondents, but is befriended by Billy Kwan, a tiny Chinese-Australian photographer and cameraman who, although the character is male, was played by actress Linda Hunt. Kwan introduces him to Jill Bryant (Weaver) and encourages their relationship, though Kwan himself is also in love with her. Bryant has advance intelligence of a possible communist takeover and advises Hamilton to leave, but he betrays her confidence and uses the information for a story. Kwan is killed in a protest against Sukarno, whom he had previously admired, but Bryant and Hamilton are ultimately reunited and escape.

Relations between the three central characters mirror the complex intrigues and balances on the Indonesian political scene. Sukarno had ruled Indonesia since independence in the forties and had cemented an alliance with the military and the communists in the fifties in the face of covert CIA support for insurrection and continued Dutch and British political involvement in the region. He survived an attempted coup on 30 September 1965, for which the communists were blamed and which was ruthlessly put down by the army. The Communist Party had been extremely powerful with several million members, many of whom were now summarily executed, as were many Chinese nationals and Indonesians who were simply caught up in the lust for blood. Estimates of the number dead range from eighty thousand to a million. There has been continued debate over the truth behind the attempted coup, whether it genuinely was a communist plot or whether it was engineered by the military, possibly with CIA help, to provide an excuse to kill communists and eventually ease Sukarno from power. The ascendant forces were now the military and the Muslims.

That was the background against which the film was set, but cast and crew did not expect to find elements of their historical drama staring them in the face as soon as they stepped off the plane in the Philippines. Even the Americans who are used to seeing police with guns were shocked at the weaponry all around them. Ayatollah Khomeini had taken power in Iran three years earlier and Islamic fundamentalism was increasing throughout Asia. Actors found armed guards on every floor of their hotel and were assigned personal bodyguards. In the villages the film-makers experienced suspicion, fear and open hostility. But it went beyond that. 'Soon we began getting bomb threats and mysterious messages from people calling themselves Islamic patriots,' says Gibson. 'Either they were really extremists who felt that if we weren't allowed to film in Jakarta there must have been a good reason, or they might just have been cranks. Who knows?'

MGM was obviously worried, the White House was alerted and the CIA became involved, along with local security forces. Producer Jim McElroy felt that they should not take the threats too seriously, but they were clearly upsetting the cast and crew, although Gibson seemed laid back about it. 'I wasn't really frightened,' he says. 'They gave us too many warnings to ring true. Still, I was glad to get out. We were only making a movie

and it wasn't worth croaking over.' Despite all the effort that
had gone into finding and setting up locations in the Philippines,
Peter Weir decided to pack up and resume shooting a few days
later in Australia.

'I got a phone call,' says Gibson. 'It was about an hour
before we left actually. They asked if I was in the room. I said,
"Who's this?" They started asking me if I was brave. I said,
"Whatcha want to know that for?" The phone was snatched
off me by the bodyguard who started yabbering down the line
in Tagalog, which is the native tongue . . . So two weeks before
we were scheduled to wrap, we just packed our bags and took
off. We missed the plane too, unlike the hero I play, and had
to spend the night in an incredibly sleazy airport hotel with a
noisy casino occupying the top three floors. Ironically, much
of the footage we shot later in Sydney looked more authentic
than the Philippine locations.'

There were other more mundane problems for Gibson too.
Weaver is several inches taller than Gibson and could not be
expected to crouch down in their scenes together, as John Phillip
Law had done on *Attack Force Z*. Gibson had to wear special
platform shoes, like Elton John in *Tommy*. Weaver is basically a
Method actress and Gibson admits it took him a while to adjust
to her style of working. Weir had planned a steamy sex scene.
Weaver was happy to do it, but Gibson had qualms and it was
dropped. 'You don't need all that graphic stuff in a love affair,'
says Gibson. 'It's all a romance. If you have hot breathing and
that kind of thing it doesn't work.'

Guy Hamilton was probably Gibson's most challenging role
to date. He was a much more realistic character than Max, but
did not offer the scope that the slightly retarded Tim had done.
Hamilton was an ordinary guy, caught up in events which are
much bigger than himself, the significance of which he does
not really see. 'It is not one of those films which assaults the
senses, like *Mad Max* or *Star Wars*,' says Gibson. 'It actually
asks you to think a little bit. And to help you along, as an aid
or a crutch to this process, you had Guy Hamilton who, like
a member of the audience, keeps asking: "What's going on
around here? What's with this dwarf? Things are happening
to me, but what?" . . . He seldom initiates anything.'

Although Hamilton comes from Australia, his father was an American who died when he was a boy, increasing his sense of dislocation in the world at large. 'He is like a person taking a journey – things happen to him. He's involved but he's got that trait that cuts it off, very surface. That's his weak point, incapable of love, I think, which I can understand. I was like that for years until all of a sudden I snapped out of it – that's what made me get married.' Gibson did not find it easy to develop his character and deliberately held back on his performance, an approach that works well, brings out the incomprehension of the character and lets Gibson's own natural screen presence work for him.

Gibson, one of his own toughest critics, reckoned the film fulfilled expectations. 'But I wouldn't have said that until I saw it a couple of times,' he said. 'You can miss a lot on the first viewing.' Reviews were mixed, though Nick Roddick raved about it in Britain's *Monthly Film Bulletin*. 'It is Weir's most accomplished film to date,' he wrote, 'very much in the grand manner . . . The whole enterprise has something of the feel of a classic mid-period Hawks.'

Weir cleverly intertwines themes and ideas in *The Year of Living Dangerously*, themes of friendship and betrayal; belonging; seeing and not seeing – ultimately symbolised by the injury to Hamilton's eye. The confusions and uncertainties are embodied in the strange, unnerving character of Billy Kwan. The viewer, like Hamilton, is unsure, at least at first, whether to take Kwan's friendship at face value or whether there is some hidden motivation, perhaps political or sexual. This feeling of unease is intensified by the fact that Kwan is played by a woman, though viewers could easily watch the film and not realise that. Nor can the viewer be certain whether the main villain is Sukarno or imperialism or fate. Nothing is ever that straightforward in Weir's movies. He showed the terrible waste of life in *Gallipoli*, but he also celebrated the naive idealism of many of the men, caught up, like Guy Hamilton, in historic events they did not understand. In the earlier film, Archy Hamilton and Frank Dunne served to personalise the bigger picture. Although, in *The Year of Living Dangerously*, Guy Hamilton, Bryant and Kwan mirror relations between the political forces, it is difficult for the viewer to regard them as embodying the bigger picture in quite the same way; for the simple reason that they are white, they are representatives of the West. *The Year of Living Dangerously* works as romantic adventure and character drama, and does give some insight into the Indonesian political situation, but at the end of the film the viewer is much more interested in the fate of Guy Hamilton than that of his communist driver Kumar or indeed the country and people of Indonesia as a whole.

It did only modest business at the international box office, though Hunt won the Oscar for best supporting actress for her performance as Billy Kwan. Gibson was branded a new sex symbol. Sigourney Weaver led the way by saying he was the most gorgeous man she had ever seen and others were quick to agree. But as often as American reviewers commented on his sex appeal, interviewers would remark upon his continued awkwardness in person. 'Gibson squirms . . . his answers are laconic,' wrote one. 'A fidgety, hesitant young man who is not particularly articulate,' said another.

At this stage in his career Gibson still maintained he wanted to alternate cinema and theatre and he had already committed himself to play Biff in Arthur Miller's *Death of a Salesman* on the Sydney stage before beginning *The Year of Living Dangerously*. 'After a film, I'm dying to do some theatre, and after theatre, I'm hanging out to do a film,' he said. 'I find the constant change refreshing and one helps the other.'

If it had not been for *Death of a Salesman*, he would probably have made his American film debut in *Once Upon a Time in America*. Sergio Leone, who had made Clint Eastwood a star in his spaghetti Westerns, wanted Gibson for one of the two lead roles in his epic about Jewish gangsters. Leone eventually made it with Robert De Niro and James Woods instead. More than a gangster film, *Once Upon a Time in America* explores themes of friendship and betrayal over several decades, continually switching between different periods. The studio butchered it for its American release, but the longer European version is now regarded by many as a masterpiece. I was part of an expert panel set up in 1996 to determine the greatest films of all time and we seriously considered it for No. 1, before placing it at No. 5. It is fascinating to speculate how it might have turned out with Gibson in it.

*Death of a Salesman* was probably the most prestigious stage production in which Gibson appeared. Playing opposite him, in the role of his father Willy Loman, was Warren Mitchell. He is best known as the working-class racist Alf Garnett in the English television sitcom *Till Death Us Do Part*, but Mitchell had already proved himself the definitive Loman in the National Theatre production in Britain and had been named best actor in the London theatre awards.

Film reference books can tell a reader, or indeed a writer, that such and such an actor was excellent in such and such a film and the reader, or writer, can check on video. With plays, even the professional theatre historian or drama critic often has to accept someone else's judgement. I have never seen Gibson on stage, but I did see Mitchell as Loman before he went to Australia. It was one of the greatest stage performances I have ever witnessed, an incredibly poignant and moving portrait of a man who is not so much a has-been as a never-was, a man who loves his sons and yet cannot communicate with them. Gibson compared Mitchell to Olivier, feeling that much of his power was drawn directly from his experience of life.

*Death of a Salesman* was widely labelled the 'theatrical event of the year' in Sydney, though it was not a particularly happy production. Mitchell was getting $5,000 a week, Gibson was on $2,500 and there was resentment from other actors who were getting something closer to $200. The critics thought Mitchell was wonderful; Ken Healey in the *Canberra Times* went so far as to say Mitchell had transformed his view of a character he previously had not cared about at all. But they were divided on the merits of Gibson's performance. H. G. Kippax of the *Sydney Morning Herald* called it superb. 'Gibson gives us, for about half the performance, acting that is deceptively bland, yet with tensions lightly but insistently intimated, mysterious and uncomfortable. In the second half the undercurrents of frustration and self-realisation begin to swirl.' Healey, however, wrote: 'There is much more to the troubled Biff than Gibson is able to capture and convey.' He was not alone in that view. The production played to full houses, but henceforth Gibson was to turn his back on the stage and concentrate on film.

Hollywood was now pursuing Gibson. A fee of $2,500 a

week may have seemed enormous to most Sydney stage actors but it was nothing compared to the sort of money Gibson could earn in films. He had committed himself to making *The Year of Living Dangerously* before *Gallipoli* and *Mad Max 2* came out, and even then he was getting about $100,000. Now he could demand as much as ten times that figure in Hollywood and he was taking his time to decide his next move. He did not necessarily simply want to sign up with the highest bidder; he wanted a role that would give him a fresh challenge. 'I'm a terrible procrastinator,' he told one American paper. 'I'd like to work here of course but only if the work is good.'

In February 1983 it was reported that Gibson had agreed to appear in a film called *The Running Man* for a fee of US$1 million and ten per cent of the gross. He was to play a Las Vegas taxi driver who finds a briefcase containing $2 million and takes off for London, pursued by gangsters. No sooner had the reports appeared than rumours began to spread that he was pulling out of that film, that he was going to do a remake of *Mutiny on the Bounty* and that MGM/UA would take the virtually unprecedented step of suing him for breach of contract. Gibson had a long meeting with studio boss Freddie Fields, who had backed *The Year of Living Dangerously*, and Fields announced an amicable solution: Gibson would make *The Running Man* after the *Bounty* film, with shooting on the former starting in late 1983.

In August 1983, shortly before shooting finished on *The Bounty*, MGM/UA announced that *The Running Man* had been postponed again, until 1984. Why? Because Gibson was going straight from *The Bounty* to make *The River*, which had to be shot in winter. He would do *The Running Man* after that. That same month, it was reported that Gibson was going to co-star with David Bowie in *Burton and Speke*, about the British African explorers. A few weeks later it was reported he was going to co-star with Diane Keaton in a drama called *Mrs Soffel*, for MGM/UA. After *The River*, he duly linked up with Keaton. He made neither *The Running Man* nor *Burton and Speke*. There was a film called *The Running Man* a few years later, with Arnold Schwarzenegger, but it was a different project. The 1989 film *Mountains of the Moon*, however, was simply *Burton and Speke* under a different name, with Patrick Bergin and Iain Glen in the roles once assigned to Gibson and Bowie.

Over the years Gibson was to become famous for procrastination and unrealised projects, though sometimes producers would fuel this process by linking his name to films before getting a response from him or even approaching him. In August 1983 Gibson's Australian agents went on record as saying he had been offered the chance to become the new James Bond after Roger Moore announced he was handing back his licence to kill when he finished *Octopussy*. Gibson's spokesman said he turned it down because he did not want to tie himself to a series when he already had 'too many' other projects. Nevertheless, producer Cubby Broccoli was said to be reluctant to take no for an answer. Gibson's name would continue to be linked with Bond even after Timothy Dalton was hired, and it was reported that Gibson would take over after Dalton stepped down in 1994.

I asked Michael G. Wilson, Broccoli's stepson who took over the mantle of Bond producer, to clarify the situation. He says: 'We never spoke to Mel Gibson, we never offered him anything. Back in 1986 the guy who ran the studio had a conversation with Mel Gibson for doing two pictures . . . That was the only conversation in the whole history of Bond. We weren't involved. It was just extra-curricular and he would come back and tell us, "Well, Mel may or may not be interested."' Certainly the reply sounds authentic. However, in the murky world of espionage, Wilson may not have known everything. At one point Joel Silver, producer of the *Lethal Weapon* films, had been interested in buying the rights to Bond, wanted Gibson as 007 and was involved in covert discussions of the possibilities.

Having considered several lucrative offers from Hollywood as his next project after *The Year of Living Dangerously*, Gibson decided not to do any of them. Instead he opted for a British film, *The Bounty*, the great David Lean epic that never was. The project had been developed by Lean, the Oscar-winning director of *Lawrence of Arabia*, and written by his regular collaborator, playwright Robert Bolt. They had been inspired by a book that cast a new light on the principal characters of Captain (actually Lieutenant) Bligh and his mutinous officer Fletcher Christian.

Charles Laughton had played Bligh as a sadistic tyrant and Clark Gable portrayed Christian as a dashing adventurer in the Oscar-winning classic of 1935. Their performances continued to provide the public perception of Bligh and Christian, despite a 1962 remake with Trevor Howard and a curiously foppish Marlon Brando.

The new film aimed to tell the true story of the mutiny for the first time. It would be shot largely on location on the Polynesian islands where the events took place, with a budget of US$25 million, a full-size reconstruction of the *Bounty* and a superb cast that included Laurence Olivier and emerging stars Daniel Day-Lewis and Liam Neeson. Gibson would play Fletcher Christian and share top billing with Anthony Hopkins who was Bligh.

The film had a long and complicated history. It constitutes two chapters, running to forty pages, of Kevin Brownlow's biography of David Lean, and even then the fact that it was eventually made with Gibson and Hopkins is relegated to a note in an appendix. Lean had been fascinated to discover in Richard Hough's book *Captain Bligh and Mr Christian* that Bligh was one of the eighteenth century's greatest navigators and a relatively benign captain. 'The difficulty is you don't quite know why they mutinied,' Lean told Brownlow. Whether that difficulty was ever sorted out in any of the drafts is unclear, but viewers of the finished product may come to the same conclusion.

Warner Brothers agreed to put up a budget of about $17 million and announced the project in June 1977. But Lean decided it was such a good idea that he wanted to turn it into two films, one dealing with the mutiny, and the second with Bligh's court martial, at which he was exonerated, and the life on Pitcairn Island of the mutineers and the Tahitians who went with them, and how they ended up killing each other. By the end of the year the project had passed to the independent Italian producer Dino de Laurentiis and was announced as two films, *The Lawbreakers* and *The Long Arm*. The budget was now $40 million. That deal collapsed the following year.

Lean and Bolt argued bitterly over the second script and other writers were approached after Bolt collapsed with a serious stroke in 1979. Melvyn Bragg adapted Bolt's screenplays into a single script, called *Pandora's Box*. He read various accounts of the mutiny and concluded Christian was simply 'a shit'. Lean disliked Bragg's script and continued to revise Bolt's work himself. But Lean eventually abandoned ship and de Laurentiis wound up at the helm again. Not only did de Laurentiis go back to Bolt's script for *The Lawbreakers*, he stuck with Lean's choice of Anthony Hopkins as Bligh. Gibson took the role that had been intended for Christopher Reeve, the American actor best known as Superman. Australian Roger Donaldson was a strange choice as director. While Lean had impeccable qualifications as a master of epic cinema, Donaldson's background was in low-budget New Zealand films, most notably *Smash Palace*, the drama of a middle-aged man who cracks up when his wife leaves him.

Initially Gibson was unenthusiastic about another *Bounty* film and inevitable comparisons with previous Fletcher Christians. He really wanted to do something original. 'At first I said no to the offer of playing Fletcher Christian,' says Gibson, 'but when I found out they intended to make a film of the whole other story and one that would set the HMS *Bounty* story straight, I signed the contract the same day the script arrived.' He was surprised to discover the truth about Fletcher Christian. 'He was only twenty-two when the *Bounty* sailed from England . . . and had already been to sea with Bligh twice before. In this movie, you can see both points of view. Christian isn't a great hero and Bligh isn't a complete villain.'

Gibson visited Christian's home in the Lake District, inspected original records and even took his research to a psychiatrist so they could discuss Christian's personality. Gibson also worked on his accent with a voice coach. While critics and public have regularly praised Meryl Streep's accents, Gibson has never received the recognition he deserves, perhaps because his accents sound so natural that you very quickly forget about them. Gibson believed Christian's youth was an important factor in his rebellion against his former friend, combined with his love for a Tahitian princess and the easy-going lifestyle on Tahiti.

Polynesia had changed since 1789 and the film-makers found local women reluctant to strip to the waist for the cameras. No sooner had they managed to persuade the women it was essential than an order arrived demanding two versions of every scene, because American television would not show naked breasts. Having been talked into taking their tops off for the sake of native authenticity, the women refused to put them back on for the sake of American hypocrisy. 'Finally we decided to just do it all bare-breasted,' says producer Bernard Williams. There was particular controversy when it was revealed Tevaite Vernette, who played Christian's bare-chested lover, Princess Mauatua, was still at school at the time of filming and her scenes had to be arranged around her school timetable.

The film took four months to shoot, with locations in England and New Zealand as well as Polynesia, and cast and crew became fractious, if not mutinous, at being away from home for so long. For much of the time they were stuck on Tahiti's smaller neighbour Moorea. Gibson was drinking heavily, literally mixing beer and whisky. 'That stuff is like liquid violence,' he says. On one occasion he got involved in a brawl in a bar. '*Bounty* was a difficult film to make,' says Gibson. 'It took a long time and the weather was terrible. I went mad. One night I had a fight in a bar and the next day they could only shoot one side of my face because the other side was so mucked up. If you see the film you can see the swelling in certain scenes.' He admits he was to blame. 'I'm still immature. I have a tendency to shoot my mouth off, provoke people, and I know I have to overcome that, even if it means going against natural impulse.' Hopkins, who is himself a reformed alcoholic, reckons Gibson was in danger of 'going off the rails'. He said at the time: 'Mel is a wonderful fellow with a marvellous future ... but he's in danger of blowing it unless he takes hold of himself.'

The pressures on Gibson were intensified by his realisation that, despite the promise of the film's central premise of rewriting the story of the *Bounty*, his own character had not been properly developed – the material simply was not there for him to bring to life. Minimalism worked fine for the character of Max, because Max was an icon; and his motivation was perfectly clear. Fletcher Christian was meant to be a real person.

Gibson's Christian is neither Gable's hero nor Bragg's shit, but rather a pleasant, though weak-willed, young man. Bligh blames Christian, Tahiti and the 'degenerate natives' for the mutiny. But Christian's motivation is never entirely clear; scenes of him splashing about topless in the sea with Mauatua fail to elevate their relationship from youthful infatuation to grand passion. Finally Gibson took it upon himself to rework the mutiny scene. 'I ended up having to virtually rewrite the scene myself the morning we were to shoot it. I had to, there was nothing in it when I got the script. I thought, 'What am I going to do here?' The character was lacking and the only place to do something was in the mutiny scene.' Gibson noted that both Bligh and another eyewitness had said that Christian was distraught and in tears at the actual point of mutiny. 'I figured the way to play that was by flipping out,' says Gibson. 'I didn't tell anyone what I was going to do. After the first take, the director Roger Donaldson ordered extra cameras. Obviously, I couldn't do it many times. This was primal scream time.' But Christian's emotional outburst and determination to protect Bligh from the other mutineers is at odds with his recent behaviour, and with the rest of the film.

For all the weaknesses in Christian's character, both in terms of personality and script, he does remain a more attractive character to contemporary audiences than Bligh. Bligh seems to have been a superb seaman and a benign captain by eighteenth-century standards – he decides against executing three deserters. On the other hand he seems an appalling man by twentieth-century standards – he has the deserters flogged, the duty officer is flogged and another seaman is due to be flogged for insubordination when the mutiny occurs. Donaldson shows Bligh sweating alone in bed while his men are having a good time on the island. The scene is too far removed from one at the beginning of the film where he is shown as loving husband and father, so the viewer can interpret it only as one of sexual repression. Our gut reaction to the man is repulsion, despite his navigational skills in an open boat when cast adrift with his supporters 3,600 miles from a friendly settlement. Historically, the case against Bligh is compounded by the fact that this was not the only rebellion against his authority. There were two others, including one in 1808 when he was Governor of New South

Wales, though eventually he rose to the rank of vice-admiral. Christian was probably murdered on Pitcairn, though there were reports that he returned to London.

The film has several exciting sequences, including the attempt to round the Horn, and is never less than interesting, but it lacks the sweep and scope of epic cinema and the focus and clarity of good character drama. Pauline Kael in *The New Yorker* said: 'This *Bounty* isn't different enough from its predecessors . . . We want more background and narrative detail to give meaning to the action, and we want more characterisation . . . With Bligh as no worse than ambitious, repressed and somewhat harsh, and Christian as a moody flower child who's drugged on love, we have no particular interest in either.' She was right. *The Bounty* was extensively advertised on American television, but flopped badly. Gibson featured prominently in magazines and newspapers as part of the hype, and, although few people seemed interested in seeing the movie, there was general agreement he was now a major Hollywood star. The fact that he had still not made a film in America was irrelevant.

# 7

# THROUGH A GLASS DARKLY

After weighing up dozens of lucrative options for his first American film, Mel Gibson surprised everyone yet again. Having rebuffed Hollywood's approaches once, to make *The Bounty*, he again turned down everything they had to offer. This time he decided that what he really wanted to do was a film he had not been offered and whose director did not want him. *The River* was the story of a poor American farmer and his family battling against the elements, the banks and big business to hang on to land that has been in his family for generations. Gibson personally lobbied for the role and even doorstepped director Mark Rydell to argue for it.

Rydell, who had just directed Henry Fonda and Katharine Hepburn to the Oscar podium in *On Golden Pond*, was impressed by Gibson's determination. 'But what do you do with a thick Australian accent in the American Midwest?' he said. 'The worst thing to happen in a picture about an American farmer is having someone who doesn't sound authentic.' Gibson pleaded for time to work on the accent. 'I don't know why he was so eager for the role, except maybe he saw a lot of Tom Garvey in his father.' Tom Garvey struggles to hold his family together. He is deep in debt to the bank and his crops are endangered every time it rains and the neighbouring river threatens to burst its banks. He leaves his wife and children to run the farm while he works in a city steel mill. The story does parallel that of Hutton Gibson, who acquired a smallholding in upstate New York and left the family to look after it while he went off to work on the railroad. Within a couple of years of making *The River*, Gibson would become a real-life farmer himself when he bought a cattle farm in Victoria.

'A few months later Mel called from London,' says Rydell. 'He was planning to stop in California on his way to Tahiti for *The Bounty*. His Tennessee accent was perfect. His persistence, even obstinacy, made him ideal for the role.' Gibson spent six weeks researching his part by getting to know farmers, but he always felt comfortable with the character and admits the biggest challenge was the accent. 'I had to get the vocal rhythm to correspond to his physicality . . . He's very uncomplicated: he works on the land and gets a reward for that from the land . . . He has a particular kind of pride of not having to answer to anybody, any employer; he's God-fearing, a bit hot-headed and certainly not cynical.'

Gibson appears (to these untutored Scottish ears) not only to have mastered the Tennessee accent but to speak it as if he had been doing so all his life. His character Tom Garvey is not exactly a talkative chap anyway. There are great chunks of film with little or no dialogue and Gibson is called upon to express himself not in words but in gestures and emotions, which he does superbly. Here is a character, in marked contrast to Fletcher Christian in *The Bounty*, that Gibson does inhabit. His family were with him on location near Kingsport in Tennessee, he was happy off set and assured on it. Unlike so many top Hollywood actors, Gibson looks comfortable in mucky overalls on a farm. He looks desperately uncomfortable with his collar sticking up slightly and his tie not quite straight when he visits the bank. You can sense mounting agitation in the way he shifts in his seat. Garvey is like a volcano ready to explode.

'Hard-working guy, Tom Garvey,' says local businessman Joe Wade (Scott Glenn) as he flies over his flooded farm near the beginning of the film. The opening sequence itself is a triumph as the camera moves from a wide shot of the river to a boy who stops fishing when he hears distant thunder, and hurries homewards as the sky darkens and rain falls. By the time he reaches his farm it is hammering down. Night follows day. Day follows night. Silently the family work to strengthen the levee that will hold back the river. Tom Garvey's bulldozer overturns and he is trapped, in danger of drowning. His wife Mae (Sissy

Spacek) and son pull him free, but the river has broken through. They rescue livestock and a few personal possessions. And as the tired, muddy family tramp away from their farm, the waters rise to swallow the ears of the corn. The opening sequence lasts more than ten minutes and contains hardly any dialogue.

Unusually for the director of a mainstream Hollywood movie, Rydell is not afraid to slow the film down and hold up the narrative in order to establish the mood of the piece. The story concerns Wade's attempts to get hold of Garvey's land for his own big business schemes, but the film's greatest strength is its empathy with the man of the land. As Kim Newman said in *Monthly Film Bulletin, The River* has 'a commitment to the soil worthy of a Soviet film'.

The Garvey farm was created on land near Kingsport. The ground was cultivated, crops were planted and the flooding was real, though the film-makers were not relying on the weather for it. Tennessee Valley Authority and army engineers worked out damming arrangements and released enough water to raise the river level five feet. This was the second successive film in which Gibson found himself filming in wet, uncomfortable conditions. 'We were fighting cold and winds and floods all the time,' he says. 'Some days we worked in mud all day.' Rydell also had to direct various animals, and not just cows in background shots. In one of the toughest scenes, Spacek's character has to provoke a bull into charging the piece of farm machinery under which she is trapped. Her family are away, her arm is stuck and she is bleeding badly, so she hopes the bull may dislodge it. 'We had two animals, one of them a "killer bull" that had killed a rodeo cowboy and then turned over the ambulance that came for him,' said Rydell. 'There is no such thing as a trained bull.'

He also needed a deer to wander into the steel mill where Garvey is working. The men surround it, they look into its eyes and let it go. Garvey had not known when he took the job that the regular workforce were on strike. After the dispute is settled, the scab labourers are left to make their own way out of the plant. The regular workers encircle them, look in their eyes and let them go. A woman with a baby in her arms spits in Garvey's face. At the end of the film Wade hires men to break down Garvey's levee, but Garvey recognises one as a colleague from the scab workforce at the mill. At last he finds eloquence. 'You're on the wrong side,' he says. 'We've been on the wrong side before . . . Don't tear me down. All I've got is what's growing in these fields.' And the man takes the controls of a bulldozer and pushes Wade's expensive vehicle into a hole in the levee. Wade himself plugs the last hole, with a warning that he will win in the end.

Critics praised Spacek and to a lesser extent Gibson, though the film itself got decidedly mixed reviews, partly because many critics are uncomfortable with the notion of melodrama as a legitimate form. Rydell predicted both Gibson and Spacek would win Oscar nominations and that Gibson would be *the* star of the eighties. 'He has the roughness of a Steve McQueen or a Paul Newman and the sensitivity of a Monty Clift,' he said. 'He's an absolutely riveting performer.' Gibson, a retiring, modest man by nature, began to get embarrassed when Rydell decided it was not sufficient to compare him to some of cinema's greatest stars but felt it necessary to say that Gibson was more exciting than McQueen, Henry Fonda and every other actor he had directed.

*The River* did better at the box office than *The Bounty* but, given that its subject is the vagaries of farming, it is ironic that it should find itself part of a glut of such produce. Farmers were having a tough time, with foreign imports, government regulations and complex finance arrangements adding to their traditional worries. They were in the news and *The River* came out at much the same time as two other prestigious farm films, *Country* and *Places in the Heart*, and it did not do as well as had been hoped. The rule of thumb for mainstream Hollywood films is that they should cover their production costs in the North American market and *The River* fell well short of its $16 million cost.

After *The River*, Gibson felt he needed a break. But he did not take one. Two years previously he was working for $100,000 a film. Now his asking price was $1 million. But he was not sure how long it would last and wanted to lay the foundations of financial security for his growing family. He already had three children and Robyn was pregnant again. After *The River* he nurtured the dream of buying a farm. And he had the chance of a meaty role in a drama with Oscar-winner Diane Keaton, to be directed by Gillian Armstrong, the Australian who had directed his old classmate Judy Davis in *My Brilliant Career*. 'I was drawn to the romantic nature of the story,' he says. 'It's the right mixture of realism and romanticism.' He and his family trekked from the Deep South up to Toronto, to begin a physically gruelling winter shoot on *Mrs Soffel*.

He plays Ed Biddle, a prisoner on Death Row, who becomes something of a pin-up, with young women gathering outside the jail to protest his innocence. The role provided him with the vehicle for an exceptionally intense, powerful performance. But he was suffering from chronic fatigue, having had only one week at home in Sydney in a year. 'I just got into town, climbed off the plane, slept for a week and then got back on the plane,' he told journalist Paul Mansfield on the set of *Mrs Soffel*, while chain-smoking and knocking back beer after beer. 'I just want a breather. But I'll get to the end of it, with a little despair. I won't go right off the edge.' Mansfield's interview appeared in *Age* in Australia on 28 April 1984. That same day Canadian papers carried the news that Gibson had been arrested.

It was towards the end of a shoot which had been plagued by budget rows, studio politics and the vagaries of the weather. 'They kept me hanging around,' Gibson says, 'used me every few days only. I was going crazy. My wife and kids had already packed off to Australia.' He found consolation in liquid form. In scenes that were reminiscent of the film, Gibson ended up in a cell himself, and young women gathered outside the courthouse to voice support when Gibson appeared on a drink-driving charge. Gibson had been arrested by Toronto police after failing to stop at a red light and crashing into another car. Randy Caddell, the other driver, raced to confront his assailant and was alarmed to discover he had been hit by the Road Warrior, though he later recalled Gibson assuring him he was for love, not war, and suggesting they go for a beer together. Police intervened, Gibson was detained for a short period and then released.

In court a week later he pleaded guilty to charges of driving with more than the legal limit of alcohol in his blood. It had been suggested that he faced six months in jail as part of a crackdown, but the judge decided a $400 fine and a three-month suspension of his driving licence would suffice. Fans shouted 'We love you, Mel' and he signed autographs outside the court. Subsequently the film company gave Gibson a driver-cum-minder and co-star Matthew Modine and his wife moved into Gibson's house to keep him company in the evenings.

Director Gillian Armstrong told me of her concern. 'Mel was going through a very bad personal time,' she says. 'We were very worried about what he was getting up to at night, because he was missing his family and drinking too much . . . He was running wild in Toronto at night. I'd like to say that my first feelings would be always for the personal welfare of an actor, but at the same time, sure, you don't want your actor turning up the next day with a black eye or something like that because they got in a fight in a bar.

'I think all the pressures of his stardom really hit him just around the time that he did *Mrs Soffel*. All of a sudden, from having an ordinary life, he couldn't go down the street, and people came up to him wherever he went.' Armstrong believes his workload was also a factor. 'I would now say that I would never take an actor who was doing three films in a row. I think it's too much. People forget what an emotional journey any actor goes through in any film . . . But of course I wanted him. There was no one else who was going to be right for Ed Biddle.'

Armstrong, like Gibson, was a product of the Australian film boom, though they had never met, and his casting was not her idea. She already had one major star in Diane Keaton and the studio, MGM, had given her the go-ahead to cast an unknown as the male lead. It was the film's original producer, Scott Rudin, who pressed her to consider Gibson. She screen-tested several young Americans, some of whom are now superstars in their own right. 'I ran the best five screen tests one after the other. And then straight after that I ran a reel from *Mad Max 2* and he just jumped off the screen . . . There's quite often a push from the studio to cast someone who is as handsome and sexy as Mel and often it's wrong for the part. But for this part it was actually very important because the real Ed Biddle had a fan following . . . He was meant to be terribly attractive and charismatic. So all those qualities that Mel has were right for the part. Plus I needed someone who was a wonderful actor . . . Even though we were very worried about him outside hours, during the shooting time he was very professional.'

Gibson and Keaton seemed a curious combination. While Gibson had made his name as Mad Max, strong, silent, violent, Keaton was playing Annie Hall, neurotic, witty, urbane. The long-term partner of Woody Allen, Keaton was the consummate intellectual performer. It had taken Gibson some time to connect with Sigourney Weaver and Sissy Spacek on previous films. Those experiences helped him develop a good working relationship with Keaton.

She plays the title character, the highly strung, seemingly very prim wife of the prison warden. She falls in love with Biddle and not only helps him and his brother Jack (Matthew Modine) escape but runs off with them, to the horror of turn-of-the-century Pittsburgh society. Much of the drama of the film is in the dynamic between the two characters. The relationship develops in lengthy dialogues between Keaton and Gibson. 'Half the battle when you work with someone is feeling easy with that person,' says Gibson, 'and knowing each other wants to do well. And she's very helpful. I mean she does stuff that works and therefore you can do nothing but return it.'

Keaton was clearly attracted to Gibson and in some comments seemed to have difficulty separating herself from her character. 'It was great to be in love with him,' she said. 'He's just so great, it's like whaaa . . . It was tremendously exciting to do that scene in the jail with Mel when he takes the saw out of my boots, and I'm reading something from the Bible and saying "I'm nothing", and he was flirting with me, and I was thinking "Well, that's the most fun I've ever had," with Mel looking up at me like that.' There is a spark in their scenes together that makes the film work as a love story. Gibson also got on well with Modine and they manage to establish a relationship that seems to have grown out of years of familiarity and affection.

Armstrong recalls a happy, communal spirit on set, with the stars travelling to the studio in Toronto together in a van rather than in their own limousines. Gibson horsed around with the crew and Armstrong remembers one tense prison scene in which Gibson and Modine turned round to reveal they were both wearing red noses, a gag that was to become a standard part of Gibson's repertoire. 'Mel has this hideously corny sense of humour and likes to do gags and play around, sort of schoolboy humour. And that's uniquely him. The rest of the Australian race would like to say it's nothing to do with the rest of us, thank you.

'There are people who consciously become the character and don't want to have that thread broken or the mood of whatever you are shooting that day broken, so if you're doing a depressing scene they'll be depressed all day. There are people who will do it unconsciously, who you'll find on a day when they're shooting a depressing scene are depressed, and they don't even know it. And then there are people who can absolutely switch in and out of it. Susan Sarandon [with whom Armstrong worked on *Little Women*] can switch in and out of it. She can be telling a joke right up to the time the clapperboard comes down in front of her face and she can just switch, just absolutely focused, into the emotion. It could be even a tearful scene. And Mel has that . . . I actually think, underneath all that, he knows that it helps to make a relaxed set, and a relaxed set makes for better working relationships.'

The commitment and sense of purpose on set were not reflected at studio level, where executives were split over the project. In his insider account *Fade Out: The Calamitous Final Days of MGM*, Peter Bart opens the section on *Mrs Soffel* by noting that Armstrong had purple streaks in her hair, which suggested, to him, 'a rebellious punk approach'. Despite internal division, it seems the project became unstoppable when Gibson's agent Ed Limato announced: 'It's a "no" on *Running Man* and it's a "yes" on *Mrs Whatchamacallit*.' One of the MGM reservations was the title, though no one ever came up with a better one.

Bart visited the production's remote Canadian location and found the pace painfully slow. He contends the strain of Armstrong's perfectionism was beginning to take its toll. 'Even Mel Gibson had begun to show the effects,' he wrote. 'By the time the shoot was over, some $50,000 had been spent to repair damage inflicted on his rented house in Toronto as a result of the actor's after-hours tantrums.' Bart reveals studio executives even discussed the possibility of firing Armstrong. They had already removed producer Scott Rudin.

The film had been budgeted at $12 million. Casting Gibson as Ed Biddle rather than an unknown increased costs by another $1 million, but Armstrong maintains MGM wanted her to pay for him by making cuts elsewhere. Not only was she having to deal with studio politics, but the snow for which she had gone to Toronto had disappeared.

'The weekend before we started shooting there was torrential rain and a heatwave and all the snow melted . . . I had walked in snowshoes over hundreds of miles finding locations. We didn't want to put tracks because it was a period movie, so we all walked in single file in snowshoes . . . We negotiated with the studio whether they would let us send a team to find locations further north . . . We did eight days' shooting in the studio while they were debating. Then, I think about the eighth day of shooting, there was a freak snowstorm. It was so bad that we were told that none of us could actually leave the studio that night because it was a white-out and all the highways were blocked, and so everyone was going to bed down in the cell beds and in the make-up rooms. They took a small group to local motels once the storm had calmed down. Overnight there was enough snow back on our locations to give us about five days of shooting.'

*Mrs Soffel* was based on a true story and, as well as shooting in Canada, Armstrong intended to use the real location of Allegheny County Jail in Pittsburgh. But she came under intense pressure from MGM to drop the Pittsburgh scenes to save money. 'Mel actually rang MGM at one time and told them to leave me alone and get off my back,' says Armstrong. 'I didn't ask him to do that.' She got her Pittsburgh scenes. 'We filmed for twenty-four hours nonstop,' she says. 'We filmed all day and all night. They thought that was the best thing; if we only entered once and only left once. And we were filming with convicted murderers and hitmen, who were all in period costume, playing extras.' She shot inside and outside the jail.

The film opens with an exterior of the grey prison and the cold, snowy streets, on which a woman prays for the Biddle brothers. It moves to a close-up of Keaton's eyes and then cuts to a darkened stairway and the sound of a woman's scream. Mrs Soffel's children play at prisoners and jailers in a corridor. 'Please don't kill me,' says the younger boy. 'I'll never shoot anyone again.' He crashes into a barred door, beyond which, out of the darkness, appear the Biddle brothers. A guard reports the children to their father. The guard calls them 'little criminals', the father suspends sentence. Their mother has been sick in bed for three months for no apparent reason, but decides she wants to get up and distribute bibles to the prisoners, including the Biddles, who have been convicted of the murder of a man during a hold-up, though it is popularly believed their partner was responsible.

She gives Ed Biddle a handkerchief after he is hurt in an altercation with a guard. It has a flower on it. They decide it is a violet. Biddle flirts with her, but he also argues with her, engaging her on a philosophical level. She talks to him of Heaven. 'Can you see me up there floating around on a cloud playing my harp for all the saints?' asks Biddle, despair in his voice and eyes. He forces himself to laugh, but it is a bitter, joyless laugh. 'I picture Heaven as a place of peace,' says Soffel. 'Death would be peace,' says Biddle. But Soffel is patient and persistent. Biddle encourages her attraction to him, and even writes a poem about the violet for her, hoping she will help them escape.

Gibson wore little make-up for the film, except a facial scar. For much of the time he lurks in semi-darkness and his face is partly obscured by bars. There is little action in the first half of the film, which could readily be performed on stage, but then the Biddles break out and head for Canada across a snowy landscape that is almost blinding after the darkness of the prison scenes. We realise now that Biddle has not simply been exploiting Mrs Soffel and that he is determined to take her with them even though she slows them down.

She makes him promise he will kill her rather than let their pursuers take her back. He confesses his guilt, which is compounded by his responsibility for the fate of his innocent sibling. When the moment comes, Mrs Soffel presses Biddle's gun against her chest. Biddle tells her he loves her and kisses her and, choking back the tears, he shoots her. But the final irony is that the Biddles, who desperately wanted to live, are killed, while Mrs Soffel survives and returns to Allegheny a prisoner, though no longer the timid, sickly creature she was. When an official insults the memory of the Biddles she slaps his face and walks defiantly towards her prison cell.

MGM/UA released *Mrs Soffel* at the end of 1984 to qualify for the Oscars. The reviews were positive. Pauline Kael of *The New Yorker* said: 'Mel Gibson, who miscast can seem a lightweight, is superb here. Much wirier than in his earlier roles, he's convincingly passionate, shrewd, relentless. There's concentrated emotionality in this performance . . . He's like the young Henry Fonda, but with a streak of something darker, more volatile, and more instinctively knowing.' Newspaper reports suggested Gibson might be Oscar-nominated for both *The River* and *Mrs Soffel*, despite the impossibility of getting two nominations in a single acting category – the performance which attracted more votes would go forward to the final ballot. At the end of the day he was nominated for neither. It is possible his vote was split between the two performances and he might have been nominated if only one or other film was in the running, though that is conjecture. Spacek was nominated as best actress for *The River*, but lost to Sally Field, star of *Places in the Heart*.

*Mrs Soffel* was less popular with the public than the critics. It is undoubtedly one of the darkest films ever made, so dark that at times it is difficult to see exactly what is happening. The darkness of the film matches the bleakness of the story; it is not easy or particularly pleasant viewing. After the box-office disappointment of *The Bounty*, *The River* and *Mrs Soffel*, Gibson needed a hit.

'I think probably having that lack of commercial success with *The River* and *Soffel* maybe gave him a jolt,' says Armstrong, 'and obviously, with his agent, was encouraged to do the action films.' Armstrong and Gibson remained on good terms after *Mrs Soffel*. She was never aware that her sex affected their relationship in any way, though she adds he was shy with women generally. They have discussed the possibility of other projects together. 'I would really like to see him push himself and do a really difficult part,' she says. 'I think some of the things he has done in the last few years have been easy . . . He should be up there getting Academy Award nominations now as an actor, as well as a director.'

She remembers Gibson was interested in the technical side of filming during *Mrs Soffel*, but adds: 'If you had asked me then on *Mrs Soffel*, would he be directing one day? I would have told you I don't know, because at that time he was partying a lot more and directors don't have a chance to do that. He stopped the partying and kept himself busy with work, which is probably a healthier thing to do. I think he doesn't like to stop; he's got to keep doing something . . . He really has pulled his life together.'

Despite public indifference to his most recent films, at the end of 1984 Americans voted him one of the ten 'most watchable' men in the world, along with President Reagan. He also topped a US poll of three hundred newspaper and magazine editors, arranged by a lipstick manufacturer, to determine the stars with the most kissable lips. And readers of *Glamour* magazine in the US voted him the thinking woman's crumpet. Gibson felt ambivalent about his status as a sex symbol, feeling it detracted from his acting achievements, and he reiterated his distaste for sex on screen. 'To me sex appeal means they want to go and watch what I'm doing – and that's good. But you are not going to get to people, ultimately, by ripping your clothes off and showing them your frontals.' He later said that he would not do 'noises' either.

He took about three months off after *Mrs Soffel* and spent time with his family at home in Sydney. 'You've got to take time off and dig a ditch or something,' he said. 'You do something physical so your mind can work      other things, otherwise you exhaust your resources. I mean, three films in a row . . . you become a basket case.' Nevertheless he fitted in a string of interviews in Sydney. Some interviewers chose to play down the 'tired and emotional' state in which they found him. Geraldine O'Brien of the *Sydney Morning Herald* was not among them and began her report by noting the two empty Moët bottles.

At one point Gibson apparently forgot why he was there and, sensing her irritation, started going on about how boring he was. His public relations minder assured him he was not boring. 'I'm a creep,' Gibson told O'Brien. 'No, you're not,' the

PR woman told Gibson. He explained that as an actor he was 'pretty fucking good', but he was poor at 'verbal communication' – 'I can't articulate shit, but I know shit' – and that the interview was an obligation to promote the film. The PR woman said that was showbusiness and Gibson sang, 'There's no business like dog's business.' He tap-danced, offered to lie on the floor so O'Brien could walk on him and asked her if she thought he was a creep. 'You're right,' he said when she did not reply. 'I am a creep. Yeah. Print it.' When she did, Gibson was furious.

A few months later on the set of *Mad Max Beyond Thunderdome* he discussed the O'Brien piece with David Wallace of *People* magazine. 'I have a bad habit of saying embarrassing things,' he said, and then he did it again. 'I don't want to be doing this interview. I don't even want to be making this film. It's just a piece of shit. Don't print that.' But you cannot tell an interviewer that your new film is 'a piece of shit' and expect him to pretend he has not heard. *People* ran the comment, but Gibson's truculence throughout the interview did not stop the magazine dubbing him the 'sexiest man alive', a description that was picked up in countless other pieces and which came to haunt him.

Gibson had been won over to the idea of another *Mad Max* film before starting *Mrs Soffel*, because he felt director George Miller had come up with something that was a dramatic departure from its predecessors in terms of concept and which significantly developed Max's character. *Max 3* is by far the most ambitious film in the series, both in its special effects and in its vision. Miller, who hired George Ogilvie to co-direct it with him, had not considered a third *Max* film until his writing partner Terry Hayes mentioned an idea for a story about an isolated tribe of feral children, waiting for their leader to return. Miller felt it would work as a *Mad Max* film, set not three or four years after *Max 2* but ten or twenty.

*Max 3* goes beyond a post-apocalyptic wasteland to a world that is beginning to evolve again into different communities, each with distinct social structures and ethical codes. There is the tribe of feral children, there is the feudal society of Bartertown, there is Underworld, with which it has to co-exist, and there is Max to bring them all together. *Max 3* had to embody philosophical themes while at the same time remaining a mass-market action adventure. Miller filmed it, with a budget of about $8 million, in the Sydney area and the barren opal-mining region of Coober Pedy in a remote part of South Australia where many of the miners lived in underground houses. It was another long, uncomfortable shoot. Several of the team collapsed from heat exhaustion at Coober Pedy and the boredom and strain began to get to Gibson.

The producer of a television commercial for Japanese beer once praised Gibson's dedication when he drank seven or eight cans in a row without complaint. 'Even when we offered to fill the cans with tea or another substitute drink he refused.' On *Max 3* Gibson was downing several beers before breakfast, carrying on through the day and ending up in some potentially disastrous confrontations with the tough local residents. The miners' wives were delighted to play host to the man with the most kissable lips in the world; the miners perhaps felt they had something to prove to their women by taking on Mad Max. Fortunately Gibson had some equally tough stuntmen on his side of the bar. They say Gibson showed no fear and one confrontation in an underground bar ended only when a stuntman stuck the inebriated Gibson over his shoulder and took him back to his quarters, where he was locked in.

George Miller told me it was not a happy shoot. 'I think that was his most tormented period,' he says, 'when he was grappling with the notion of success and he was drinking and being pretty wild and disgruntled about everything. *Mad Max 1*, you know, we were all raw, we had no idea what we were doing and I guess he was just learning, and *Mad Max 2* was a chance to make up for the lack of resources on the first one. By the time he did the third one he was already a big star internationally.

'It was a very difficult time because I had just lost my partner Byron Kennedy [killed in a helicopter crash]. The film was almost a kind of – just getting in and doing something, just to keep my mind off grieving . . . I didn't have, perhaps, time to think about anybody else or even what Mel was going through, but I know he was drinking a hell of a lot and, you know, pissed off with doing interviews . . . He was never rude to me or anybody on the set, but I know it was going on in the background.'

By the time the film came out, Gibson was insisting he no longer drank in bars. 'I'm a non-violent person,' he said, 'though I have to admit I've been a wild boy in my time. I used to get into pub fights at an average, I'd say, of two a year . . . I could never walk away.' During the making of *Max 3*, Gibson clearly had incredible amounts of nervous energy for which he had to find an outlet and, despite the presence of a small army of stuntmen, he did the combat sequence in the Thunderdome himself.

'Mel was better at doing all that stuff than his stunt double,' says Miller. 'I remember we were in Broken Hill a day or two before we were shooting *Mad Max 2*, we were going for a walk, just talking about the role and stuff, and he walked into a lamppost, fell backwards, clutching his face and moaning. And I thought, "Oh my God, he's really hurt himself" and "What are we going to do about the film? We shoot tomorrow." And I bent over him and said, "Mel, Mel," and tried to pull his hand away from his face. I thought he was in bad pain and then he just laughed and he showed me how he did it, where he did this slapstick fall where he timed it so it looks like he hits his head on the lamppost, but of course the impact comes from his foot.

'Mel is like a natural actor. He has to act . . . It's just what he does. He's never still. He's always practising physical gags and stuff. He'd always be doing a trick with coins rolled across the back of knuckles or reflex tricks or imitating people on the set or doing sort of slapstick falls or things like that. In a way I think he'd just been an actor all his life. These were just ways to exercise his natural gift. By the time he'd got to the third film he'd already picked up a hell of a lot of craft.

'By the third film he'd spent a lot of time on set instead of going off set when he wasn't required and after a while he knew extremely well what the camera did. He was technically very adept. I learned on the first film that he would often leave his best moment or performance in rehearsal, while he was waiting for the other actors to catch up. And so I knew after the first film to make sure that Mel did hold back a bit in rehearsal and I knew I had to get the other actors and everyone out there – the rest of the other technical variables – up to speed, so that we could get it in the early takes. By the third film I think he understood that, so it wasn't wasted in rehearsal or in the early takes. He knew he had to pace himself to get the best moments. So he was an extremely efficient actor.

'He's one of those actors that, you know, a nanosecond before you say "Action" is kidding around and stuff like that, he completely just becomes the character and then the moment you call "Cut" he starts kidding around again. There's not a lot of Method in that traditional way the word has come to be used . . . He just had a craft sense, you know. Some actors just aren't interested in it and just basically don't even watch dailies. But Mel would watch dailies. And he had a real sense of what was happening beyond just the performance . . . I knew then he would direct.'

Gibson once again delivers a focused, compelling performance in *Mad Max Beyond Thunderdome*, which is a much better film than anyone might have expected, given the difficult circumstances under which it was made.

It begins with an airborne camera swooping across a desert towards a dust trail that turns out to be a caravan being pulled by a team of camels. Only when the driver is knocked from his seat does the viewer realise the camera represented the view from an approaching small aircraft, piloted by none other than a pith-helmeted Bruce Spence, who was the Gyro Captain in *Max 2*, and is playing someone called Jedediah in *Max 3*. He has the same comic, but dangerous, personality as the Gyro Captain and yet seems to be a different character, partnered by a pith-helmeted son, very much a chip off the old block. Jedediah makes off with the caravan, while his son pilots the plane, leaving the caravan driver behind in the sand. The driver, swathed in black robes and turban, gets to his feet and the audience realises Max is back.

He makes his way to Bartertown, which looks like a futuristic twist on Pier-Paolo Pasolini's medieval films – dirt and bare flesh and incipient damnation. It is a fledgling free-market society, where everything is traded from a drink of water to a human life, and where disputes are settled in a semi-spherical gladiatorial cage called Thunderdome. Tina Turner, dressed in chainmail and a hairstyle that looks like a dead sheep, plays its ruler Aunty Entity and delivers not so much a character as a rock and roll

Mel Gibson's grandmother Eva Mylott was the family's first international star.

A smile for the camera, but Mel Gibson (top left) was bullied at school and desperately unhappy after the family moved to Australia.

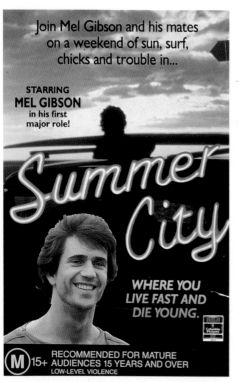

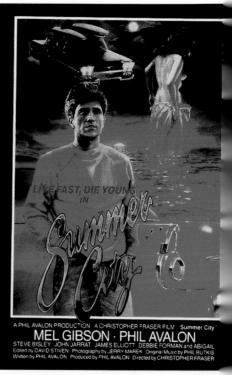

Gibson's film debut was in a supporting role in *Summer City*, though he was elevated to star billing when he became famous.

In 1979 Gibson co-starred in the play *Waiting for Godot* with another future Oscar winner, Geoffrey Rush.

Gibson did extensive research and talked to veterans for the powerful First World War drama *Gallipoli*.

*The Year of Living Dangerously* proved an apt title, for Gibson and co-star Sigourney Weaver received death threats.

Gibson was still at drama school when he won the lead in the ambitious, low-budget action movie *Mad Max*.

After failing to make the breakthrough in America, Gibson returned to Australia for a third *Mad Max* film.

Gibson went straight from *Mad Max Beyond Thunderdome* to another hit series –
*Lethal Weapon*, with Danny Glover.

Walking the dog was more fun than a love scene with Patsy Kensit in *Lethal Weapon 2*,
according to Gibson.

Gibson slept in his dressing room, going home only at weekends, so he could focus on the challenge of *Hamlet*.

Gibson has big problems with the New York traffic in *Ransom,* another big box-office hit.

Gibson came close to nervous breakdown on *Braveheart*, but the end result was an
international hit and an Oscar triumph.

Wife Robyn accompanies Gibson to showbiz occasions, but to the kids he's not a Hollywood superstar, he's simply Dad.

performance. Her authority is challenged by Master-Blaster, a silent giant with a brilliant midget on his shoulders. Brawn and brain, they run Underworld, on which Bartertown depends for its energy, methane from pig shit. Aunty agrees to get Max's possessions back for him if he will help in her power struggle. Max fights Blaster in Thunderdome, where they bounce from the roof, suspended on elasticated cords, towards a variety of weapons, including chain saw and mallet. But Max refuses to kill Blaster when he unmasks him and sees he is mentally handicapped. Having broken the law of 'Two men enter, one man leaves', Max is driven into the desert to die.

The Thunderdome sequence may be stylish and well executed, but it is also very violent and unpleasant, particularly in its use of a mentally handicapped character. The tone of the film changes completely when Max is discovered by Savannah Nix (Helen Buday) and dragged back to the idyllic, waterside settlement of the tribe of feral children, whose ages range from infancy to teens, and who are awaiting the return of their leader, Captain Walker. 'I finded him,' says Savannah. 'It's Captain Walker.' In sharp contrast to the capitalism and violence of Bartertown, the children's society is founded on co-operation, with designated hunters and gatherers, underpinned by their distinct religious beliefs and rituals.

There are similarities with William Golding's novel *Lord of the Flies*, in which a conch shell becomes a symbol of order and entitles the holder to speak and be heard. Here a frame of sticks, which looks like a cinema screen, serves the same purpose. 'I'm looking behind us now, across the count of time, down the long haul into history back,' says Savannah, and she tells of the 'poxyclypse' and Mr Dead and how Captain Walker and his people took to the sky but were jumped by a gang called Turbulence. The survivors found a place for which they had 'the hots', but they missed the 'high-scrapers' and Captain Walker set out to find the way back, while the rest waited and went on waiting.

In the third part of the film Max returns to Bartertown with Savannah and some of the tribe, rescues Master and escapes, with Aunty in pursuit, which provides the context for another chase sequence, this time involving a train. Master, Savannah and the children end up with Jedediah in his plane, while Max charges at their pursuers to give them the chance to take off. Aunty just looks at him, dismisses him with a laugh as nothing more than a 'raggedy man' and leaves him, once more alone in the desert. The others fly over the ruins of Sydney. At the end of the film they have established a new community there. 'Every night we does the tell,' says Savannah. 'So we member who we was and where we came from, but most of all we members the man who finded us ... And we lights the city, not just for him, but for all of them who are still out there, 'cos we knows there'll come a night when they sees the distant light and they'll be coming home.'

Critics admired the special effects, stunts and some of the set pieces, but many were uncomfortable with the episodic structure and uneven tone. It is not so much a film in three acts as a trilogy within a single film, with the inherent danger that critics and/or paying public would instinctively compare the different sections to the detriment of two of them. There were complaints that the first part was too violent, the second part too slow and the third part too similar to *Max 2*. Miller has drawn from a myriad of influences to create something rich and unique, even if it never quite gels. Despite its flaws and its production problems, it became the major worldwide hit for which Gibson had been looking.

# 8

# LETHAL TAKINGS

Mel Gibson turned his back on movies after *Mad Max Beyond Thunderdome* and bought a 600-acre beef farm in the Kiewa Valley, a part of Victoria that reminded him of Scotland. In the past year and a half he had worked in snow and desert, water and mud, freezing cold and tropical heat. He had been arrested for drink-driving in Canada, fought with islanders in Polynesia and clashed with miners in South Australia. To borrow a couple of lines from *Mad Max 2*, he had become a shell of a man and it was in the Kiewa Valley that he learned to live again. He threw himself into the physical challenges of working the farm without hired hands. 'It's just a little old farm, with a few head of cattle on it,' he said. 'I don't know where their bodies went.' He even learned to castrate bulls, though he needed help with that. He was a new breed of cowboy of whom John Wayne might not have approved, for he rode the range on a motorbike rather than a horse.

It took him a long time to recover from the strains and excesses of the previous eighteen months. A naturally untidy person, he was still finding it difficult to organise his personal life. In February 1985, for the second successive year he failed to submit his tax return on time and was fined $100 and ordered to pay $18 costs. He was continually exhausted, sought specialist advice and it was eventually discovered he had a yeast infection in his blood. He was told to lay off sugar, carbohydrates, coffee and, not surprisingly, alcohol. He devised a drink consisting of liquidised carrots, celery, beetroot, red pepper, garlic and ginger. He slimmed down by twenty pounds and gradually built up his fitness and energy levels again. He enjoyed life on the farm and even thought about packing in acting. He held out for a year and a half.

Hundreds of scripts came his way during that time, but the one that lured him back was a thriller by a young writer called Shane Black, with a strong emphasis on character. 'Lethal Weapon is one of the best scripts I've ever read,' said Gibson. 'And, believe me, I've read a lot of scripts in the past few years. This writer hadn't been spoiled or influenced by the system. There is a stimulating rawness about his work.'

The film centres on two LA cops. One, Roger Murtaugh, is a middle-aged man, with a nice family, nice home and even a small boat. He is a model citizen, though in a neat twist on stereotypes he is also black. He is brought to the screen by Danny Glover, who had recently starred in Steven Spielberg's The Color Purple. The other cop, Martin Riggs, lives with a dog in an untidy trailer and is considerably younger – though he mentions that he was serving in Vietnam in 1969. There is no other reason to suspect Gibson's character is older than Gibson, who was thirteen in 1969, though the script does make it clear Riggs has always been exceptional. A special forces veteran, an expert shot and a master of martial arts, he is the lethal weapon of the title, though the term is used jokingly by his new partner. Gibson undertook an intensive programme of weight training and instruction in unarmed combat before filming began.

He was, however, attracted principally by the fact that Riggs is no superman but a vulnerable individual who takes incredible risks not because he is brave but because he does not care. His wife has been killed in a car crash. It seems this was an accident, there is no target for vengeance, and Riggs reacts to his loss very differently from Max. We first see Riggs smoking in bed, forcing himself to get up to get a beer from the fridge. Riggs sleeps naked, though Gibson was still not showing his 'frontals', despite shouts of 'turn round' from women in cinema audiences.

Riggs's manic humour, another element that attracted Gibson to the role, is illustrated when he pretends to want to buy drugs from three dealers. Told they will cost 'a hundred', he coolly starts counting out $100 in small bills. The dealers explain they mean a hundred thousand. Riggs puts his hand to his head and says he cannot afford that on his salary. He has a better idea: he will take the drugs for nothing and they can go to jail. The dealers call him crazy. He laughs uneasily and asks if they 'want to see crazy', repeatedly slapping himself, poking one of them in the eyes, slapping another and drawing his gun before they can react. One of the crooks manages to get a gun to Riggs's head and hold him hostage. Riggs pleads with back-up officers to shoot his assailant and, when they do not, he pleads with the assailant to shoot him, finishing off by head-butting him in obvious frustration.

Gibson was attracted by the idea of comedy in tragedy. He went on patrol with LA police and talked to Vietnam veterans. 'I used their experience for the Riggs role. I never killed anybody, although I can imagine how it could be. We've all wanted to kill someone at one time in our lives.' But he also felt there was something 'Chaplinesque' about Riggs. He improvised with the character, inspired by Chaplin, by Shakespeare's use of humour as light relief and specifically by the Three Stooges in his routine early in the film with the small-time drug dealers.

Back at the trailer, while Christmas music plays on television, he drinks and ponders a photograph of his dead wife. He loads his pistol, puts it to his forehead and then in his mouth, his expression of determination turning to one of despair at his failure to pull the trigger, as Bugs Bunny appears on television extolling the joys of Christmas, a second successive Gibson film to feature Bugs – one of the tribe of feral children had a Bugs Bunny toy in *Mad Max Beyond Thunderdome*. Riggs is the opposite of Max. Where Max bottled up his emotions, Riggs lets them flow out of him in rivers of tears.

He gets back the will to live when he becomes involved in trying to break a high-level heroin import business, run by veterans from Air America, the CIA operation that traded in rice, people and drugs during the Vietnam war and which would provide the subject for a subsequent Gibson film. The veterans decide to reactivate former contacts.

Gibson said at the time: 'This thing is going to work as an action film because it has a strong basis, a strong foundation. You are going to care about all the action because you care about the characters.' Journalists who visited Burbank Studios found Gibson more relaxed than ever before. 'This is the most enjoyable set I've ever worked on,' he told one. 'Everyone is just goofing off. But we are getting really good stuff because it's being done in a really good spirit. Then again maybe it's just me, because my attitude has changed.' It was the first time Gibson had stayed in Los Angeles for more than a few weeks; he rented a house and his family were with him during the three-month shoot. Although he had previously been scathing about Los Angeles, he found that, after the rigours of Moorea and Coober Pedy, he was enjoying the experience of working in LA and returning home to his family at the end of each day, almost like an ordinary working man. He described himself as 'replenished'.

Director Richard Donner, whose previous credits included *The Omen* and *Superman*, was very keen to get Gibson for the role, though he had feared he would not be able to prise him away from his farm. 'I think there is a lot more depth to Mel than he admits to, and we have found this out. He is not just an action kid who does these *Mad Max* things, not that I don't enjoy those . . . But it is amazing what he has going for him – his discipline, his theatre background, his training. It's all there and you feel it every time you work with him . . . Study Mel Gibson's face – something comes out of his eyes. The dynamics are just amazing . . . he's got a twinkle, a wondrous sense of humour. His chemistry with Danny is phenomenal.'

Donner had been sure Gibson would be good in the part, but it was not until they shot the scene where Riggs attempts to kill himself that he realised just how good an actor Gibson really was. There was room only for the cameraman in the trailer with Gibson, and Donner watched on a monitor outside. The scene was so tense, and Gibson so convincing, that Donner began to worry.

'I couldn't believe what Mel was doing . . . Things rushed through my head. Did Mel ask the armourer or special effects guy to 'put one in there to give me motivation'? I tell you I was terrified as Mel started to choke on the barrel, his finger tightening on the trigger. I was torn between rushing in and stopping the scene in case there was a shell in the gun, and getting this amazing performance. I was literally glued to watching the video screen. The crew was spellbound. A couple of the girls were choking, beginning to cry behind me.

'I figured we had what we wanted and was about to call "Cut" into the radio mike that went to the cameraman's earphones. But Mel kept it going, adding a few final tears of frustration and mental anguish as he wept openly, apologising to a photo of his dead wife. I can tell you I breathed out loud when he stopped the performance and I called a meek "Cut" to the operator. I rushed into the van and hugged Mel, told him it was great, fantastic. He looked around, shook his head. "Want to try another one for safety?" he said to me quite innocently, wiping a real tear from his eye. I gave him another hug and said, "You were perfect . . . we've got it."'

A couple of years later, Gibson told a rather different version of the story to Lynn Hirschberg of *Rolling Stone*. He said that in the original script Riggs contemplated overdosing on sleeping pills, but Gibson argued that was 'pussy' and that 'the macho way out' was for him to shoot himself. Gibson continued: 'It was a weird little scene . . . It was a hair trigger. And I knew they had put a real bullet in there.' Was Gibson uncomfortable? 'No, I was extremely happy.' Really? 'Absolutely. I really enjoyed it. I was ecstatic.'

Donner was slightly surprised how easy Gibson was to work with. He described him as 'the most exciting thing that's come into my life', they became close friends and over the next ten years they would make another four films together. Nevertheless, Donner recognised that Gibson had his darker side too and was prone to mood swings. 'Mel has a lot of anger and hostility in him,' he said. 'He bottles it up well, but there have been times when I've seen the pot start to boil over, and I know enough to back off and get others to back off.' Donner probably came as close as anyone to getting to the heart of Gibson's personality when he said he was just a 'big kid'.

Some critics expressed concern about the violence in *Lethal Weapon*, though most praised Gibson's performance and some singled out the scene where he considers suicide. The film grossed $65 million in North America alone, almost twice as much as *Mad Max Beyond Thunderdome*, and ended up as one of the ten highest-grossing films of the year. Gibson had at last proved he could attract a mass audience in something other than a *Mad Max* film.

After *Lethal Weapon*, Gibson went back to Australia and spent another year on the farm, or rather farms, for he expanded his domain with the acquisition of a neighbouring property. He became a regular farmer out in the fields all day chasing calves on his motorbike. 'You zero in on this little critter, and you can beat him on the bike, but he takes a lot of weird turns and you have to second-guess him . . . And his mother is very cross about the fact that you've got her youngster, so you've got to keep an eye on her, because you're bent over this calf, exposed like the new man in Cell Block C.'

He seemed to have the politics to go with his red neck and endorsed Robert Taylor, a trucker who stood as an independent right-wing candidate in the federal election even though, as an American, Gibson could not vote. 'I'm responsible for bringing five little Australians into the world,' he said. 'What have they got to look forward to in the future? It doesn't look like a hell of a lot . . . I have to speak up about what's happening to this country before it's too late.'

Gibson's uncompromising politics have marked him as a man apart in the more liberal environment of Hollywood. He has been critical of trade unions and high taxes. But it is not just on economics that he has appeared right-wing; his social views have been shaped by the Christian fundamentalism he inherited from his father. He has made it clear he has no truck with gay liberation and feminism, while calling for tougher action on crime. In *Lethal Weapon*, after Murtaugh's daughter is kidnapped, Riggs says to him: 'We do this my way: we shoot, we shoot to kill.' Gibson stressed that he was not endorsing Riggs's way. 'I'm not advocating police taking on villains in street blood baths,' he told one reporter, 'but I back capital punishment 100 per cent . . . It's a sick, violent world out there and a humane form of capital punishment is a valid way of dealing with that sickness.' One liberal cause he has embraced is the environment, giving up disposable nappies, aerosols and tuna, and planting one thousand trees near his home.

Gibson attended a rally at the Wodonga Showground where

Taylor railed against 'child abuse, drug abuse, suicide, pornography and the AIDS thing'. Then Gibson returned to Hollywood to play a drug dealer in *Tequila Sunrise*. 'It's not a pro-drug film,' he said. Others were not so sure. Warner Brothers had already attempted to persuade writer-director Robert Towne to turn the protagonist from a retired drug dealer into a numbers racketeer, and when that failed they wanted him to deal only in cannabis. But Towne insisted the character's past involvement in hard drugs was vital. Harrison Ford was lined up, only to drop out, apparently because of his concern over the film's stance on drugs.

'Things don't quite match up, and that's what appealed to me about the script,' said Gibson. 'The script doesn't deal with good and bad, but shades of grey in between.' Gibson was to play Dale McKussic, 'Mac', a Los Angeles drug dealer who is now trying to go straight. 'Here's a man who has a very illicit lifestyle and has had an unsavoury career. Yet he always tells the truth and deals honourably with people ... He's retired from drug dealing, but nobody wants him to retire ... It was one of those scripts that you just kept turning the pages. It demanded a second read.' And indeed a second viewing to work out what was happening, and I do not necessarily mean that pejoratively.

Robert Towne is one of the best and most intelligent writers in Hollywood. It was his wife who suggested Gibson as Ford's replacement and Towne sent him the script after seeing him in *Lethal Weapon*. Towne had previously written *Chinatown*, the brilliant thriller in which Jack Nicholson's detective takes on a sleazy little sex case and gets caught up in a web of murder and corruption. *Chinatown* was a film whose rich complexities can be fully appreciated only on repeated viewings. *Tequila Sunrise* was ostensibly a thriller about cops and drug dealers, combined with a romance in which two men, one a drug dealer and the other a cop, compete for the affections of the same woman. The drug dealer is supposedly retired, but he helps set up a minor drugs sale for a lawyer friend, one of whose customers has paid his bill in cocaine. The Drug Enforcement Agency do not believe he has retired and are not above trying to frame him.

Towne said: 'The most dangerous thing you can do with that

issue is to make *Cocaine Fiends* or *Reefer Madness* [notoriously crude propaganda films], because then it removes it from the world of reality . . . When you show how it can be in context of our normal lives, then you can suggest the damage it does. We can't deal with Dick Tracy kinds of good and evil, because it's just more complicated than that.' Gibson maintains the film conveys the idea that drugs destroy the fabric of the family and invade friendships, without the need for his character to say it in words. 'I like the idea of conveying an emotion or idea that isn't right there in the dialogue,' he said. But it is illegal drug dealing, not drugs as such, that destroys the fabric of the family and invades friendships in the film.

*Tequila Sunrise* is not really about drugs. It is primarily about friendship, and being a romance, about love, and, finally, it is about betrayal. Mac and the head of the local drugs squad Nick Frescia were kids together. The role of Frescia went to Kurt Russell, star of *Escape From New York*, after Towne had considered Kevin Costner and Dennis Quaid, and his close friend Warren Beatty, upon whom the character was partially based. Frescia confesses he would have been busted for marijuana down in Mexico along with Mac, except he was off swimming at the time and Mac took the rap. Nick sabotages DEA plans to arrest Mac. There is a woman, Jo Ann Vallenari (Michelle Pfeiffer). No one seems sure where she fits into the scheme of things but both men romance her and much of the action, or inaction, centres on her restaurant. The DEA know that a big-time drugs dealer called Carlos is coming to LA. He saved Mac's life long ago in a Mexican prison and only Mac knows what he looks like. A high-ranking Mexican cop (Raul Julia) arrives to help the DEA. But the high-ranking Mexican cop is Carlos. How a drugs dealer worked his way up to run Mexican police anti-drug activities is never explained, nor is the film's title, which seems to relate only to its Mexican plot elements and Towne's pretty shots of the sun.

Whereas repeated viewings bring out the richness of *Chinatown*, they serve only to confirm the flaws in *Tequila Sunrise*. The film quite deftly draws inspiration from classic Western themes of the gunfighter trying to quit his former life, and of two strong men, on opposite sides of the law, pursuing the same woman. But whereas the relationships between the three main male characters have the richness and complexity of time behind them, Vallenari's role seems awkward and contrived, as does the film's determination to place so much of the action in her Italian restaurant.

Although this was Gibson's second successive thriller, it is a much more cerebral film than *Lethal Weapon* and is not for those with short attention spans. It is clear Gibson was continuing to push himself creatively in his choice of work. *Tequila Sunrise* promised much. Mac and the other characters get endless opportunities to articulate their feelings and their motivations, but Towne never does quite face up to the moral questions posed by Mac's past. We are expected to see Carlos as a villain because he is a drug dealer, but accept Mac as a hero despite the fact that he used to be a drug dealer, is enjoying the benefits of his crimes and is still prepared to help out a friend with a deal. Reviews were disappointing but it was another hit nevertheless, grossing $41 million in North America; and the industry was accrediting its success not to its distinguished writer-director but to Mel Gibson.

*Lethal Weapon 2* was under discussion even before the original opened. The first film cost around $20 million and grossed $65 million in the US. The second film cost $30 million. One single sequence, in which Gibson pulls the stilts from under a luxury house, cost about $500,000. And it lasts less than ninety seconds on screen. The expense was a huge gamble. Received wisdom was that sequels generally worked on a law of diminishing returns, and the summer release schedule was jammed with them. *Premiere* magazine was predicting *Lethal Weapon 2* would end up behind *Ghostbusters II*, *Star Trek V* and various other films. 'Not Lethal enough to bump off the big guns,' it predicted. But *LW2* took $147 million in North America and ended up the third highest-grossing film of 1989, behind *Batman* and *Indiana Jones and the Last Crusade*.

Gibson was reportedly on $4 million and a share of receipts. He was now sufficiently well off to add to his property portfolio, complementing his Australian holdings with a house in Malibu, the seaside community just outside Los Angeles, which has provided homes for several Hollywood stars. Gibson's family were with him during *LW2* and he was shooting in the LA area. Gibson had it made, even if the film bombed. 'When I first read the script I thought we were in trouble,' he said. 'But as we'd knock it off every day, it just changed. I've never improvised so much in my life. It was fun, a free-for-all.' He entertained colleagues with puns, renditions of 'Edelweiss' and Jewish impressions, utilising a coffee filter as skullcap. He also shot an anarchic video record of production for the HBO American TV channel.

*LW2* opens with a close-up of Gibson as Martin Riggs, screaming with delight and pounding the roof of his car as he and his partner Roger Murtaugh pursue – you've guessed it – a drug dealer. 'God, I love this job,' exclaims Riggs. At one point he even chases the drug dealer's car on foot, he jumps on it and demands to see a driving licence and insurance. Riggs has obviously emerged from his suicidal phase and the film immediately establishes a much jokier, more upbeat tone than its predecessor.

Riggs is still crazy enough to dislocate his shoulder to win a bet that he can get out of a straitjacket, but he is now sufficiently composed to discuss his wife's fatal road accident with his partner's wife Trish. Riggs still lives with his dog in a trailer, where he is seen laughing away at the Three Stooges on television, though he appears to have become a part-time member of the Murtaugh family. At one point Riggs tells their colleagues that Murtaugh's daughter will be appearing in a television advert, despite Murtaugh's discomfort, which intensifies when the family sit down to watch it and discover it is an advert for condoms. Riggs tells Murtaugh not to worry about the reaction at work because his information to workmates about the advert 'will have gone in one ear and out the rubber'. This, presumably, is an example of Gibson's improvisation.

The funniest performance is that of Joe Pesci as a camp, hyperactive, motor-mouthed accountant called Leo Getz. 'Whatever you need, Leo Getz.' He is prepared to give evidence against the drugs gang for whom he has been laundering money, and Riggs and Murtaugh are assigned to protect him.

In the opening sequence the drug dealer escapes but has to leave his car behind and the boot turns out to be full of gold

Krugerrands. He subsequently reports the loss to his boss Arjen Rudd (Joss Ackland), who is exploiting his position as a South African diplomat to run a drugs operation. 'It's not your fault,' Rudd calmly tells his underling. 'Sometimes these things don't go as planned.' And then he signals discreetly to his lieutenant, Pieter Vorstedt (Derrick O'Connor), who shoots the man dead. The scene is reminiscent of the sort of punishment meted out when minor villains fall short of expectations in James Bond movies.

Riggs and Murtaugh realise Getz must have been working for the same gang as the driver they had been pursuing and follow up his leads, with Getz helping. One of the best sequences is when Getz creates a diversion to allow Riggs to infiltrate Rudd's offices. He tells an official he has a friend who wants to emigrate to South Africa, the official is enthusiastic until Getz introduces Murtaugh, who explains he wants to go to South Africa to support the oppressed black majority.

Riggs has a romantic relationship with a South African secretary, played by Patsy Kensit, the actress and singer who survived the debacle of *Absolute Beginners*. The film includes one of Gibson's more explicit sex scenes, though he later revealed there were 'hundreds' of people present, including his wife, and claimed to have had more fun walking the dog. Kensit's character is killed by Vorstedt, who tells Riggs that he killed his wife too, in an attempt to kill him. Riggs is then trussed up in a straitjacket and thrown into the sea. Big mistake, of course. Riggs and Murtaugh meet up at Rudd's house, and Riggs instructs his partner to 'just go in and shoot those fuckers' when Riggs gives a signal, which turns out to be when he attaches a cable from his truck to the stilts supporting the house and pulls it down.

Director Richard Donner had used a real house on Mulholland Drive for some scenes, but the $350,000 house that is pulled down was specially built in the hills near Six Flags Magic Mountain theme park. It took ten weeks to put up and just seconds to bring down. Neither of these houses could be used for the interior shots where the house starts to vibrate, so Donner spent a further $100,000 on an elaborate vibrating set at Burbank Studios. The collapsing house was built with 'break lines' throughout the walls and floors, at which points explosive bolts were placed. Donner used multiple cameras, some of them unmanned, to ensure he got the best footage possible in the only take there was going to be.

Riggs and Murtaugh track the South Africans to the docks and virtually wipe them out. But Rudd manages to pump Riggs full of bullets before turning to Murtaugh and claiming something called 'dipp-low-ma-tick eem-you-ni-tay'. Murtaugh shoots him anyway and orders Riggs not to die. Riggs tells him he is beautiful, asks for a kiss and is obviously going to survive to fight another day. Gibson had said he was attracted to *Lethal Weapon* by the fact that Riggs was no superman. Clearly by the end of the sequel he is.

Joss Ackland, the veteran British actor who plays Rudd, recalls the shoot as great fun. 'It was jokes all the way really. And Mel, to work with, is a joy. He's so professional and at the same time always full of humour . . . It's very rare that someone as good-looking as that is such a good actor . . . And it was, I may say, quite a rare thing to work with someone in the States of that age who wasn't totally narcissistic and selfish.'

Gibson encouraged everyone to improvise and Ackland claims credit for Glover's quip that the villains have been de-Kaffir-nated. 'A lot of the dialogue sort of sprang up at the last minute during the take,' says Ackland. 'Whenever one makes a movie, whatever you do, the important thing is to know it backwards, and then when you get to the scene, and suddenly something happens differently, then you do that. That's what Mel did. He seized the moment.' Ackland had not seen the first *Lethal Weapon* film. 'I'm not a great action movie fan,' he says. 'Bruce Willis and Schwarzenegger leave me cold, quite honestly. But there was so much humour in the script, and even the violence was jokey. It couldn't really be taken seriously.'

But many people did take it seriously and there was considerable debate over it. The body count rivalled that of the Bond films, and while Hollywood villains usually make one last attempt to shoot the hero, simply to justify the hero's own action in killing them, there is no such conscience-salving device here. Rudd is executed in cold blood. One villain is killed by a flying surfboard and Murtaugh kills another two with a nail-gun.

Richard Guilliatt argued in London's *Time Out* magazine

that the film tapped the American obsession with crime but replaced the moral ambiguities of *Dirty Harry* with jokes. 'In contrast to Harry Callahan, Riggs is a zany wise guy, whose vigilante ethic is never questioned. He's pure hero.' Gibson clearly got annoyed when Guilliatt persisted with the same line of questioning during an interview. 'Good guys and bad guys, it's been the same since Hamlet,' said Gibson. 'What the hell's the difference? Hamlet goes in and kills people because they did something to him. He's a vigilante . . . You're getting serious about it. And that's a fashionable mode at the moment. And it's bullshit.'

The British censor James Ferman would not approve the film uncut, even for over-18s, though other countries took a much more liberal view and children could see it in the United States, if accompanied by an adult.

Much of the violence is rooted in the absurd, physical comedy of the Three Stooges, but the Three Stooges did not have machine-guns. There is an underlying nastiness which the humour cannot entirely disguise and which detracts from *LW2*'s style and energy. Pesci is nothing short of brilliant, a wonderful foil to Gibson and Glover. He is never still, tagging along behind them like a dog, stealing every scene in which he appears. And Ackland makes for a ruthless, exotic villain worthy of Bond, even if he is an outrageous stereotype that prompted complaints from South African officials.

Ackland had been appearing in British films since the forties, but it was *White Mischief*, a drama set in Kenya during the Second World War, that landed him the part. 'You know what the Americans are like,' he told me. 'Kenya is in Africa and this is South Africa, so that is how it happened.' His previous credits included *The Three Musketeers*, *Saint Jack* and, on television, *Tinker, Tailor, Soldier, Spy*. 'I find it a bit infuriating, in fact. I have done an awful lot of work and people know me from *Lethal Weapon 2* more than anything else, simply because the whole world has seen *Lethal Weapon 2*, everywhere you go, whether it's Mexico or the Bahamas or up in the Himalayas . . . It was a bit of old nonsense, but it was enormously successful nonsense.'

Rob Cohen and John Badham, prospective producer and

director of *Bird On a Wire*, visited the set of *Lethal Weapon 2* and sat drinking cappuccino while waiting for their opportunity to interest Gibson in their comedy-action movie about a man who has been in hiding for fifteen years when suddenly, in the course of a single day, two hitmen track him down and the girlfriend he has not seen for a decade and a half turns up by chance at the garage where he is working. He claims to be someone else, but she returns for a second look just in time to rescue him, and they end up on the run together, pursued by gangsters and police.

*Bird On a Wire* was just one of hundreds of projects offered to Gibson around this time. Producer Jerry Weintraub developed a big-budget motor-racing film called *Champions* specifically for him and lined up Tony Scott, director of *Top Gun*. It fell through and Scott went off to direct Tom Cruise's racing picture *Days of Thunder* instead. For years Gibson had been developing projects in Australia with *Gallipoli* producer Pat Lovell, including *Tetley*, a comedy adventure, scripted by Lynda La Plante who wrote the *Widows* television series; and an adaptation of the Australian writer George Johnston's book *Clean Straw For Nothing*, which would have reunited him with Gillian Armstrong and Judy Davis.

Lovell nursed Gibson through drinking bouts and hangovers, stuck him on a flight home to Robyn when the excesses of the Cannes Film Festival proved too much and accompanied him to high-powered business meetings in Hollywood where he felt ill at ease and disconcerted everyone by throwing peanuts in the air and trying to catch them in his mouth. Gibson discovered he enjoyed Hollywood more than he expected, and, during the making of *Lethal Weapon 2*, announced he was pulling out of Gibson Lovell Productions, without a single project coming to fruition. Lovell refuses to discuss the experience.

Cohen and Badham did not even have a script to show Gibson. Not an entire script anyway. It was in the process of being rewritten in the original, the central character was a sixties radical who had gone underground – the film's title is taken from a seminal Leonard Cohen song of the period. But several films with similar sixties plot elements, including the excellent *Running On Empty*, had done disappointingly at the box office. The script was now being reworked to make the central character a small-time drugs smuggler who provides evidence against two corrupt federal agents and has a series of false identities under a witness protection programme. Cohen's song was retained, for his namesake believed its title conjured up the image of a bird exposed like a target.

In managing to set up a meeting, Cohen and Badham had already got further than most who wanted to see Gibson's name above their movie title. Cohen had been executive vice-president of Motown's motion picture division at twenty-three and produced *Mahogany* and *The Wiz*. Badham's previous work included *WarGames*, *Short Circuit* and, most notably, *Saturday Night Fever*. Nevertheless, they still had to hang around in the middle of the night, waiting for Gibson to fit them in when he had a few minutes spare.

Years later Cohen recounted the details for me of that first nervous meeting with Gibson. 'I showed him half the script, which was all I had, and Badham talked a little about what he wanted to do with the movie and I could see that the meeting wasn't really going particularly well. You know, you're looking for the common ground and we hit on the fact that he and I were both involved in cattle-breeding programmes, because my wife's family are cattle ranchers and Mel is very active in big-time cattle ranching. We were both interested in the low-fat, lean beef, Limousin beef, and different breeds, so he and I started to talk about cattle and we made this sort of nice connection, because I don't think he expected anybody else in Hollywood to be interested in this sort of thing.

'And I said to him before we left, about two o'clock in the morning . . . "You know, Mel, the movies that you've had great success in are the movies that either have action or some good female counterpart. And I understand that you're thinking of doing an all-out comedy." And he said, "Yes, that's right." And I said, "Well, I think *Bird On a Wire* gives you an action format, with a lot of opportunity to use your natural humour and a woman to play against."

'He read the first sixty pages and he and his wife Robyn really seemed to like it and everybody in his camp seemed to like it. We got the other sixty pages and we had this terrible day where in the morning we heard he was passing and then in the afternoon we got a call saying he had decided to do it.' According to Cohen, Gibson was unconcerned that yet again he was playing a character with a background in drugs. Cohen says: 'He was relatively innocent. Basically he was a kid who liked to fly aeroplanes and who got involved with some bad characters.' The back-story is simply a plot device to get the two central characters moving.

Goldie Hawn's agent lobbied for the female lead. Gibson was now at the stage where he could approve or veto co-stars. Hawn had not had a major hit since *Private Benjamin* in 1980, and she was ten years older than Gibson. Gibson knew Hawn through Kurt Russell, her partner and Gibson's *Tequila Sunrise* co-star, he liked her and felt she would heighten the comedy and fun within the film. *Bird On a Wire* shot on location in Canada, Gibson moved his family up to Vancouver and when *Lethal Weapon 2* opened Warner flew journalists up from the United States for interviews.

*Bird On a Wire* is not that far removed from *Lethal Weapon 2* in its combination of comedy and action, except the balance is tipped towards the former and the tone is lighter. In his first scene, Gibson's character Rick Jarmin plays a trick on his boss, who leans on the car under which Jarmin is working and brings it crashing down. The boss grabs Jarmin's legs which come away in his hands and Gibson emerges laughing from the other side of the car. 'You can't say you never pulled anybody's leg before,' he quips.

Hawn, however, has to attempt to establish her character as a successful lawyer-businesswoman at the outset, though she soon has the opportunity for her trademark kooky comedy, which entails much screaming where one might normally expect acting. An early car chase differs from *Lethal Weapon* and *Mad Max* in that Gibson starts off upside down, with Hawn's foot on his face, attempts to take over driving, sits on her shoulders and winds up with her legs round his neck.

The car chase is followed by a motorbike chase and an aircraft chase. Jarmin has been wiped from FBI computers by a corrupt agent, and the two men against whom he gave evidence are now on his trail. In the original script, Jarmin revisits a whole series of past lives, but in the rewritten version he revisits only two. His return to a hairdresser's salon to pick up an address book affords the chance for some half-hearted mincing, which annoyed gay activists. Jarmin subsequently goes back to a farm just because it is near. The final showdown takes place in a zoo and involves apes, big cats and piranha fish.

There are no particularly memorable lines and the film depends on the strength and energy of the central performances. Angie Errigo's comments in *Empire* were typical: 'This is nonsense of the most derisory sort . . . But Hey! Who cares? Mel looks absolutely scrumptious and is far more amusing than the writers deserve, Goldie's Awfully Cute, and together they make a very appealing, almost persuasive couple.'

Gibson seemed fairly in tune with the critics when he described the film as 'a piece of fluff'. On the question of Hawn's credibility as a high-flying lawyer, he said: 'I forgot about the lawyer bit. You can't hook into it like that. It's not that kind of film. It's full of huge holes in the plot . . . It's a very surface kind of effervescent entertainment piece.' Gibson and Hawn refused to do a sex scene, insisting it would undermine the tone of the film. Nevertheless he had no objection to showing everyone his bum again and the film was another big hit, grossing $71 million in North America.

Cohen got to know Gibson well during this time. 'Mel is an incredible nexus of contradictions,' he says, 'which is why he's so interesting as a man and also on screen. He has a lot of nervous energy, there's a certain shyness to him, and yet there's an aspect of him which is the class clown of the sixth grade. You know, there's days where he's throwing condoms filled with water, tied up as water balloons, as you walk onto the stage, and he's running around on top of the make-up trailer like a schoolboy. And then there's the Mel that's got a dark and extremely soulful side. And then there's the Mel that's very aware that he's one of the most handsome men on the planet. And then there's the Mel that wants to be taken seriously as an artist.' Cohen believes Gibson is ultimately a mixture of the religious and the profane, haunted and driven by demons inherited from his father.

Cohen acted as second unit director, as well as producer. 'I directed him in several of the action sequences and we were talking about our desires to be fully-fledged directors in our own right.' Gibson was uncomfortable with his status as a Hollywood star, but Cohen argued Gibson could use it to further his ambitions as a director by insisting he would only act in a film if he could direct as well. 'I really felt there was a quest in the man to get on to something big . . . A lot came together for him in *Braveheart* that was beginning to percolate back when we were doing *Bird On a Wire*.'

Cohen, who went on to direct Sean Connery in *Dragonheart* and Sylvester Stallone in *Daylight*, had seen the *Braveheart* script before Gibson was attached and reckoned the religious imagery was challenging and the final graphic scenes of execution and torture were going to be particularly problematic for whoever directed it. Then he heard Gibson was doing it. 'I knew *Braveheart* was the perfect story for him,' he says.

*Bird On a Wire* came in the middle of what was becoming another movie-making binge for Gibson and was followed almost immediately by *Air America* and three arduous months of filming in remote parts of Thailand, during which the 500-man crew suffered everything from extreme boredom to mystery viruses and earthquakes. Thailand was doubling for Laos during the Vietnam war. It was supposedly neutral but in reality the Americans were prepared to take extreme measures to promote their interests there.

*Air America* was conceived as a black comedy in the style of *Catch-22*, in which an enterprising American officer sets up a commercial company and eventually accepts a contract from the Germans to bomb his own men. The absurd lengths to which the CIA would go to preserve alliances with the Laotian military were to be illustrated by the provision of aircraft and pilots to transport the local warlord's heroin – at a time when the drug was tightening its grip on Western society, young Americans were dying and US law enforcement agencies were doing all they could to stop the flow into the country. The big difference between M&M Enterprises and the use of American planes for German bombing and Air America and the use of American planes for heroin transportation is that the latter actually happened.

While President Nixon was insisting the US had no combat

troops in Laos, the CIA had secretly built up the largest civilian airline in the world, transporting everything from pigs and people to napalm and heroin, on the basis that the drug trade was essential to finance the Laotian military. It was yet another example of Tricky Dicky's duplicity and intrigue. Writer Richard Rush was attracted by both the nefarious politics of the enterprise and the spirit of adventure of the men who flew the aircraft, from tiny single-engined planes to transporters that looked like gigantic pregnant guppies.

The part of Gene Ryack, the older of the two main pilots, was originally intended for Sean Connery, with the younger role of Billy Covington passing between Bill Murray, Jim Belushi and Kevin Costner. Gibson was approached to play Covington, read the script and turned it down. 'The attitude was entirely too black,' said Gibson, who was honing comedy skills of a somewhat lighter variety. John Eskow, who scripted the Clint Eastwood comedy *Pink Cadillac*, was hired to rewrite Rush's script and described the revised project as 'a fun, zany thing for the whole family, with laughs aplenty and big things blowing up'.

Gibson signed up for $7 million and a share of the takings. However, he felt he was too old to play Covington and opted for the role of Ryack, a veteran who has 'gone native', married a local woman and is trading guns on the side to finance his retirement. Covington is a newcomer, recruited to Air America after being sacked as a radio traffic reporter when he flies his chopper right down into a jam and gets involved in an on-air confrontation with a lorry driver. As Covington the film-makers hired Robert Downey Jr, a gifted actor who subsequently won an Oscar nomination for *Chaplin*, but whose career has been blighted by drugs, culminating in his arrest in 1996 for drink-driving and possession of heroin, crack, cocaine and an illegal revolver.

Director Roger Spottiswoode was going to have to spend months making a film in the Golden Triangle with a man with a drug problem and another who only seemed able to keep his drink problem under control when his wife and family were with him – and they were not going to be.

*Premiere* magazine recalled the first meeting on the set between the stars. Downey said to Gibson: 'I don't know about you, but I'm the kind of actor who doesn't sit around bullshitting about character motivation. I say we just go out and kick some ass.' And Gibson replied that that was his approach exactly. Except Downey had been joking, because he is the kind of actor who sits around worrying about character motivation. Downey gave up drinking and smoking, and, despite being in the Golden Triangle, stayed off drugs during the shoot. He lost weight and worked out rigorously, though he would often turn up late on set.

The film was an enormous undertaking. It had a budget of $35 million; a crew of 500 divided into four units using as many as 15 cameras; and 26 aircraft borrowed from the Thai air force. They were shooting in temperatures of over 100°F, in a country inhabited by poisonous snakes and dangerous drug dealers – one of whom was reportedly placated with Gibson's autograph.

On the first day in a hill-tribe village, the tribesmen began drumming just as Spottiswoode was about to shoot. One of the villagers had died and, despite pleas from the production team, the drumming continued all day. For a scene in which Ryack and Covington are captured by tribesmen, Spottiswoode needed rain. The village shaman told Spottiswoode it would rain. But the forecast was fair, so Spottiswoode arranged for his own downpour. Just as the crew turned their hoses onto the set, the rain came. The shaman correctly predicted it would last only one hour and would be followed by an earthquake, which was the first of three during production.

Ryack takes Covington under his wing, so to speak. Covington is shot down. General Soong comes and retrieves his drugs but leaves Covington and his companions, at which point Ryack picks up Covington, they are shot down for a second time and end up in the hands of the hill tribesmen. In one of the film's funniest sequences Ryack tells his captors they were ripped off when they traded a cow for such old guns and asks if they have tried them in the rain. One of the tribesmen pulls the trigger with his gun aimed at Ryack. Nothing happens. 'For all-weather guns at rock-bottom prices . . .' says Ryack, launching into a sales pitch.

*Air America* has some delightfully black moments, including the CIA plan to drop extra-large condoms from aircraft to make the locals think Americans have very large penises and must therefore be extremely formidable men. And it goes some way towards capturing the weirdness of the pilots' existence and the world they inhabit: drinking, arguing and shooting lizards on a crazy golf course that represents American culture exported to the Orient; and radioing an advance order for lobster at Nino's Restaurant (where two dinner-jacketed Laotians, one tall and thin, one short and fat, sing 'Horse With No Name') not knowing whether they will make it back without being shot down.

But alongside the strain of surreal black comedy is a second variety that borders on slapstick and revolves around a visiting senator and the general, whom the senator initially mistakes for an airport porter. General Soong is played by Burt Kwouk, who was Cato, Inspector Clouseau's houseboy, in *The Pink Panther* movies.

The script was undergoing continual revision throughout the shoot, relations on set became increasingly tense, particularly when Gibson was refused leave to attend the birth of his sixth child. Stuck in a strange land on an unhappy set without his family, Gibson began drinking heavily again. The film shot throughout October, November and December 1989 in Thailand, resumed shooting in Los Angeles after a Christmas break and finished with a month at Pinewood Studios in England, so production spanned two decades. Even then, the film-makers seemed unsure of what they had got and eventually deemed it necessary to recall Gibson and Downey to shoot a new ending, after Gibson had made *Hamlet*.

Ryack defends their involvement in the drugs trade by saying no one has won a war in the region without controlling the opium and argues they are simply pack mules. Covington attempts to blow up the refinery, but fails. Ryack, obviously under the moral influence of Covington, dumps his cache of arms to make space in his plane for refugees who are stuck between two armies in a battle zone. He plans to recoup his losses by selling the plane – 'The US doesn't exist in Laos and neither does this plane' – and the film closes with Frank Sinatra singing 'Come Fly With Me'.

British journalist Christopher Robbins, whose book inspired

the film, claimed *Air America* was a trivial travesty, Air America's veterans were unhappy, critics were dismissive and box-office returns were disappointing. *Air America* is underrated. It is both funny and engaging, but it never truly fulfils the potential of its central grotesque absurdity and is undermined by its sentimental, feel-good Hollywood ending. Gibson told one journalist off the record that he hated the way the film finally turned out. Which seems slightly ironic, given that his objections to the darkness of the earlier script were a key element in moving the project towards 'a fun, zany thing for the whole family, with laughs aplenty and big things blowing up'.

# 9

## TO BE

Zeffirelli is one of the great names in the arts. In a long and glittering career he has worked in opera and theatre, and occasionally film and television, with Callas, Olivier, Visconti, Dali and Domingo. In the late sixties he filmed Shakespeare's *Romeo and Juliet*, with teenagers in the title roles. It was not just a hit, but the fifth biggest of 1969 in North America. We are talking about a film whose success was on a par with *Wayne's World* and *Mrs Doubtfire*. Zeffirelli had earlier filmed *The Taming of the Shrew* with the battling Burtons. Casting is not quite everything for Franco Zeffirelli, but everything else flows from it.

He nurtured plans to complete his Shakespearean film trilogy with *Hamlet*, arguably the greatest play ever written. He had already directed it in the theatre, where the uncut text lasts more than four hours. It is a classic revenge drama and yet it is more than a revenge drama. Hamlet is the archetypal modern man, who dwells upon the nature and consequences of intended actions, and in so doing fails to act. He cannot bring himself to kill the uncle who poisoned his father, bedded his mother and took his crown. He considers killing himself instead – 'To be or not to be: that is the question.' He does nothing but talk. It is a play of 'words, words, words': *Hamlet* made it into *The Guinness Book of Records* with the 11,610 that he delivers. And yet by the end the stage resembles the final scene of *Reservoir Dogs*.

The part of Hamlet demanded a man who was one of the best actors of his generation. Zeffirelli demanded he must also be a film star whose presence in the role would automatically take Shakespeare to a new mass audience. Zeffirelli wanted an actor who could not only carry off Hamlet's intellectual musings but could also explode into violent action. Sean Connery had the box-office clout Zeffirelli wanted, he could explode into action and, although public and critics had difficulty in disentangling Connery from Bond, his other films revealed an exciting and accomplished actor. But by 1970 he was already forty. Zeffirelli wanted a younger man.

Years passed. Perhaps the man for whom Zeffirelli was looking simply did not exist. And then he saw *Lethal Weapon*. Martin Riggs is driven, by the death of his wife, to thoughts of suicide. He puts his revolver in his mouth and steels himself for death. In the darkness Zeffirelli smiled and said to himself the words: 'To be or not to be.' He had found his Hamlet. The only problem now was convincing Mel Gibson he could play a part that brought Laurence Olivier an Oscar and Daniel Day-Lewis a nervous breakdown.

'I spoke to his agent, who is a good friend of mine, Ed Limato in Hollywood,' says Zeffirelli. 'And the man almost fainted when I told him.' Limato was extremely dubious. *Hamlet* would be an enormous risk not just for Gibson, but also for Limato, whose share of Gibson's escalating fees was sufficient to maintain a very comfortable lifestyle. Nevertheless, Limato set up a meeting between Gibson and Zeffirelli over Sunday brunch in an LA hotel. Gibson later recalled Zeffirelli's opening words when they met, a salutation perfectly in keeping with Zeffirelli's great sense of theatre: 'Something is rotten in the state of Denmark,' Zeffirelli declared.

Gibson takes up the story: 'He was like a comedian coming out on stage and provoking the audience to shout "How rotten is it?" And the guy replies, "Let me tell you, it was so rotten . . ." Then he told me how *Hamlet* was a play about spies, listening to each other all over the place.' Zeffirelli outlined his vision of a *Hamlet* for the young people of the 1990s, not just pretty words but an exciting drama of sex and violence. 'The brunch became lunch,' Zeffirelli tells me, 'and the lunch became tea in the afternoon and the tea became dinner and supper until eleven o'clock of the same day we had been talking for seven hours, eight hours, and decided we were going ahead with it.'

'It wasn't a question of deciding to do it,' says Gibson. 'Why shouldn't I do it? It was like someone drawing a line on the ground and daring me to step over that line. It was a question of whether I'd pick up the challenge or let it go by.' The popular perception of why Gibson should not be playing Hamlet was suggested in newspaper headlines like 'Mad Max to play Crazy Dane', 'Lethal prince' and 'Alas, poor Mel's Hamlet'. The public, and more particularly the press, associated Gibson specifically with action movies, most recently with a little light comedy thrown in. They did not associate him with Shakespeare, great drama or even great films.

Many in Britain and America had forgotten, or never seen, *Tim* and *Gallipoli*, which had earned Gibson two best actor awards in Australia by the age of twenty-five. He had drifted into roles that were earning him a fortune but no longer provided the artistic challenge of earlier work. 'I have cruised through a couple of films, I have to admit, and it shows,' he said. 'You want to cringe at the rushes and beg them to cut away to anything.' Zeffirelli may have seen in *Lethal Weapon* an actor who could deliver *Hamlet* to a new generation, but Gibson's Hamlet was not simply from *Lethal Weapon* untimely ripped. Gibson had been a classical stage actor, with glowing reviews for *Death of a Salesman*, *Waiting For Godot* and *Romeo and Juliet*. He had read and memorised Shakespeare's sonnets for pleasure and now he was being offered the chance to play his greatest role by the one man who had succeeded in taking Shakespeare to a truly mass audience in the second half of the twentieth century. Gibson was not going to say no.

Gibson read the play ten times in ten days. 'It's shifty stuff. So many ways to do it, none of them safe. Contradictions everywhere. Nasty twists and turns. Hellish. And on top of everything, the great, great lines. Shakespeare was like a tennis champion serving ace after ace. How could I possibly hit them back?' Gibson was simply coming to the same conclusions as countless Shakespearean scholars had done before him, albeit he expressed them differently. He read various commentaries on the play and found a different interpretation in each.

'Figuring *Hamlet* is like looking for Bigfoot. I just gotta take my best shot,' said Gibson. 'Hamlet, as I see him, is in one hell of a depression. He's a man of action, but he can't act. He knows Claudius killed his father, but he can't face it. Even after he gets the evidence, he keeps chasing his own tail, playing word games, pretending to be crazy. And all the while his emotions build up and up. Then the dam bursts. But at the wrong time and over the wrong people. He calls his mother a whore, he breaks Ophelia's heart, he murders Polonius, a harmless old fool, and doesn't seem to give a damn.

'He's exquisitely sensitive and savagely cruel. He's a minefield of contradictions and ambiguities, no sense of proportion, no sense of timing. For someone so rational he's incredibly volatile. The man is a living time bomb, and that's how I decided to play him.'

Much was made of Gibson doing the film for a fraction of his usual fee, which was variously put at anything from union minimum to $1 million. Although the film's budget was reported at the time as being between $15–30 million, Zeffirelli says it was about $10 million, a minuscule sum for an international production, with location shooting, specially constructed period sets and costumes, and a starry cast, although most were coming from the stage and were therefore comparatively cheap. This was at a point in Gibson's career when Limato might well have been asking for $10 million to pay for his client alone.

'Hamlet is for love,' said Gibson. But not only did he have a back-end deal, which would start paying dividends when the public came to see the film, he had also become involved financially in the film. He set up Icon Productions with Bruce Davey, the Sydney showbiz accountant he had met a decade earlier. So *Hamlet* formally became a Franco Zeffirelli film and an Icon production; for Carolco, the big independent company whose roster included *Rambo* and *Terminator*; for, in turn, Warner Brothers, who were putting money into *Hamlet* and would distribute it in the United States.

The name Icon seems to play on Gibson's religious outlook, his self-deprecation and his penchant for punnery, that old combination of the spiritual and the profane. Bruce Davey became executive producer of *Hamlet*. It was a Shakespeare film, it was a Zeffirelli film, but it was also very much a Gibson-Davey film. 'I wish I had a money man like him,' says Zeffirelli, maintaining he was still waiting for money he was due more than five years after the film came out.

After *Air America*, Gibson had two months in which to prepare for *Hamlet*. He did not perhaps realise the enormity of what he was doing until he had lunch with Paul Scofield and Alan Bates. They had both played Hamlet on stage, night after night, exploring the nuances and contradictions, the sensitivity and savagery, that could possess an actor. Now they were playing supporting roles to Gibson – Scofield, the ghost of Hamlet's father, and Bates, Claudius, Hamlet's uncle. Gibson admits he was intimidated by the company.

He took fencing lessons, he learned to ride, he tinted his hair and he grew a beard, about which he would continue to swither right up to shooting. He did not want 'to put an accent on like an accessory', but worked with a voice coach to effectively neutralise his own accent. Glenn Close, the American actress who moved from stage to films that included *Fatal Attraction* and *Dangerous Liaisons*, was to play his mother. She is only nine years older than Gibson, but Zeffirelli argued that Gertrude could have had Hamlet at twelve and he wanted them to be very close in age to accentuate the sexual attraction. Zeffirelli had tried to get Sean Connery to play Hamlet's uncle, before settling on Alan Bates, one of the leading young British actors of the sixties. The rest of the cast were English. 'There was an unspoken agreement for everyone to try and meet up in the middle,' says Gibson. But it was not simply a question of accent. Gibson discovered the British actors enunciated much more clearly than most Americans, who he feels have a tendency to mumble to stress their naturalism. But no one mumbles their way through *Hamlet* and gets away with it. Gibson gave up smoking and embarked on a programme of breathing and vocal exercises.

Like an athlete preparing for the Olympics or James Bond about to set off on a particularly daunting mission, Gibson had to prepare every part of himself, physically and mentally, and acquire new specialist skills in an extremely short time for what was going to be the biggest challenge of his professional life.

Zeffirelli found Gibson committed but very tense. And he would remain tense throughout filming. 'He realised how dangerous it was,' says Zeffirelli. Gibson showed his parents around Shepperton Studios, where interior sets had been constructed. He had rented a large house in the south of England and pulled his family around him for support.

Most of the early shooting, however, was in Scotland. Olivier had shot at Elsinore itself. But Scandinavian castles lacked the primitive, sinister atmosphere Zeffirelli wanted. He was keen to shoot in Scotland, and told me, in my capacity as *The Scotsman*'s film correspondent, he needed 'a castle where you get familiar with the idea of a tragedy – something rotten in Denmark'. I suggested the dramatic clifftop ruins of Dunnottar Castle, near Aberdeen. He also used Blackness Castle, near Edinburgh, and Dover Castle.

There was an alternative plan to shoot in Hungary, but Gibson and Zeffirelli both favoured Scotland. The country and its people had left a lasting impression on Gibson on his only previous visit, en route from the United States to a new life in Australia more than twenty years earlier. Zeffirelli had never been to Scotland before September 1989, though he was taught English by a Scotswoman when he was a child in Florence. She introduced him to the works of Shakespeare. And during the Second World War, after a period fighting with partisans, Zeffirelli joined up, in an unofficial capacity, with the Scots Guards.

Zeffirelli had problems with Scottish weather when he returned to Dunnottar in May 1990: it was too sunny. Some actors just seemed to flow into their characters, while Gibson struggled simply to remember the lines, or so he said. Gibson was piecing together a very physical Hamlet, a riposte to some of the aesthete characterisations of the recent past. 'He didn't want to have a double,' says Zeffirelli. 'He did everything himself, actually some very dangerous scenes when he was galloping like mad on the stony beach at Stonehaven [near Dunnottar].' According to Gibson, he was given a horse that ran on rocket fuel. He jarred his back so badly that he had to take time off and has had recurring back problems ever since.

Zeffirelli pushed Gibson hard. They lay face to face on the ground at Dunnottar with a skull between them going over

and over the 'Poor Yorick' speech, filming take after take
after take. Gibson told documentary film-maker Ruth Jackson:
'Franco is obsessive with every minute detail, every garment,
every image, every visage.' His co-star Helena Bonham Carter,
who plays Ophelia, noted that Gibson seemed 'petrified' at
first, chewing nicotine gum constantly. He never relaxed,
and he began to question Zeffirelli's judgements. *Hamlet* was
proving an enormous emotional challenge for Gibson as the
film progressed and cast and crew moved from location to
location and into the studio, where Gibson had a bed installed
in his dressing room. He would sleep there during the week and
return to his family only at weekends, determined to focus on
his performance.

Zeffirelli and Gibson argued over key scenes. Looking back,
Zeffirelli considers Gibson one of the easier stars with whom he
has worked. But then you have to bear in mind that he is used to
working with people who are quite literally prima donnas. 'We
had our differences,' he says, 'but I don't recall that experience
as harder than the one I had with the Burtons or Maria Callas
or Anna Magnani . . . Like marriages, there are moments when
you don't agree, or you quarrel, or for a couple of days you just
go into a tantrum. That's absolutely normal.' It may be normal
in opera, or in Italian marriages, but it is not quite so common
in Hollywood films.

George Miller had once pressed Gibson to restrain his
performance, much to Gibson's chagrin. Gibson had gone on
to become an extremely expressive, rather unrestrained actor
in his most recent films. Zeffirelli wanted Gibson to let it all out
and it was Gibson who was arguing that Hamlet was not that
sort of man; that they should remember he was from Denmark
not Italy. He telephoned *Bird On a Wire* producer Rob Cohen
to talk through his problems, though the idea of phoning the
producer of a fluffy Hollywood comedy to ask advice about
*Hamlet* seems crazier than casting *Mad Max* in the first place.
He could not sleep at nights for worrying about *Hamlet* and
he told Jackson that sometimes he felt like shooting himself.

'You're in every scene spitting the stuff out nonstop,' says
Gibson. 'It made me kind of nuts for a while. You get very
insecure playing a part like that. I felt unsure, frustrated, but

not frightened.' He was internalising his acting perhaps more than ever before, speaking not only with the text but also with his eyes, intense pools, in whose depths lay pain and confusion, madness and latent violence. And yet, when required, Gibson was more physical than any other Hamlet had ever been.

Helena Bonham Carter had bruises on her neck after one scene with Gibson, but the most difficult scene was the one in which Zeffirelli brings out the sexual attraction between Hamlet and his mother. Hamlet pushes her onto the bed, his whole body thrusting in sexual rhythm as he rails against her betrayal until finally she silences him by kissing him full on the lips. It is an extremely emotional scene, with both characters in tears. 'This is pretty intense stuff,' said Gibson. 'I'd like weeks to work on this, but if you're in the middle of a shoot and the money clock is running at more than $100,000 a day, the pressure is on and you just get out there and shoot it.' It took five days to film. Glenn Close was so exhausted she did not have the energy to get up between takes, but at the end of it she felt deeply refreshed by the experience, as if all the tears and sweat had washed the impurities out of her body.

Gibson was sewn into his costume for the climactic sword fight with Laertes and was sweating off ten pounds a day, but he found it easy after some of the emotional challenges of the previous three months. It was one of the few points where he could introduce a little low-brow physical comedy into the film, pretending his sword is too heavy, winking at Gertrude, sneezing in another character's face, trotting round the circumference of the ring out of Laertes's reach. It is the comic interlude before the mass slaughter that ends the drama with the death of Hamlet, Laertes, Claudius and Gertrude.

'As I began to fight for Hamlet I started to understand him,' says Gibson. 'His main problem was that no one understood him. The court all thought him mad and this caused him to have doubts about himself, but throughout the play he is the sole voice of sanity. Suddenly, in the thick of the fight – with no time to think, only to react – and completely absorbed in Hamlet's actions, I am him.' To be or not to be? To be.

Those who had predicted that Gibson would not be able to rise above the mayhem of *Lethal Weapon* and *Bird On a Wire* were to be surprised at the quality of his performance. Zeffirelli had cut the play to two and a quarter hours, dropping whole sections and reordering others. He dispensed with the politics, focused on the sexual elements, played up the violence and introduced some unscripted comedy. But there was no sense of gimmickry in any of this. It was skilfully done within the limits of what would be classified a 'straight' rendition of *Hamlet*.

Jonathan Romney in *Sight and Sound* described the film as 'set-text cinema Shakespeare' and suggested 'a touch of Hollywood excess would have been welcome'. He argued Gibson's performance stood honourable comparison with his distinguished co-stars, and then went on to describe it as 'excessively august: as if he were trying above all to live down the flightier connotations of his usual image'.

Critics were generally positive, with some extremely enthu-siastic reviews. Vincent Canby of the *New York Times* thought Gibson's Hamlet 'strong, intelligent and safely beyond ridicule'. David Robinson of the London *Times* said Gibson's diction shamed young British actors. 'He excels too in intelligibility,' Robinson wrote. 'Even Olivier was not above relying on the music of his voice, and fudging any unclear meaning that could have been the muddle of some 17th century printer. Gibson has clearly ferreted out the sense of everything he has to say. His lines are clear, comprehensive and alive. Without losing the poetry, the soliloquies have the natural air of a man musing to himself.' Gibson and Zeffirelli, thinking back to Dunnottar, may have been amused to read Robinson's comment that 'even "Alas, poor Yorick" sounds as though it is uttered for the first time'.

Several critics, however, carped about how conventional the film had turned out. Angie Errigo in *Empire* congratulated Zeffirelli for his coherent adaptation and abbreviation of the text and praised Gibson for the thought, vigour and humour of his performance, but said she had hoped for more audacity and thought the overall film dull. Having ridiculed the idea of Mad Max playing Hamlet, sections of the press seemed disappointed Gibson had delivered a fine, classical interpretation of the part.

Despite his doubts and difficulties, Gibson was proud of *Hamlet* and it was rushed out in the United States in December

1990 to qualify for Oscar consideration. He made a teaching video with LA schoolchildren. Gibson's mother Anne, who was diabetic and had been ill for some time, died without getting the chance to see the finished film, though she had seen rushes while the film was in production. *Hamlet* did reasonably good business, grossing $21 million in North America, though that was only half as much as *Romeo and Juliet* two decades earlier.

There was considerable speculation that Gibson would get at least a nomination for best actor, as Kenneth Branagh had done the previous year for *Henry V*. One might have thought Gibson's achievement, in the face of widespread scepticism, and the PR job he had done for Hollywood would stand him in good stead. In the event the best actor short list was Kevin Costner (*Dances With Wolves*), Robert De Niro (*Awakenings*), Gerard Depardieu (*Cyrano de Bergerac*), Richard Harris, a surprise nominee for *The Field*, and Jeremy Irons, the eventual winner for *Reversal of Fortune*. Only *Hamlet*'s art direction and costumes got nominations, and neither won awards.

Zeffirelli believes Gibson succeeded in making *Hamlet* accessible for young audiences. 'He brought something that I've never seen in any other actor playing Hamlet . . . This man is real.' Gibson says: 'I don't think I pulled it off. I don't think anyone's pulled it off, not even Olivier . . . I gave it everything I had. What isn't there, isn't in me. It's the hardest acting I've ever done, far and away. It's taught me a lot about myself and what I can do. It's changed me and I suspect it's changed the direction of my career. I know now what it's like to work with great material. So why settle for less?'

Gibson was exhausted by the run of four films that culminated in *Hamlet*. The last time he had tried to do a string of films back to back he wound up drinking too much, brawling and being arrested for drink-driving. There were no such problems on *Hamlet*. Gibson was by no means teetotal at this point, but he seemed to have much more control of himself. His family had been in England during the shoot, even if Gibson had become obsessed with his character and started sleeping at the studio. Gibson did make one curious comment in the *Hamlet* documentary when he said: 'If your personal life is unhappy –

and whose isn't from time to time – that can help you do good work, because you're trying to get away from that so hard that you throw yourself into your work.'

Gibson was regarded very much as a family man and the comment was delivered in the context of how important it was for him to get back to his family at weekends. Out of context it might seem a rather stark admission that he has not always been happy at home, to the extent that he was glad to get away for a while. By Hollywood standards the Gibsons certainly seemed to have a very stable and enduring relationship. They had now been married ten years, Gibson insisted he believed in fidelity and attempts by tabloid newspapers to link him with other women had been few and insubstantial.

After *Hamlet* he planned to retreat to his farm in Victoria 'to lead my own life instead of someone else's'. There were Robin Hood projects all over the place and Gibson was linked with one of them. But Kevin Costner was about to begin shooting another version and in any case Gibson had serious reservations about a second successive medieval drama. He told journalists in Los Angeles: 'I'm going to take off ten months or a year, if for no other reason than people must be getting sick of the sight of me.' He wanted rest and recuperation.

But Gibson was never the sort of man who would be content doing nothing for long. His interest in farming provided him with the opportunity for hard manual labour and an alternative business venture. He ploughed some of his wealth into a ranch in Montana and in October 1990 he travelled to Modesto, a small agricultural city, east of San Francisco, to buy cattle. In Modesto he got involved in an incident that would cause him serious embarrassment more than two years later when details – and photographs – appeared in tabloid newspapers around the world.

Gibson's drink problem was never simply that he drank too much, but that he drank too much in public bars. It was the macho Australian way of drinking. 'I'd wake up in the morning with no idea where the hell I'd been the night before,' he said, by way of hostage to fortune. In Modesto he was basically picked up by three local women, with whom he shared a drunken evening, much of it in public. But his real misfortune on this occasion was that one of them had a camera.

Photographs were finally published in January 1993, including shots of Gibson cuddling the women. He certainly looked drunk, but the pictures seemed otherwise innocuous. Other shots, however, appeared to show him sniffing and drinking from one woman's high-heeled shoe. The pictures were accompanied by a text worthy of a Mel Gibson comedy. 'I just love your shoes,' he supposedly proclaimed. 'You don't understand, I really LOVE your shoes.' According to one witness, Gibson got down on his knees, removed one of the shoes which had been the subject of his attraction, held it to his nose, enthused about 'the scent', licked it, put it in his mouth, panted like a dog, growled, barked and howled, ordered vodka, poured it into the shoe and drank it and then sucked the stiletto heel.

According to one of the women, Gibson went home with her . . . and met her father, who devised a practical joke whereby he would get his secretary to come over and Gibson would jump out of a closet with no clothes on, with the apparent intention of giving the secretary a surprise. 'You don't forget a movie star running through your house buck naked.' This was comedy of a very high order indeed, though Gibson and his lawyers were not laughing. They attempted to stop publication of the pictures, which enabled *Globe* to slap on its front page the final enticement to its readers that it was printing 'bombshell photos married hunk tried to hide'.

Tabloids were understandably prepared to fork out large sums of money for the pictures. Gibson's representatives wanted the pictures, but did not want to join a bidding war for them. The scenario of Gibson having the chance to acquire compromising pictures of himself for a large sum enabled the *News of the World* to headline the story as 'sex blackmail' and talk of 'a cruel extortion plot', before repeating every detail under an 'exclusive' tag. Gibson's spokesman was quoted as saying: 'He's not denying the drinking, but is most definitely denying that any sexual adventures took place.'

The whole incident seems funny, surreal and rather trivial in itself. Gibson was not maintaining a mistress, he had simply got himself embarrassingly drunk. But the incident was not a

one-off and underlined the continuing seriousness of Gibson's
drinking and consequent lack of self-control. It is perhaps
fortunate that two years elapsed before publication and that
Gibson was forewarned and could prepare Robyn for headlines
about 'heel-raising frolics'. By the time the story was published,
Gibson had joined Alcoholics Anonymous and was teetotal.

In 1995 Gibson told Andrew Billen of the *Observer* that he
did not even remember being photographed in the bar. 'All I
was doing was drinking out of a shoe or something . . . It is
quite funny in retrospect.' He said he used to drink to loosen
up, but by this point he had not had a drink in five years.

Gibson took his time before signing up for his next film. He
was still insisting in February 1991 that if the *Lethal Weapon
3* script did not come up to scratch he would not do it and
spoke vaguely of returning to theatre or trying his hand at
directing a low-budget feature. A fee of around $10 million
may have helped persuade him of the *LW3* script's merit. The
project seems to epitomise opportunism. Gibson would again
be teamed with Danny Glover and his entire screen family;
Joe Pesci was brought back simply because he had proved so
popular in *LW2*; and Rene Russo, a model who had recently
turned to acting in *Major League*, was recruited to provide
both romantic interest and a fresh counterpoint to Gibson's
character.

*LW3*'s opportunism is perhaps best highlighted in the spectacular opening sequence in which Riggs decides to defuse a car
bomb himself without waiting for the experts. Murtaugh, who
has only eight days left until he retires, is reluctantly dragged
along. They no longer have conversation, just banter. Every line
strives to be funny, if not in content then in delivery, as Riggs
literally gets his wires crossed and makes light of the fact that
he could be about to kill them both and blow up a multi-storey
building. As it happens, they have time to get clear, but the
building explodes. Or rather implodes. This was the City Hall
in Orlando, Florida. And it really was demolished.

Florida Film Commission wrote to producer Joel Silver before
filming began in October 1991 to notify him of the planned
demolition and invite him to film it for use in the story. Director
Richard Donner says: 'When we first learned of the implosion,

we thought it would be great, but didn't know where to put it. At the end of *Lethal Weapon 2* we'd pulled an entire house down. When this opportunity was presented to us, our screenwriter Jeffrey Boam suggested starting this picture off with a bang.' The special effects team took weeks to rig up the building with glass, cork and paper that would spew from the windows to create the illusion of a bomb blast. The demolition itself took just thirteen seconds. 'Oops,' says Riggs as the building comes down behind him.

Performances are as slick as the production values, with Gibson and Glover putting on the characters of Riggs and Murtaugh like old slippers and improvising around the script. Most of the filming was done in Los Angeles, so once again Gibson could go home at night. Despite the glossiness, *LW3* has the feel of an old serial as they move from set piece to set piece. After their ill-fated effort at bomb disposal, they are returned to uniformed patrolman duties. Riggs stops a young man for jaywalking, Murtaugh asks if he needs back-up, the astonished young man begins to argue and Riggs whips out his gun.

No sooner has the jaywalking incident concluded than an armed robbery just happens to take place right in front of them. The robbery just happens to be carried out by a couple of members of a gang run by Jack Travis, a vicious ex-policeman, who is captured on video when he shoots the individual apprehended by Riggs and Murtaugh. Travis escapes but Pesci's character, Leo Getz, who is now working as an estate agent, trying to sell Murtaugh's house, just happens to recognise Travis on the video, having arranged ice-hockey tickets for him. The coincidences do not matter terribly much, for Riggs, Murtaugh and Getz have by now become the Three Stooges and the plot is simply a vehicle for gags, jokes and explosions.

Rene Russo plays Lorna Cole, a hard-boiled Internal Affairs officer who has been investigating Travis. She and Riggs take an instant dislike to each other of course – because they are so similar. Russo manages to produce the same slightly manic expressions and deliver her lines in the same clipped fashion as Gibson. After a violent encounter with the villains, Riggs and

Cole go back to her place where it transpires she has a Three Stooges computer game; they compare scars (a scene lifted straight from *Jaws*), and suitably aroused by such esoteric foreplay they make love.

Riggs still needs his fix of human suffering to get him really mad and it is in the nature of things that Something Bad must happen to Cole. Mrs Riggs was killed before *Lethal Weapon* began. Patsy Kensit's character was killed in *LW2* and her killer explained, just for good measure, that he was responsible for Mrs Riggs's demise too. Cole is shot, but survives, so Riggs can tell her he loves her in a variation on his final scene with Murtaugh in *LW2*. Cole's shooting, however, was just a sort of booster, for Riggs has already been motivated by the killing of a young colleague – on his twenty-second birthday no less.

Reviews ranged from poor to lukewarm, but are best summed up by the word irrelevant. *LW3* was formula cinema. It knew what it was trying to do, it did it well and expected its return in dollars and pounds rather than good reviews and Oscar nominations. It became the second highest-grossing film of 1992 in North America. Takings of $145 million were just short of *LW2*'s figure. It was No. 3 for the year in the UK and No. 2 worldwide, behind *Basic Instinct*, with a gross of more than $300 million.

*Forever Young* is the story of a test pilot who volunteers to be frozen in a secret experiment in 1939, after his lover is involved in a road accident and he is told she will never come out of a coma. He is defrosted in 1992, begins to age rapidly, but eventually discovers his old girlfriend is still alive. The script reminded Gibson of old romantic movies from the thirties and forties that he had seen and enjoyed as a boy, particularly *Random Harvest*, in which Ronald Colman is a shell-shocked First World War officer who blanks out his recent past, whereupon his wife becomes his secretary, until years later it all comes back to him and he rediscovers true love. 'The premise is just extraordinary, corny, really corny,' says Gibson. 'You think, oh my God, this can't be happening, but it works.'

Gibson was annoyed that he had failed to see the potential in *Ghost* and passed on a script that became one of the highest-grossing films ever, despite a wooden performance from Patrick Swayze. It had proved there was a huge audience for romantic fantasy and Gibson believed *Forever Young* could tap the same audience, while expanding his range as an actor. Warner Brothers paid $2 million for Jeffrey Abrams' script *The Rest of Daniel*, for Icon to develop as *Forever Young*. Warner had made the *Lethal Weapon* films and had long nurtured their relationship with Gibson, providing space at their Burbank lot for Icon's offices. Accountant Bruce Davey became producer and Gibson hired Steve Miner, who had made *Soul Man* and *Warlock*, to direct; but it was Gibson who was calling the shots.

Gibson was aiming the film primarily at women; he believed men would enjoy it too, though he felt many men were uncomfortable discussing love and emotions. 'I'm a romantic at heart,' he said. 'But I don't go around saying it very often. I'm even a bit ashamed to be saying it now. I'm not the most articulate guy. I think a lot of men from Australia are not too good about expressing their feelings.'

His character Daniel McCormick sits alone in a diner rehearsing a marriage proposal but cannot bring himself to deliver the lines when his girlfriend Helen (Isabel Glasser) shows up. She is knocked down as she leaves the diner. Gibson – the sexiest man in the world – admitted he could identify with McCormick's nervousness. 'I would work myself up to asking a girl out but would never do it . . . I had just as much trouble proposing to my wife as I did proposing in the movie.' He said he was touched by the film and eventually did get around to saying 'I love you', presumably to Robyn. 'Maybe if the men watch this movie, they'll be moved to say "I love you" before it's too late, because life is so uncertain.' On the other hand he also suggested Stevie Wonder's song 'I Just Called to Say I Love You' provided a 'way of saying it – without having to say it'. It also says something about his lack of musical taste.

McCormick is yet another Gibson character motivated by loss. This time there is no one to kill and McCormick neither sticks a gun in his mouth nor does he ponder the nature of being. He is frozen in what looks like an old vacuum cleaner. The early part of the film captures the style of the late thirties and the spirit of classic romantic movies. As McCormick slips into his own personal ice age, he sees himself kissing Helen one last time, on a cliff top, with a red biplane flying past.

The film cuts to the nineties, and quickly establishes a very different tone. This is a world of precocious brats, single-parent families, domestic violence; a world where badly behaved kids play around in an old military warehouse and interfere with the oversize vacuum cleaner, stuck away in a corner after its inventor was killed in a fire. A cold, naked Mel Gibson emerges. There are of course enormous comic opportunities in a man who has missed out on fifty years of technological change, but the film seems strangely reluctant to exploit them. Although McCormick is nonplussed by a man telling him to leave a message and 'squealing' in his ear, he has previously had no problem using a push-button payphone.

McCormick is taken in by Nat (Elijah Wood, who had built up a CV which, by the age of ten, included *Avalon*, *Radio Flyer* and *Paradise*), and his mother Claire, played by Jamie Lee Curtis. The daughter of Tony Curtis and Janet Leigh, she came to the public's attention when she was stalked by a masked psychopath in the first two *Halloween* movies. When she went to open the door to McCormick in *Forever Young*, she found Gibson standing there in an ice-hockey mask with a knife in his hand. (Actually the serial killer with the hockey mask was Jason Voorhees from *Friday the 13th*, two instalments of which were directed by Steve Miner.)

Gibson's character ages fifty years towards the end of the film. Make-up artists do a good job in producing loose skin around his face. Greg Cannom, who also did make-up for Francis Ford Coppola's *Dracula*, said: 'We wanted a Cary Grant look. The problem was his eyes. They are so piercing.' Despite affecting a stoop, Gibson also retains the powerful physique of a man in his thirties beneath loose-fitting clothes, and although his hair turns grey it remains as plentiful as when his character was in his prime.

Jill McGreal in *Sight and Sound* declared *Forever Young* 'a risible failure'. 'Never sure what kind of film it is meant to be, it starts off as comic-strip action, careers into buddy-buddy and turns into tearjerker before the plot gets going. By the time the action jumps to 1992, it's become a kid's movie, and en route to the finish it's alternately an action adventure, slapstick comedy and romantic drama.' Most reviewers were in broad agreement. It is true the central romance is never sufficiently developed to maximise the impact of Helen's accident and McCormick's consequent depression, the middle section of the film is slow, and Curtis seems uncomfortable, which is not surprising given that the film-makers appear unsure whether they want her character to be an alternative romantic interest or not.

The film gathers momentum tremendously towards the end. Nat and Claire have to rescue McCormick from hospital before the authorities get to him. There is a chase and Nat and McCormick end up airborne, in an old plane rather than on a bicycle. The final reunion between McCormick and Helen is clever and effective. McCormick has aged so rapidly that he is now much the same age as she is, and they embrace on the same cliff top on which they were last seen in 1939. Either one may expire at any moment, but at least they have that moment together.

The flip side of Jill McGreal's argument that *Forever Young* does not know what sort of film it wants to be is that it is aiming to exploit various genres at once. Critics have terrible problems with films that do not neatly slot into one genre, films such as *Highlander* and *Blade Runner*, both of which also play with intertwined notions of love and time. *Forever Young* is hardly in *Blade Runner*'s league, but it was not without its strengths, not the least of which was Gibson himself. A North American gross of $56 million was not bad for a failure, particularly a risible failure.

# 10

# NEW DIRECTIONS

There is perhaps a sad irony in the readiness with which Mel Gibson identified with the severely scarred title character of *The Man Without a Face*. With his blue eyes and good looks, Gibson has been branded the sexiest man alive, whereas Justin McLeod was the victim of a car crash and fire, which left the flesh on one side of his head looking as if it had melted. It is not that McLeod has no face, but that he has a face so disfigured that it becomes an object of fascination for those who see it. 'I have to cope with what he had to cope with,' Gibson insisted. 'I can walk down the street and see people do a double-take and stare just as though I had two heads. The way you look can be a blessing or a curse.'

Both Gibson and McLeod have been victims of unwanted public attention and gossip and have attempted to retreat into their own private worlds. 'I've often felt reclusive, just like he does,' said Gibson. 'I know what it's like to want to leave and just shut it all out.' For a Hollywood star, Gibson does lead an exceptionally reclusive life, though he has shared it with his unusually large family, whereas McLeod is a loner, living by himself in a spooky cliff-top house.

Gibson also saw aspects of himself in Chuck Norstadt, the awkward, pre-pubescent boy who gets to know McLeod, first as a reluctant tutor and then as a friend. The film is set in 1968, when Gibson was twelve, much the same age as Chuck. Chuck is an outsider, who comes from a broken home and whose ambition is to go to military academy. In 1968 Gibson had just moved to Australia and found it difficult to fit in –

though he had a stable family background, and he hated the old-fashioned school to which he was sent, run by Christian Brothers with strict military discipline.

Isabelle Holland's source novel had been optioned several times before Canadian TV writer Malcolm MacRury adapted it. His agent forwarded the script to Gibson, knowing he was looking for a small-scale character drama for his directorial debut. MacRury recalls their initial meeting was an uncomfortable affair, particularly for Gibson, who was suffering such severe recurrence of his back pain that he summoned an assistant to massage him as they spoke. After about an hour of this, he had to call out a chiropractor and abandon the discussion.

*The Man Without a Face* was budgeted at around $10 million, the sort of figure which by this stage Gibson could demand as his salary as an actor. It focused on the relationship between Chuck and McLeod, with the story of the latter's past gradually emerging as the relationship develops. The secondary focus was the relationship between Chuck, his mother and his two half-sisters. Gibson felt comfortable with the milieu and scale of the project. To keep costs down, he was taking Directors Guild minimum salary of less than $120,000. However, the film was being made by his own production company, Icon, with his partner Bruce Davey again acting as producer.

Despite his identification with McLeod, Gibson did not intend to play the character himself. He reckoned directing would be challenge enough and approached William Hurt and several other actors. But for one reason or another, they knocked him back. It got to the point where the finance was beginning to look shaky if the film did not get under way. Rather than postpone the project, Gibson decided to play McLeod himself. It meant not only that he would have to split his attention between directing and acting, but that he would have to spend three hours in make-up every time he wanted to step in front of the camera. The small-scale, low-budget character drama had suddenly become a major challenge.

'It was like a three-ring circus,' says Gibson. 'Getting up at five in the morning to put the prosthetics on, going out and winding up shots and then actually being in it was certainly not easy . . . I directed with my make-up on, but whatever I had to do to make this film I was prepared to do. When I first read the story I couldn't put it down. I knew it was tremendous and it fired my imagination. I was really moved by it because it has a lot to say about tolerance.'

McLeod has lived just outside a New England town for seven years without ever becoming part of the community. He is regarded as a freak by local adults and children alike. It is rumoured he writes pornography for a living, or that he killed his wife, or boyfriend, or that he is, horror of horrors, one of the Kennedys. It takes another misfit, young Chuck Norstadt, to penetrate his defences. Chuck has failed his entrance exam for the military academy which his father attended. When he discovers McLeod used to be a teacher, he asks him to help with his studies.

McLeod tests Chuck's resolve by first asking him to dig holes around his property. Gradually a friendship develops between them, but Chuck does not tell his mother about McLeod. During a row, his elder sister tells him the truth about his father – that he committed suicide in a mental hospital. His mother is away and he turns to McLeod for comfort, spending a night at his house. His mother is horrified, for it transpires McLeod served three years in prison for 'involuntary manslaughter' after his car crashed and a pupil, with whom McLeod was allegedly having an improper relationship, was burnt to death.

The film shot in Maine, where Gibson rented a cottage for himself and his family. He would spend a long day on set, watch rushes in the evening, return to the cottage and watch television to relax (TV apparently having taken the place of alcohol) and finally get to sleep, according to Gibson, at 'four or five in the morning'. Obviously he was not getting much sleep, though if one accepts Gibson at his word, bearing in mind that he said he got up at five, he was getting no sleep at all. 'I remember talking to my assistant director and going to sleep in the middle of a conversation,' he says, 'like when people get really old and just nod off . . . I was away with the fairies for about three days there, right in the middle of the film, when it wasn't under my control. It was too much. I had a million things to do.'

Nevertheless it appears to have been a relaxed shoot. Gibson rode around the set on a hobby-horse and issued directions in a variety of funny voices, ranging from old-time Westerner Walter Brennan to cartoon character Elmer Fudd. The cast nicknamed him 'Demento Boy'. 'If you have a happy crew and joke a lot, you get twice as much work done,' said Gibson. Nick Stahl, who plays Chuck, was making his feature film debut, and his role was actually bigger than that of co-star Gibson. 'Mel jokes a lot and makes me feel that I'm not messing up,' he told Allen Barra of the *New York Times* when he visited one of the locations. 'He takes all the pressure off me.'

Margaret Whitton, who plays Chuck's mother, told Barra: 'Mel is remarkably open to the ideas of other people involved. He's not a theorist or an ideologue. He sees film as a collaborative process. He's going to be a very good director, and that shouldn't surprise anyone. He's a very good actor, and good actors know how to direct themselves.' Gibson said: 'That side of the camera I feel I know something about, so that's what I'm sticking to, the acting. I feel safer with that than trying to be Orson Welles my first time out.' He says he picked up ideas on lightness of touch from Richard Donner, shock tactics and economy of time and money from George Miller and the 'artsy' side from Peter Weir.

The film begins with an ambitious dream sequence in which Chuck imagines himself carried on the shoulders of his peers at a military academy graduation day. In one striking shot the parade appears to march right over the camera, giving the audience a worm's-eye view. Gibson achieved the shot by putting the camera behind a hinged Perspex ramp which lowered as the parade approached it. Chuck begins to panic and observes that there is a face that he cannot see 'out there beyond the edge of the crowd'. The crowd falls silent and Gibson's camera whisks from one sullen, slightly menacing face to another. The whole sequence opens and closes with caps rising and falling through a blue sky.

For all that this is a small-scale character drama, scripted by a TV writer, Gibson demonstrates considerable directorial flair and confidence right from the outset. His style is, for the most part, simple and uncluttered, with the focus on the characters and the sense of time and place, though he returns to the graduation dream at the end of the film, replaying it for real. Advised to discontinue his relationship with Chuck, McLeod has moved away from the neighbourhood. But when Chuck graduates, he notices there is a figure, watching, out there beyond the edge of the crowd and he raises a hand in acknowledgement.

This is also an important film for Gibson as an actor, for it is arguably his first true character role, though McLeod is not really a man without a face. Early in the film, Chuck is seen reading a comic about the *Batman* villain Two-Face and the film's make-up artists seem to have taken Two-Face as their model. One side of McLeod's face is horribly burnt, but the other side remains pristine film star and there is no escaping the fact that McLeod is the Man With Half of Mel Gibson's Face.

It is a strange relationship in which McLeod persists in calling Chuck by his surname, but Gibson develops and defrosts his character with little touches, such as his enjoyment in the literal play-acting when he comes to teach *The Merchant of Venice* and in the way McLeod rushes to check Chuck's mock exam paper as soon as Chuck is out of the door.

*The Man Without a Face* grossed $25 million in North America, low compared to other Gibson films but a respectable figure considering the budget. More importantly, it established Gibson as a proficient and imaginative director and further enhanced his reputation as an actor. 'It really looks as if he'll have a career off the pin-up board,' said Alexander Walker in the London *Evening Standard*. 'Patent sincerity is augmented by considerable skill,' said Derek Malcolm in the *Guardian*. 'Gibson gets excellent performances from his cast, and himself contributes a determinedly unstarry portrait.' Malcolm enthused about the detail of the family quarrels, the praise for which he attributed to MacRury's script, though Gibson drew inspiration from his own childhood.

Gibson told Rachel Abramowitz of *Premiere*: 'I had a brother and sister who used to fight like cats and dogs . . . Finally my dad had enough. They were in the middle of one of their tirades, one of their venomous little spats, throwing things and breaking things . . . And he grabbed both of them by the neck and he banged their heads together really hard. I mean, it sounded like the Three Stooges. They were nearly unconscious. And he said he didn't want them to talk to each other for six months . . . Finally when the ban was lifted, they were friends, and they have been ever since. It was a perfect lesson.'

Although Gibson hated school, he has old-fashioned views on discipline and a very conservative political outlook. A liberal academic is a figure of fun in *The Man Without a Face*. But many viewers may feel the beauty of the relationship between Chuck and McLeod and of the film itself is undermined by the ultimate goal, the supposed happy ending, of a place at military school. Many would agree with Chuck's mother's comment that such places are fascist and unnatural. Some feminists also criticised the film as misogynist. Gibson responded by saying the concept of political correctness made him sick.

'Directing was more difficult than I thought it was going to be,' he later admitted. 'It's a lot more involved, especially if you are directing yourself . . . It drove me crazy because it was too much to do. I had to wear too many hats . . . If I directed another film, I wouldn't be in it.'

Gibson had fulfilled one ambition by directing *The Man Without a Face* and his next film would fulfil another. For years he had wanted to appear in a Western. In 1984 his name was linked with a possible remake of John Ford's *My Darling Clementine*, in which he was to have taken the role of Wyatt Earp, played by Henry Fonda in the original. Burt Reynolds would have directed the film and played the other major role of Doc Holliday. Reynolds was rated Hollywood's top box-office draw at the end of the seventies and beginning of the eighties, but by 1984 his popularity was waning and the team-up with Gibson never happened. Gibson was also keen to do a film called *Renegades*, in which he would have been a bounty hunter. It looked set to shoot in 1991 and Julia Roberts, who was emerging as one of Hollywood's top actresses after *Steel Magnolias* and *Pretty Woman*, was lined up to co-star. But it was to be another five years before Gibson and Roberts worked together, on *Conspiracy Theory*.

Gibson was disappointed when *Renegades* fell through and he and Davey immediately set about considering other options. It was Davey who suggested they investigate the possibility of a big-screen version of *Maverick*, the television Western series they both remembered fondly from childhood. Hollywood was only just beginning to realise the potential of film versions of old television programmes. By the time *Maverick* reached fruition, *The Addams Family* and *The Fugitive* had become major hits. '*Maverick* was screaming out at us,' says Gibson. 'He was a great character. He had flair, but was also flawed. He was charming and had a terrific sense of humour.'

*Maverick* had been one of the most successful of the many TV Westerns that aired in that period and it had been made by Warner Brothers, with whom they had such a close relationship. Unlike most TV Western series, its central character, Bret Maverick, was neither cowboy nor lawman. Neither was he tough or brave, but rather a devious and cowardly gambler. Maverick's cynicism and humour contributed to the subversion of stereotypes of Western heroes and villains, a process that was accelerated on the big screen by the spaghetti Westerns in the sixties.

More than a hundred hour-long episodes were broadcast between 1957 and 1962, with James Garner as Bret Maverick. Garner had already made several films and was in demand for more, so the producers introduced Jack Kelly as his brother Bart and latterly Roger Moore as his cousin Beau, to give Garner more free time. In the seventies the short-lived *Young Maverick* went to the extent of making the central character Beau's son Ben, in other words the original Maverick's cousin once removed.

By 1963 Garner was sharing top billing with Steve McQueen and Richard Attenborough in *The Great Escape* and he successfully played a variation on his Maverick character in *Support Your Local Sheriff* in 1969. His television private detective series *The Rockford Files* was enormously popular in the seventies. Proposals for a film of *Maverick* never got off the ground, though Garner's Cherokee production company revived the character in a series called *Bret Maverick* in 1981.

Icon and Warner Brothers agreed to develop *Maverick* as a feature film. It is normal for the director to hire the stars, but on this occasion the star hired the director, Richard Donner, with whom he had worked on the three *Lethal Weapon* films. To write the script, Gibson approached William Goldman. His volume of memoirs *Adventures in the Screen Trade* is one of the wittiest books ever written about the film industry and it provided Gibson with an invaluable insight into how Hollywood works when he arrived as a young star. But the approach to Goldman was not motivated simply by Gibson's enthusiasm for his memoirs. He was the man who scripted *Butch Cassidy and the Sundance Kid*, whose blend of drama, action and comedy very much appealed to Gibson.

Goldman produced an intelligent and witty script, with three main parts – Bret Maverick, gambler Annabelle Bransford, and Marshal Zane Cooper, all of whom are making their way to a high-stakes poker game on a Mississippi riverboat. Gibson would play Maverick of course; Meg Ryan, star of *When Harry Met Sally*, would play Bransford; and the role of Cooper was intended for Paul Newman, who had brought Butch Cassidy to life twenty-five years earlier.

Both Newman and Ryan dropped out, however, the former to make *The Hudsucker Proxy* and the latter to spend time with her baby. Kim Basinger and Jodie Foster were discussed as possible replacements for Ryan. Donner felt that, although she was an extremely talented actress, there was nothing in Foster's performances from her child prostitute in *Taxi Driver* to her FBI agent in *The Silence of the Lambs* to suggest she could be light enough or sexy enough for the role. Foster wanted to do a comedy and, despite having won two best actress Oscars, was prepared to audition for the part. By the time she signed up, there were just three weeks to go before filming began and other commitments meant Foster would miss the first ten days.

*Maverick* became a 'Who Was Who' of the Westerns. James Coburn, one of the original *Magnificent Seven*, plays the substantial supporting role of the riverboat commodore, and numerous Western veterans make cameo appearances in the big poker game, including Doug McClure, Trampas in *The Virginian*, Henry Darrow, Manolito in *The High Chaparral*, and Robert Fuller from *Laramie* and *Wagon Train*. Gibson and Donner talked long and hard about the possibility of having James Garner in the film, but felt it would be insulting to ask him to play anything other than Maverick – though it was not as if no one else had ever borne the name Maverick over the years. The loss of Paul Newman forced them to reconsider the role of Cooper and Garner jumped at the chance.

Gibson continued to gather old friends around him, including Vilmos Zsigmond, the cinematographer from *The River*. Geoffrey Lewis, the policeman in *The Man Without a Face*, became the banker in *Maverick*; Art La Fleur, one of the *Air America* pilots, became a poker player; and when Maverick pulls down the mask to expose the face of a bank robber, it is the features of Danny Glover that are revealed. Maverick is unsure whether he recognises him or not and eventually shakes his head. Between takes cast and crew played poker and Gibson and Garner practised gunplay and card tricks.

It was an eye-opener for Foster. She admits that when she first arrived, she felt everyone was simply too happy. 'I didn't really trust it. It's specifically a studio comedy mentality – they come to work basically to have fun. It's not about delving into the abyss. I usually go to work for totally different reasons . . . I've chosen a path that makes me always kind of professionally serious, and it's such a relief . . . to actually let your private personality be reflected in your work as well, instead of just the opposite.' She had started in lighter roles, and as a child star with Disney in the early seventies she had worked with James Garner on a Western called *One Little Indian*. She soon entered into the spirit of the film. Aware of Donner's initial doubts about her casting, Gibson was extremely helpful.

It was the beginning of a lasting friendship. Gibson has at times seemed awkward in his relations with other big stars and, perhaps even more surprisingly, with women as a gender. But Foster was easy company, and Gibson, and his wife Robyn, could feel assured there was no sexual danger in the relationship. Donner maintains Gibson and Foster share 'the same gross sense of humour'. Foster described Gibson as 'the kind of guy you just want to protect . . . I think that's his secret weapon, that he is so incredibly vulnerable and unaware of himself . . . All he does is spend time doing magic tricks for people or trying to think of things that will make them squeal or disgust them. He listens in a way that's kind of innocent and he disarms you because he is so unthreatening. He's like your best buddy immediately.'

The film shot over fifteen weeks in Arizona, Oregon, various

Californian locations and at Warner's studio at Burbank. The
film is picaresque and episodic as Maverick moves from one
adventure to the next on his way to 'the big game'. It opens,
in the style of the spaghetti Westerns, with an extreme close-up
of a dark, moustached face. The image seems to shiver in the
heat. Donner cuts to a shot of a rope and follows it downward
to the figure of Maverick: one end is tied round his neck, the
other end is tied to a tree – the only one in an otherwise barren
landscape. Maverick is sitting on his horse. 'Almost got hung
myself once,' says the moustached figure, the mischievously
named Angel, played by Alfred Molina who served as the
villain at the beginning of *Raiders of the Lost Ark* too. 'Didn't
care for it much.' As a parting gesture he throws down a sack,
from which a snake begins to emerge.

Maverick's voice-over declares it has been a shitty week from
the beginning and the film flashes back to his arrival – on a
donkey – in the picturesque town of Crystal River, which the
film-makers built on National Parks land on the shore of Lake
Powell in Arizona. He is owed money by the local banker, but
the bank is shut and he becomes involved in a poker game where
he first meets Angel and Annabelle Bransford. He breaks his
losing streak and deprives an apparently dim-witted youth of
a sizeable pot, but the youth suggests they disregard the hand
because his mind was not on the game. It emerges the youth is
the gunfighter John Hardin. Maverick placates him by handing
over the money, which prompts Angel to ask Maverick if he
has always been gutless. 'For as long as I can remember, at
any rate,' says Maverick. 'My old pappy always used to say,
"He who fights and runs away can run away another day."'
Maverick stands up and begins to explain how he would have
no chance against a gunfighter. His eyes, eyebrows and arms
are up and down all over the place, and suddenly, in a flash,
his pistol is in his hand, a feat he repeats several times, for, as
he observes, it just will not stay in its holster. Gibson manages
to switch from comic to manic in an instant and there are some
extremely funny throwaway lines and surreal notions in this
lengthy early sequence.

Maverick believes that if he thinks of a card hard enough he
should be able to cut straight to it in a deck. 'That would be

nothing short of magic. Of course it didn't always work. As a matter of fact it had never worked.' He meets Bransford again on the stage, where an argument between them is interrupted by the gallant Marshal Cooper. 'My feeling is that if there weren't any women none of us would be here,' he announces. Maverick has to climb out and bring the horses under control when their ancient driver finally expires. They meet a missionary party and retrieve money stolen from them by outlaws disguised as Indians, just as a party of real Indians shows up.

The Indian chief Joseph (Graham Greene who played the thoughtful Kicking Bird in *Dances With Wolves*) is an old friend. Maverick is the only one who speaks the Indian language, so he persuades his travelling companions he is offering himself up as a human sacrifice for trespassing on sacred land, whereas he really goes with Joseph because Joseph owes him money. At the Indian settlement, Maverick rides a bicycle (as did Goldman's Butch Cassidy) and Joseph explains the war paint and incessant drums are to entertain a rich Russian tourist, who insists Joseph go around saying things like 'How, white man' when he would rather speak French. 'I'll get your money just as soon as I've changed some roubles into dollars,' he tells Maverick. They devise a plot whereby Maverick pretends to be an Indian and the Russian will pay for the honour of hunting him.

Having earned $1,000 from that ploy, Maverick is waylaid by Angel and strung up from the tree we saw at the beginning of the film. He escapes when a branch breaks, and eventually reaches 'the big game', where Cooper is responsible for security. The finalists are Bransford, Angel, the Commodore (Coburn) and Maverick, who realises the dealer is in league with Angel and the Commodore. Needing the ace of spades for a royal flush, he insists Angel should personally deal him a card from the top. Against all odds, it is the ace of spades and Maverick wins half a million dollars.

But that is not the end, for *Maverick* has more final twists than any other film in motion picture history. If you have not seen the film and do not want to know the final sequence, skip to the next paragraph. Twist number one: Cooper makes off with the cash. Twist number two: Cooper and the Commodore were partners. Twist number three: the Commodore double-crosses

Cooper and intends to kill him. Twist number four: Maverick turns up and takes the cash. Twist number five: Maverick is enjoying the good life in a bath house when Cooper reappears. Twist number six: it turns out Cooper is Maverick's father, therefore Garner is playing Maverick, which is a neat twist on the complex genealogy of the television series. Twist number seven: Annabelle Bransford turns up and takes the money. Twist number eight: Maverick has kept half the money in his boot and announces he will enjoy retrieving the other half.

The early episodic structure nicely mirrors the TV series, and the device of relating most of the episodes in flashback from the lynching scene leaves the viewer looking forward to the resolution of that scene, as well as enjoying the action as it unfolds. But given that the script is otherwise so witty and inventive, the resolution of Maverick's predicament by way of a broken branch is a serious anti-climax. The latter part of the film hinges on the poker game, won by Maverick's royal flush, which leaves the viewer waiting to find out how he knew the top card was the ace of spades. But there is no explanation other than that it was magic – a reference to the earlier comment about being able to cut to a specific card but ignoring the fact that Maverick did not cut the deck, Angel dealt the card. And, for all its earlier sureness of structure, the film simply does not know when to stop.

Goldman's script gave Gibson by far the most amusing material he had ever had, though he continued his usual practice of improvising, so it is difficult to determine where Goldman ends and Gibson begins. Gibson maintains his Maverick is essentially the same as the fifties version, though the humour has been updated: 'Good or bad, my sense of humour does bleed through. You can't help it when you're as mad as I am.' Goldman is loyal to the spirit of the original character. In fact he has managed to create a West where not only is Maverick crooked, virtually everybody else is too.

It grossed over $100 million in North America, where Gibson was voted the most popular actor in an *Entertainment Weekly* poll a few months after its release. Interestingly, he topped neither the men's nor the women's votes. Harrison Ford was No. 1 with men and Tom Hanks with women. But Gibson's appeal across both sexes made him overall No. 1. The film's success and Gibson's pre-eminence in Hollywood prompted early talk of *Maverick 2*, but Gibson was becoming increasingly wary of getting caught up playing the same roles over and over again. He was still looking for fresh challenges.

At around the same time, Gibson was working on another Western, of sorts, but a film that was completely different from anything he had done before. Disney were in the process of bouncing back from the lean years of the seventies and eighties, with some of the most commercially and creatively successful cartoon features ever. Gibson followed the example of Robin Williams in *Aladdin* and Whoopi Goldberg and Jeremy Irons in *The Lion King* and agreed to provide the voice for a Disney cartoon character.

*Pocahontas* was to be Disney's first cartoon feature based on a true story. Gibson's character John Smith was a seventeenth-century Englishman who is captured by Indians in Virginia, which was of course the Western frontier at that time. *The Last of the Mohicans* is arguably a Western, though set in New York. The Western was never a fixed geographical term but rather an abstract concept, so Texas has traditionally been considered an intrinsic part of the Wild West, whereas California has not. Smith was about to be put to death by the Indians when, according to legend, Pocahontas, the daughter of the chief, ran forward and threw herself over him to stop the execution, at which point her father relented.

Disney were keen to make a love story and believed Pocahontas and John Smith would provide a dramatic adventure and a message of racial harmony, as well as a stirring romance, though the film sticks to historical fact in its refusal to marry them off and have them live happily ever after. Disney had been seriously considering an adaptation of *Romeo and Juliet*, whose ending makes *Pocahontas* seem positively upbeat.

The film is true in so much as Pocahontas and Smith existed, Smith was captured by Indians and Pocahontas may well have saved him, but almost certainly there was no romance. For a start, Pocahontas was only eleven or twelve when they met. Disney have added a few years to avoid any suggestion of paedophilia. The film's conclusion that Pocahontas belongs with her people and Smith must return to his does not sit easily with the central message of racial harmony or with the bigger historical truth about Pocahontas. After all, she married another Englishman, tobacco planter John Rolfe, with the blessing of both her father and the governor; and went with him to England, where she was received at court and where she died, possibly of smallpox, at the early age of twenty-one.

Disney are not great payers; a star's voice is not worth an eight-figure salary when many in the audience will watch the film unaware of who it belongs to. As James Earl Jones said when he voiced Mufasa in *The Lion King*: 'If you want to earn money with Disney, you buy Disney stock.' Stars voice the cartoons for fun and often for their children, for whom it may well mean more than a starring role in *Field of Dreams* or *Hamlet*. *Pocahontas* served as another lesson in Gibson's film education.

Making cartoons is an extremely lengthy process and *Pocahontas* took almost five years from its conception in 1990 to its premiere in 1995. 'It's a good deal more complicated than I would have imagined,' says Gibson. 'I was particularly intrigued by the way they create the story, which is obviously very important. I was aware of all the changes and innovations they were making as the film progressed.' Originally Disney intended that the animals should talk, as in most of their cartoons, but they jettisoned the idea to heighten the realism of the film and focus on the human characters.

Most of the voice work was done before the animation. 'It's an interesting notion to not be able to see an image and have to use your imagination to create the story and actions purely with voice in a room with a microphone,' says Gibson. 'It's like cutting off some of your senses and just using one aspect of yourself. You have to use a lot more imagination and that becomes an interesting exercise all in itself.' Disney's animators used the recordings to help them visualise the characters. The vocal performances were subtler and more sensitive than in previous cartoons and the drawings had to be more realistic.

Director Eric Goldberg says: 'Mel gave us the essence of John Smith that we wanted. He also brought a maturity to the role which added to the sense that this was a guy who actually had been around the world and done a lot of things. He gave us all that in his vocal performance and made Smith seem cavalier, yet extremely warm, sensitive and even vulnerable.' Mike Gabriel, who instigated and co-directed the film, says: 'We were very impressed with the quality of his acting skills and his ability to take a line of dialogue that might be somewhat caricatured and flatten it out. That is, he'll make it work by levelling the line instead of heightening it, which is what we normally do.'

Pocahontas looks like Irene Bedard, the actress who provided her voice. Animator John Pomeroy tried to reflect the charm and mischief of Gibson's voice in his depiction of John Smith. The character on screen is tall, thin and blond with angular, pointed features, and Pomeroy admits that as well as being inspired by the sound of Gibson he was influenced by the look of Errol Flynn. Among the other 'voice actors' was Linda Hunt, with whom Gibson had co-starred a decade earlier in *The Year of Living Dangerously*. Having played a man in that film, she was now playing a tree in this one. Disney's commitment to realism could only go so far.

The singing voice of *Pocahontas* was provided by Broadway star Judy Kuhn, with yet another singer, Vanessa Williams, singing 'Colors of the Wind' over the end titles. Gibson, however, decided to do his own singing. 'I'm a confirmed kind of shower singer,' he says. 'And that's kind of where I wanted to leave it, but I thought, what the heck, I'll give it a whack.' His singing attracted praise from *Empire* film magazine. It noted: 'The old Gibson tonsils were stretched to the limit, as *Pocahontas* contains no less than 12 tunes', ignoring the fact that Gibson sings on only two – the reprise of 'The Virginia Company' song that opens the film and 'Mine, Mine, Mine' – and he has only a few solo lines in each. He can hold a note and even inject the appropriate emotion into the note, but there is little to suggest he might be joining Kuhn on Broadway.

Gibson was heard but not seen in *Pocahontas*, while in another film in the cinemas at the same time he was seen but not heard. In *Casper*, Bill Pullman's character looks into the bathroom mirror to see Clint Eastwood staring back at him and threatening to kill him, his mother and her bridge-playing friends. The mirror image metamorphoses into first Rodney Dangerfield, who is not exactly pretty, and then Gibson. The reflection looks surprised, turns to one side and smiles in apparent satisfaction. And that is about it. But there was a third film in cinemas in the summer of 1995 in which Gibson was both seen and heard. It was called *Braveheart*.

# 11

# BRAVE START

Edinburgh is at its most cosmopolitan in the summer months. Its resident population of less than half a million is swollen by an influx of international tourists who come to savour the rich heritage of an ancient capital and enjoy the annual arts festivals, including the famous Fringe, the biggest such festival in the world. There was nothing to distinguish Randall Wallace from thousands of other Americans who thronged the streets of Edinburgh city centre in the summer of 1993. A tall, soft-spoken man in his mid-forties, whose clean-cut good looks might have suggested a career in films. He was not in films, but he wanted to be.

He made his way along Lothian Road, beneath the city's medieval castle high on its volcanic rock, and into the former church that now served as Filmhouse, an arthouse cinema complex and headquarters of the Edinburgh Film Festival, the oldest annual film festival in the world. Staff were dashing about completing preparations for a programme that would include premieres of *Naked* and *The Piano*. But Wallace was headed for the adjoining upstairs offices of Scottish Screen Locations, which had been set up to offer advice to film-makers who might be considering shooting in Scotland. The American tourist explained his name was Wallace and that he had been so excited to discover one of Scotland's great national heroes was also called Wallace he had gone away and written an epic film about him and now he would like advice on possible locations please. He was a professional writer, but none of his novels had been published in Britain and he had never had a

screenplay filmed before. Scottish Screen Locations had a staff
of three and resources were limited. They directed him towards
Stirling, where his namesake had his greatest victory, and to
the Trossachs, the scenic lands of Rob Roy, and to Galloway
in the south-west. Thousands of people write screenplays; very
few get filmed. An American tourist had discovered a story that
was familiar to generations of Scots and had written a script
that would cost tens of millions of dollars to film. No one was
holding their breath.

During the film festival I was routinely chatting to Lee Leckie,
the then head of Scottish Screen Locations, and she happened
to mention Randall Wallace's visit and gave me his phone
number. 'I would love to talk to you,' he said, 'and tell you
everything about it.' I took down the details with mounting
excitement when I heard not one but two Hollywood studios
were interested in his script. The story was standing up and
was to prove a front-page exclusive for *The Scotsman*. At the
very end of the conversation I asked Wallace if the film had a
name. 'Yes,' he said, 'the title of the movie is *Braveheart*.'

Randall Wallace had first visited Scotland in 1983 with his
pregnant wife and followed the standard tourist trail up the
Royal Mile to the castle. The visitor crosses a bridge over a
dry ditch and enters through a stone gatehouse where two
great statues of fearsome medieval warriors stand sentry. They
represent Robert the Bruce and William Wallace. The guard
said Wallace was Scotland's greatest hero and explained how
he led the Scots to victory over the English army of occupation
at Stirling, another of the great medieval Scottish strongholds. 'I
asked if he and Robert the Bruce were allies because I noticed that
their dates overlapped, that they were contemporaries,' Randall
Wallace told me. 'And he said, "No one will ever know for
sure, but some of our legends say that Robert the Bruce may
have been involved in the betrayal of William Wallace to the
English, so that Robert the Bruce was free to become king."
The greatest hero of Scotland is unknown to Americans like
myself and he was betrayed by his own people, possibly by
the man who became king and became a great king, so it was
almost like hearing that Judas Iscariot had gone on to become
St Paul.'

Randall Wallace was to make William Wallace a household name not only in America but all over the world. But at the time he was already working on a novel, a sprawling 1,500-page story of an American in the Russia of Catherine the Great, called *Love and Honour*. It took him four years to write and although he had found publishers in the United States for his two previous novels they balked at the scale of this latest work and turned it down. Wallace had family by this time, he badly needed money and could not afford the luxury of embarking on another epic historical novel without any guarantee of publication. He worked in television, writing for the series *Broken Badges* and *Sonny Spoon*, and branching out as a producer, a job which in television is closer to that of a director in films than a film producer. He produced the TV film *Thunder Boat Row*. He managed to land himself a writing contract with MGM and his unpublished novel became an unfilmed screenplay. In 1991 he returned to the idea of writing about William Wallace. He intended it as a novel, but a screenplay would be quicker, he could submit it to MGM and he could use it as an outline for the novel. 'It seemed time to pick up the story and really research it,' he says.

He began with the *Encyclopaedia Britannica* but was soon immersed in medieval texts. Blind Harry's *The Wallace* had been enormously popular and shaped the perception of Wallace as national hero. But it is little read these days. This is no sonnet, but a work to make 'The Rime of the Ancient Mariner' seem little more than a haiku; Blind Harry's *The Wallace* is about as long as this entire book and written in old Scots.

Wallace's story takes place at a time when Scotland was just emerging from the Dark Ages with some sort of national identity that united the warring tribes of Picts, Britons, Angles and Scots – who were originally Irish but who were to give their name to the new nation. It was a country far removed from the wealthy and sophisticated civilisations of the Middle East, China and the great African cities of Zimbabwe and Timbuktu. The Normans crossed the Channel from France and conquered England in 1066; their influence expanded across the border and the Scottish king acknowledged subordination to the English crown.

Little is known for certain about the early years of William

Wallace. He was born in about 1270. His father was neither a great nobleman nor a commoner, but a small landowner. He belonged essentially to the Middle Ages middle class. And Wallace's home was not the rugged West Highlands of picture postcards but Ellerslie in Ayrshire, in south-west Scotland. The Wallaces may originally have been of Norman descent, but it seems they came to Scotland from the borders of Wales and the personal name was sometimes spelt Waleys. Edward I, known as the Hammer of the Scots, no longer recognised Scotland as a kingdom in its own right; he installed his own men to run the country and his forces occupied the land.

There were insurrections in the Highlands, Aberdeenshire and Galloway before Wallace steps into the history books in May 1297 when he killed the English sheriff of Lanark, William Heselrig. Academics still argue over his reasons, but it may have been in revenge for the killing of Wallace's wife or mistress, a woman called Marion Braidfute. Wallace plagued the English with guerrilla attacks and became a figurehead for independence and by September he had amassed a considerable army at Stirling where the English army advanced to meet him. Wallace and his troops were irregular infantry. The English may have believed they would turn and run at the sight of well-trained cavalry. But rather than turn and run, they watched the English advance over the bridge across the River Forth, ran forward, engaged those who had crossed the bridge, slaughtered those who were on it and, having taken control of the bridge, cut off reinforcements. It is reported that one hundred English knights and five thousand infantry were slaughtered. Wallace had Hugh de Cressingham, one of Edward's commanders, skinned.

Wallace did not become king but took the title of guardian of Scotland. He invaded England, but the Scottish nobility were reluctant to support him, possibly fearing he would eventually be defeated by Edward, who had been in Flanders during the Battle of Stirling Bridge. Edward personally led an army north and met Wallace's forces at Falkirk, just ten miles from Stirling, on 22 July. The Scottish noblemen withheld their cavalry and Wallace's infantry reportedly fell 'like blossoms in an orchard' beneath the rain of English arrows.

After Falkirk, Wallace spent some time on the Continent and it was not until 1305 that he was captured by Edward, having apparently been betrayed by Scottish nobles. He was taken to London and tried for treason. All he said in his defence was that he had never sworn allegiance to Edward and therefore could not be guilty of treason. He was hanged, drawn and quartered – that is, cut up while still alive. Parts of his body were put on public display in Stirling, Perth, Berwick and Newcastle and his head was exhibited at London Bridge.

'*Braveheart* is a drama,' says Randall Wallace. 'I wasn't trying to write strict history any more than Shakespeare was in *Macbeth*, but I still believe I had captured something true to the spirit of the man. I didn't decide on the title really until I had come to the end of the story. I remember vividly sitting down and typing Braveheart at the centre of the title page. It was about courage and heart.' Randall Wallace is a former seminarian and is prone to talk about his 'vision'; his work is infused with a sort of mystical spirituality. 'I think the essence of the film is that freedom has a cost and it is paid in the currency of sacrifice and love.'

He submitted the script to MGM, where the head of the studio Alan Ladd Junior was impressed. Ladd had impeccable Hollywood credentials. The son of the famous 1940s leading man, Ladd had revived the fortunes of 20th Century Fox with *Star Wars* while president of the studio in the seventies and had subsequently had his own production company. It made such quality films as *Blade Runner*, *Once Upon a Time in America* and *The Right Stuff*, as well as high-profit, low-brow *Police Academy* movies. Randall Wallace hoped Ladd would not only give the go-ahead but would allow him to direct the film himself with a modest budget and a focus on the human dimension rather than the battle scenes.

Wallace always considered the ideal man for the central role would be Mel Gibson. Ladd agreed and an approach was made to Gibson, who was working on post-production of *The Man Without a Face*. Gibson wanted to finish it before considering *Braveheart*. He had never heard of William Wallace, though he used to drink in a bar of that name in Australia. When he did get round to considering the *Braveheart* script, he was intrigued by the notion of a man who could rise from the common herd to lead a nation. 'William Wallace is one of the people who have changed the course of history,' he says. 'His is an incredible story about courage, loyalty, honour and the brutality of war. The film is also an inspiring love story.' In an interview with *Premiere* magazine, Gibson described Wallace as the 'Second Coming of Christ'. As if he was embarrassed by such a grand allusion, he seemed to feel the need to bring the conversation back to earth by adding that 'he was a really straight-ahead dude', a neat illustration of the profound, spiritual Gibson side by side with the banal anti-intellectual.

Gibson was worried that he was too old for the part – Wallace was in his mid-twenties at the Battle of Stirling Bridge, Gibson was in his mid-thirties. Of course life expectancy has increased dramatically since the thirteenth century and Randall Wallace argued that younger actors simply would not have the authority to convince audiences they could command not only an army but also national devotion. Gibson went off to make *Maverick* without giving a definite answer on *Braveheart*.

Meanwhile Randall Wallace went to Scotland, visited Scottish Screen Locations and discussed the project with the Wallace Clan, an organisation dedicated to the memory of William Wallace. Their activities range from historical research to medieval fight demonstrations. Randall had renamed Wallace's woman Elizabeth because he felt the name Marion would create confusion in America with Robin Hood. The Wallace Clan were more concerned about the name Elizabeth than almost anything else in the script. It was the name of the English queen who had Mary Queen of Scots beheaded. They suggested Murron, as a variant on Marion, and Murron it became. Randall Wallace photographed mountains, castles and some of the wild Wallace men ready for action.

Randall Wallace also made a significant revision to the screenplay. Instead of ending with William Wallace's execution, the film now fast-forwarded nine years to the Battle of Bannockburn, just outside Stirling, where Robert the Bruce leads the Scots to a decisive victory that establishes Scotland as an independent country for four hundred years. A downbeat ending was transformed into a gloriously uplifting one; Wallace's death is seen much more clearly as the sacrifice that inspires Bruce, and Bruce himself becomes a more effective character in film terms.

Bruce's family were certainly Norman in origin, his father had lands in both England and Scotland and Bruce spent much of his boyhood in England. Although he had sworn allegiance to Edward, he joined the insurrections of 1297. He renewed his allegiance to Edward in 1302, joined the forces against Wallace in 1304 and finally committed himself to open rebellion in 1306 when he had himself crowned king.

In the summer of 1993, MGM and Ladd parted company and as part of his severence deal Ladd was able to choose two projects to take with him to the re-established Ladd Company. He chose *Braveheart* and intended to act as producer on it. He told me at the time: 'I have no doubt that I have chosen wisely and have very high hopes for this project.'

Meanwhile Terry Gilliam, the former *Monty Python* artist who had become a highly individualistic film-maker with the likes of *Brazil*, was well advanced with his plans for another historical drama, an adaptation of Charles Dickens's French Revolution adventure *A Tale of Two Cities*. He was pushing ahead in the firm belief that Gibson would play the tragic English hero Sydney Carton who takes the place of an aristocrat on the guillotine because the woman Carton loves is in love with the nobleman who is due for the chop, and only through Carton's self-sacrifice can he make her happy. It had been filmed before with Ronald Colman and subsequently Dirk Bogarde in the lead and is best known for the closing speech: 'It is a far, far better thing that I do than I have ever done; it is a far, far better rest that I go to than I have ever known.'

Gibson was supposedly already on board and the finance in place when Gilliam was hired to direct. 'I spent a long time working on it with Don MacPherson,' says Gilliam. 'He wrote a really wonderful script and they spent like two years on this, seducing Mel Gibson into playing Sydney Carton. And I was kind of intrigued, because I thought, of all the stars, he could actually pull it off because I think he's a good actor and can do a decent English accent.' Gilliam visited locations, envisaged shots and felt he had already made the movie in his head. 'Then

Mel changed his mind and said he wants to be a director . . . so off he went.' Gilliam told me he felt crushed, though he realised it was not unusual for a project to collapse at a late stage for one reason or another. 'I don't know how most directors put up with it, but most of them do.'

The backers were prepared to put up a budget of $60 million if Mel Gibson was in the lead, according to Gilliam. The project was repackaged with Gibson's *Bounty* co-star Liam Neeson, who had just been nominated for an Oscar for *Schindler's List*. 'We got the budget down to $41 million with Liam,' says Gilliam, 'and they wouldn't go. "Twenty-six for Liam," they said. And that was the end of the conversation.' Neeson went to Scotland to shoot *Rob Roy* instead. Gilliam's comments are a fascinating insight into the way Hollywood works and the difference between a star like Neeson and a superstar like Gibson, and just how much power the very few true superstars have. Ironically, however, one role that Gibson really wanted to play, but did not get the chance to, was that of Oskar Schindler, which Steven Spielberg gave to Neeson.

After prolonged consideration Gibson decided he did not want to star in *Braveheart* but he did want to direct it. He was inspired both by his experience of directing *The Man Without a Face* and Kevin Costner's commercial and critical success with another sprawling historical adventure, the Oscar-winning *Dances With Wolves*. Gibson was both excited and frightened at the scale of the project, and wanted to concentrate his energies on directing. Like *Dances With Wolves*, *Braveheart* mixed action with romance. Costner had made part of his film in Lakota, with subtitles in English, and Gibson discussed the possibility of filming partly in Gaelic or Scots, with subtitles. The idea met with a cool reception; nevertheless, Gaelic is used in the film, at Wallace's wedding, and Gibson used subtitles on a couple of occasions when Wallace spoke Latin, French and Italian. At this point various other star names were touted, including that of Daniel Day-Lewis. But Gibson the proven box-office star was a much more valuable commodity than Gibson the inexperienced director. The deal was that the film would be in English and Gibson could direct if he also agreed to act.

Gibson became star, director and producer of the film, which now became a co-production between the Ladd Company and Gibson's company Icon Productions. Although Ladd retained his previous role of producer, Bruce Davey, the Australian accountant who founded Icon with Gibson, became the third producer, so the balance tilted heavily towards Icon. Steve McEveety, Icon vice-president of production, became executive producer.

It is very difficult to determine a film's budget if the production companies will not divulge details, and sometimes it is just as difficult when they will. Studios can bump up the supposed cost of a film by allocating all sorts of overheads against it, but the cost is usually taken to mean direct expenses involved in producing a finished negative, and excluding the cost of prints and marketing. *Braveheart*'s budget was variously reported from $40 million to $72 million – and those figures all appeared in a single publication, the trade magazine *Screen International*.

In May 1994, the month before filming began, *Screen International* put the budget at $53 million. In September, in a location report, it used the figure $40 million, and in April 1996, in a post-Oscar marketing analysis, it put it at $72 million. There is an official figure. Long after filming was over, Gibson said categorically that it had cost $53 million, the very same figure that had appeared in *Screen International* before filming began. The specialist *Screen Finance* magazine cited a figure of £35 million, which would equate with $53 million.

But sources directly and indirectly involved in the production suggest *Braveheart* cost significantly more. 'It was a much higher budget than was on paper anywhere,' says one. *Daily Variety*, the American publication sometimes regarded as the 'showbiz bible', ran an article in March 1996 looking specifically at Icon Productions and incorporating comments from Bruce Davey and it used the figure $70 million.

While Ladd was at MGM, *Braveheart* had been provisionally budgeted to shoot on location in Scotland for about $40 million. Subsequently the Ladd Company was being backed financially by Paramount. Gibson's Icon Productions had a working relationship with Majestic Films, a British company involved in financing, sales and distribution. Majestic had provided much of the budget for *Dances With Wolves* and the plan was that it would raise funds for *Braveheart* by selling rights to the film in territories outside North America. But the *Dances With Wolves* budget was only $18 million and when Paramount and Majestic Films worked out detailed costings for *Braveheart* they found $40 million was a serious under-estimate. Even £40 million looked insufficient. With the likely cost up around $70 million, Majestic Films decided *Braveheart* was out of its league and pulled out just weeks before shooting was due to begin. Paramount, too, was wobbling. 'The proposed budget was off by nearly $30 million,' says a studio insider. 'We're a conservative company, and a company that had never done a movie whose budget started with a six, let alone a seven.'

Now totally committed to *Braveheart* and the story of William Wallace, it was Gibson who saved the film. He has said he put up $15 million of his own money. *Premiere* reported that this was essentially bridging finance, while a deal was secured in which Paramount would have North American rights and another company would buy the rights to the film in the rest of the world. Warner Brothers, the studio behind the *Lethal Weapon* series, was sounded out and said no, but 20th Century Fox was keen to improve its performance outside North America. Fox had lost out badly when it sold off foreign rights to *Die Hard With a Vengeance*. It took a close look at the financial performance of other historical adventure films, including Costner's *Robin Hood: Prince of Thieves*, and agreed to put up more than $30 million.

Gibson has said on several occasions that he was not taking any payment up front. As star and director he could reasonably have commanded a fee of $20 million – and a deferred fee of $20 million would explain the difference between the official budget and the figure which people in the industry believe was the true cost of the film.

For all the convoluted financial and production arrangements, the bottom line was that this was now very much a 'Mel Gibson Film'. There are sixteen names on the *Braveheart* poster, five of them are Mel Gibson. Randall Wallace is credited as the sole writer, though there has been some question over how much work Gibson did on the script and he certainly encouraged the

cast to try to improvise when filming got under way. Gibson
told *Premiere* magazine: 'I rejected the project because I loved
the idea but I thought the script was really corny . . . I couldn't
get to sleep because I started thinking about it in images, and
I said: "Look, let me direct it, let me change it." And me and
the writer sat down and it got to the point where I started to
really like it.' Wallace and Gibson did discuss the script at length
together; Gibson suggested some changes to clarify details of
character and motivation and Wallace made them, but the final
film differs little from early drafts of the screenplay.

Gibson's comments in *Premiere* looked as if he was claiming
credit for the final script and it would be surprising in the
circumstances if Wallace had not been just a little annoyed.
In the official *Braveheart* press notes, Gibson said: 'I couldn't
wait to turn each page and was surprised at every turn. The
screenplay had everything – heroic battles, a powerful love
story and the passion of one man's strength which fires a
whole country against its aggressors.' And when Gibson and
I discussed the script a few months after the *Premiere* article,
there was no suggestion that it had been in need of radical
revision. 'It worked as a compelling piece of cinema more or
less on the page,' he said.

Film criticism has long been dogged by the auteur theory, in
which the director is regarded as the author of the work in the
same way a novelist is the author of a novel; every aspect of the
film is regarded ultimately as the artistic expression not of the
writer or the cameraman but of the director, though actors have
to some extent retained the credit for their performances and,
curiously, in television drama the writer often gets the credit
as the most important creative element. The auteur theory is
obviously valid where a single person has written and directed
a film. Directors often regard scripts as a series of suggestions
that they can remodel in their own image; but the director does
not necessarily need to rewrite a good script in order to bring
his personality to a film. It does not undermine the achievements
of a director to acknowledge the contribution of others in his
team, for a film is usually a team effort, and the auteur theory
oversimplifies the process.

Gibson is not a writer. It may sound perverse but one of

the areas in which we can perhaps see Gibson as auteur is in his selection of the films in which he wishes to act, a process that is deeply personal and absolute. There is no doubt that he is drawn towards characters who are motivated by loss, and more particularly the death of their nearest and dearest. Max Rockatansky becomes Mad Max when his baby son Sprog is killed by bikers and his wife is left critically ill in hospital. Martin Riggs becomes a Lethal Weapon after the death of his wife. Hamlet experiences similar suicidal and murderous tendencies after the death of his father. And it is the killing of Wallace's wife that motivates him. Gibson expresses himself as an artist in the representation of Wallace as the slow-motion avenger on horseback, glimpsed between the village houses – a silent, impassive man on a heavily breathing horse, a pale rider and his name is Death.

Gibson did, however, express reservations about William Wallace's motivation when we discussed it. 'It seemed like when I read Randy's script that it was a pure script device and I said, "Oh no, not this again." But there's reason to believe that it could be true. It's referred to in some of those epic mythical poems of Harry the Minstrel and indeed some of the bona fide historians give that particular aspect of the story some credence and they say that it's quite possible that this Marion Braidfute, that he married, was killed and it was as a kind of lure to get him in because he was already on the warpath.'

He laughs at the suggestion that the selection of all these films about the death of spouses and children reflects his own personal nightmare. 'I wouldn't exactly relish the thought of losing my family. We've all got to go sometime. If you take away anything that someone holds in great value I think that person may get a little obsessive about the measures he takes to avoid that kind of thing happening again. It's like, you know, a parent who loses a child in a driving accident, or from some ailment, will sometimes become very active in promoting foundations to prevent, or research into, the disease, or mothers for drunk drivers or something like that. So it's just human nature, isn't it?'

But are family and partner more important to him than to some other actors, given the repeated selection of such roles, the durability of his marriage and the number of offspring? 'I've never given it much thought that way, that aspect, can't comment,' he says. He gives the impression that he does not think about such things. He thinks deeply but is loath to admit it. It is the Second Coming of Christ/straight-ahead dude dichotomy.

He thought long and hard about Wallace and his motivation. 'I looked in a lot of books,' he says. 'Everyone's had a crack at it. The most unbiased, truthful and, I think, probably the smartest or the most savvy account of Wallace was done by a guy called Fisher [Andrew Fisher who wrote the biography *William Wallace*, published by John Donald in 1986]. I really liked that book . . . He tries to fill in the pieces in between what is verifiable . . . I found that he kind of put Wallace's character in there, so I found that a good acting exercise.' He makes the point that he was not reading these books with a view to revising the script. 'It was just for my own interest . . . and to reassure myself.'

It is indicative of Randall Wallace's 'vision' that just as William Wallace was 'guardian of Scotland', Randall Wallace regarded himself as 'guardian of the script'. He dissuaded Gibson from amending the character of Bruce to make him less duplicitous and more straightforwardly heroic, though he would have to back down on one major scene when he got to Scotland and was faced with the combined opposition of his director and his clan chief.

Early in 1994 Gibson, Wallace, Ladd, Davey, McEveety and production designer Tom Sanders flew to Scotland and met Seroas Wallace, chief executive of the Wallace Clan, in Glasgow's Marriott Hotel. 'I was sitting in the hotel with them and I wasnae very comfortable,' says Seoras Wallace. 'And I said, "Do you want to come back to the house and we can get a good blether?" So they were like, "Yip, let's do it." It was dead funny, you know, it's just a place naebody would be expecting Mel Gibson, above a Chinese restaurant in Glasgow.' Seoras Wallace drove Gibson and Randall Wallace back to his modest tenement flat in Albert Drive in Pollokshields, an area south of the River Clyde with a high proportion of Scots-Asian residents. Gibson sat on the floor while they discussed William Wallace over a kebab. Gibson told Seoras Wallace not to be nervous. Seoras Wallace assured him that he was not nervous, but suggested that Gibson should be, intending as he was to make a film about Scotland's great hero. The two immediately warmed to each other.

'A couple of the clan folk came in,' recalls Seoras Wallace, 'but they're dead used to things. Mel Gibson was sitting on the flair and they went, "How are you doin'?" And he's like, "I am." And they're like, "Aye, well, we are too." And it's a good crack and away they went.'

Randall Wallace had included Irish troops in Edward's army and Seoras Wallace was insistent that the Irish would not have fought with the English against the Scots, an argument that appealed to Gibson, with his strong Irish roots and his knowledge of English imperialism. Randall Wallace was not sure that Edward would not have had Irish mercenaries. Gibson came up with the idea that the Irish and Scots charge each other only to stop and embrace at the point of contact. Gibson was making a film about Scottish nationalism, not Irish nationalism, but this new device suddenly transformed his ancestors from villains to heroes fighting a common cause with the hero against the oppressor.

Gibson visited the Wallace Clan's headquarters underneath the Kingston Bridge where they showed him how to fight with a broadsword. Members of the Wallace Clan were hired as technical advisers, stunt fighters, extras and drivers on the film. Several, including Seoras, whose film work dates back to Sean Connery's *Highlander*, are singled out for individual thanks on the credits.

As Scotland's one A-list film star, Sean Connery inevitably figured in media discussions of *Braveheart* and the press reported Gibson's comments that Connery was too old to play Wallace as if they were a gross insult. The *Daily Record* said: 'Hollywood's vertically-challenged heart-throb Mel Gibson was talking himself UP yesterday. And talking Scotland's home-grown star Sean Connery DOWN . . . When he was asked yesterday why a Scot such as Sean wasn't taking the lead part, he said Connery was too old . . . But there's another little matter he's overlooking about Wallace. The thirteenth-century freedom fighter was SIX FOOT SIX tall. And Mel, well . . . 'Fraid he's a mere five foot eight on a good day . . . Sean, on the other hand, has height on his side at an impressive six foot two.' But at sixty-four, Connery was thirty years older than Wallace was when he died.

What the press did not know was that Connery, the world's most famous Scottish nationalist and probably the world's most famous Scot, had been approached to play King Edward of England, Hammer of the Scots. It would not have been the first time he had played an English king. He played Richard the Lion-Heart in *Robin Hood: Prince of Thieves*. But Richard was a goodie, Edward was one of the most reviled figures in Scottish history. Connery told me he could not do it because it clashed with his commitment to *Just Cause*.

Despite the approach to Scotland's National Monument, Gibson maintains he wanted a cast of unfamiliar faces. 'If possible I would have cast Wallace like that, but it just would have been impossible to get the budget. It's best to come from no place to total believability. I have to actually fight against the baggage that I've got with me. That's the hard part of it: you have to always be recreating yourself and try to be believable when you've already been around for twenty years and people are used to you in other things. It's hard to beat the association, but you try.'

The role of Edward eventually went to Patrick McGoohan who remains a cult figure because of his roles in the television series *Danger Man* and *The Prisoner*. But that was thirty years earlier, McGoohan had become something of a recluse and even the erudite Jeff Dawson of *Empire* film magazine failed to recognise him in *Braveheart*. Gibson told Dawson: 'It was at the suggestion of the first AD [assistant director] David Tomblin, who was a great friend of his. I said, "Oh Jeeze, I remember him," because I loved *The Prisoner* and *Danger Man* and all that stuff. When I met him I remembered the young guy and he's gone down the track a bit . . . whoa, he's different. He looks really Irish, you know, with this little pug nose. He didn't have the kind of Plantagenet beak that I imagined, so we put him through the make-up and slapped on a fake nose every day.'

One respected Scottish star, who has made a mark on Hollywood and who did appear in *Braveheart*, is Brian Cox. He had played Wallace on television many years earlier and he was the original Hannibal Lektor in the underrated 1986 thriller *Manhunter* – the character which brought Anthony Hopkins an Oscar in *The Silence of the Lambs*. Gibson was very keen to get Cox and offered him the role of Campbell, the elder statesman of Wallace's band. But Cox was not impressed by Campbell nor indeed most of the other Scottish characters. 'There was a lot of heuching and hauching and standing there and pulling arrows out of your shoulder and all that kind of stoic Scottish stuff.'

Michael Caton-Jones also wanted him for his Scottish historical adventure *Rob Roy*, whose production schedule overlapped with that of *Braveheart* and which was actually going to use the same glen outside Fort William. Cox thought *Rob Roy* was a better script, with more subtle characters; nevertheless he believed *Braveheart* had the potential to be the better film because of its ambition in terms of both scale and vision. 'I said the only role I was really interested in was Argyle [the uncle who raises Wallace after the death of his father] which I thought was a really nice role because it had a point of view to it.'

Although important, it was a much smaller role and meant Cox could be in *Rob Roy* too. Gibson had no problems with that, but Cox told me he came under pressure from Caton-Jones not to do *Braveheart*. 'They didn't want people to be in both movies,' he says. 'I thought it was stupid. Scotland has two movies, it's such a nonsense to say that we don't want people to be in both.' Peter Mullan has a similar story. He says he could have taken the rest of the year off on the strength of his fees for *Braveheart* and *Rob Roy*. His schedules overlapped by three days, which would have meant missing some of the rehearsals for the latter. He believes he could have caught up, but 'the *Rob Roy* mob' insisted he choose between the two. 'What it came down to was, you're either in our gang or you're in their gang,' he says. He joined Gibson's gang.

For the roles of Robert the Bruce and Wallace's wife Murron, Gibson chose two big-screen newcomers. Catherine McCormack was a strikingly beautiful ex-convent schoolgirl, English, despite the name, with very little acting experience. Only a year out of drama school, she had done a little television and a low-budget film that had not been released in Britain. She had never even met a film star before going along to London's

Mayfair Hotel to discuss *Braveheart* with Gibson. She was understandably nervous but was surprised to discover Gibson was nervous too. And shy. She felt she had to break the ice. 'I made a couple of extremely crass and crap jokes,' she says, 'really sad jokes about hamsters and, you know, willies . . . I left thinking I would never ever see the man again.'

But it sounds like they were on the same wavelength from the start. Quite apart from her looks, McCormack has a tremendous presence and a certain strength of character that would be necessary so as not to be overwhelmed by Gibson, whom she calls Melly in press interviews.

At the time of their first meeting Gibson was thinking of getting one actress to play both Wallace's wife and the English princess Isabelle, which would have been an extremely daring move but which makes sense in terms of the script, given that Wallace makes it clear that he sees aspects of his dead wife in Isabelle. However, when McCormack met Gibson for a second time this idea had been dropped and she was in the running for the role of Murron. The French actress Sophie Marceau was cast as the princess after Gibson saw her in *Les Chouans* and *Fanfan*, another detail that undermines his attempts to maintain an anti-intellectual image. In Hollywood watching a French film is rather like reading Tolstoy or Rushdie.

McCormack says: 'I saw a script before I went back for the second interview, but he didn't ask anyone in this cast at all to read, so it was just very much how he got on with people and how he felt.' The meeting ended with the usual 'don't call us, we'll call you' message. And Gibson did. 'I got back from a long weekend and there were nine messages and this was just like number seven or something . . . I remember every word and every breath. He just said to me, "Hi, this is Mel. Phone me at the Mayfair Hotel. I may have some good news for you" . . . I thought, "Oh my God, he's found my watch." And so I phoned and he wasn't there, he had gone back to LA. He phoned later and just asked me if I'd like to play his wife and I had to think about it obviously.'

Although Angus McFadyen, the star of television's *Soldier, Soldier*, is Scottish, he was originally in the running for the role of King Edward's effeminate son, the future Edward II. It is a fascinating possibility that both Edward I and Edward II might have been played by Scotsmen, while Wallace was played by an American. McFadyen was one of the few principals who was already familiar with the stories of Wallace and the Bruce. He obviously was not going to get to play Wallace, but he was determined he would rather be Robert the Bruce than Prince Edward. He says: 'Heroes are usually presented as very passive characters who are almost superhuman, and in this situation it was like you had the birth of somebody, from very sort of meek, mild origins, who had to overcome certain obstacles and I suppose personal weaknesses in order to become the hero which he was destined to become ... He's a very confused character.

'I drank two bottles of red wine and I went [to a meeting with Gibson] and courageously put my foot down and said, "Robert the Bruce, c'est moi," and spent about an hour and a half doing monologues explaining exactly why – for the emotional reasons that I could bring to the character. And a week later the part was mine.'

Gibson cast his younger brother Donal in the supporting role of Stewart, one of Wallace's men, and he considered using one of his children to portray Wallace as a boy. 'Then I thought I'd let my boys stick to their day jobs – just being children,' he says. 'I wouldn't wish this job on any child.'

Gibson has said that he builds his characterisations from within himself and for *Braveheart* he was looking for actors he felt already had aspects of the various characters in the script, that is why he chose to sit and chat with candidates rather than go through a process of extensive screen tests in character. He wanted actors he felt could draw the characters from within themselves. The selection of several of the supporting cast was to prove one of his personal triumphs.

While he was choosing the cast, other members of the production team were busy researching the period, designing costumes and buildings, working out make-up and finalising the dark, earthy look of the film, a look that contrasted the gilt and finery of the English court with Scots who looked as if they had been moulded from the very clay beneath them.

The medieval village of Lanark and the ill-fated sheriff's

stockade were built in Glen Nevis just below Ben Nevis –
the low-roofed houses were inspired by buildings on the
now-deserted island of St Kilda. One might imagine that
Britain's highest mountain would be in some desolate and
inaccessible spot, but it is just a few minutes' drive from Fort
William, one of the principal towns of the West Highlands, and
the mountain range would afford an impressive backdrop. Less
than a month before filming began, news broke that Gibson had
decided to 'switch filming' to the Republic of Ireland. The news
was described as a 'tragedy' for Scotland, the impression was
given that Scotland was missing out completely and a fierce
political row broke out over the British government's alleged
indifference to film-making and the tax incentives on offer in
Ireland.

It subsequently emerged, however, that Scotland and Ireland
were both to be used for location filming and that tax incentives
were only one element in the decision to shoot part of the film in
Ireland. It had never been the intention to shoot the whole film
in Scotland, which does not have the necessary studio facilities.
The use of Ardmore Studios, near Dublin, was England's,
and specifically Shepperton's, loss. Executive producer Steve
McEveety told me at the time that the decision to shoot some of
the location scenes in Ireland was taken principally on creative
grounds, after considering possibilities in Scotland, England and
Ireland. 'Tax incentives were a bonus,' he said. He pointed out
that the film is not set wholly in Scotland, a significant part of
the action takes place in England.

'The logistics of an undertaking like this are huge,' says
Gibson. 'It can become a logistical nightmare and we just
found the problems a lot easier to solve over there. People say
"they went because of the incentives", but it's not true. Yes,
they do offer Section 35 tax incentives on films, but we hadn't
planned to go there, so that we more than used up any benefits
we may have gained simply by moving there, so that did not
become a benefit. What we did benefit from was an area that
had far more horses. It's very hard to find horses in Scotland
in any great numbers. We found an area underfoot that was
horse friendly, you know, because it's softer country. And we
also had the use of the reserve army, something that we tried

here [in Scotland] but I don't think the army was too interested. But the Irish government was able to, you know, fix us up with the army. Also the battlefield itself was near a race track where we could house the animals, and the army had a barracks just over the hill, so you had accommodation for all these various people and they were close together and they could walk to work practically.'

In Ireland Gibson had not only a ready supply of horses and extras, but also battlefields, castles, hotels, a film studio, an airport and a major city within a thirty-mile radius. Gibson says: 'You're talking about civilised accommodation for three thousand people and we simply couldn't find a location here that could offer us that. It was all those things.' It is perhaps just as well that the film-makers had not considered Ireland at the outset. No one dared suggest this at the time, but the hard financial logic might well have been to shoot the film entirely in Ireland.

# 12

# BRAVEHEART

Gibson sat staring into space, thinking, sometimes not thinking. The minutes ticked away and the crew and actors and extras waited. He sat and never said a word, just continued to stare into space. Everyone waited, including the 1,700 soldiers on loan to the film from the Irish army. Young lads in high spirits, many of them still in their teens, they regarded the film as a bit of a lark. No one spoke to Gibson. He was trying to figure out the next shot, but the long hours, the budget problems and the inevitable personality clashes were beginning to take their toll and he was finding it increasingly difficult to focus his mind. He was working twenty hours a day, often starting at four in the morning. Costume and make-up was a lengthy process because of the hair extensions that had to be laboriously fitted. Shooting started at eight and would go on until nine or ten in the evening. There would be a quick bite of supper before watching and discussing the rushes of the previous day's filming, by which time it would be midnight.

After *The Man Without a Face* he had said he would never direct and act in a film again. Now here he was directing and acting in a $70 million epic with an army of three thousand awaiting his next command. And all he wanted to do was sleep. The minutes ticked away. He just sat there staring into space. Some of the crew were worried about him but no one dared break his concentration, if indeed he was concentrating. An hour passed. All he wanted to do was sleep, but time was money, big money. At last he stirred. Thousands of eyes focused on him as he rose from his seat and issued his instructions. There was work to be done. He could sleep for as long as he wanted in a month or two.

Filming had begun on the other side of the Irish Sea, in Glen Nevis, on 6 June 1994. It seemed an eternity ago. Although scenes are almost never shot in the sequence in which they appear in the finished film, shooting on this occasion did begin with the film's opening section of Wallace as a boy. So Gibson did not initially have to juggle his directing and acting duties. He was full of nervous energy. After months of preparation, this was it. Machines belched out mist to supplement the natural variety that already shrouded the 4,400-foot mountain, above the fertile river valley. Glen Nevis is not like the rugged, heathery glens found elsewhere in the Highlands, but a fertile and surprisingly flat valley of open pasture, with alder, rowan and birch dotted along its length. The hubbub of the crew suddenly died and the landscape was silent. A surge of pure pleasure ran through Gibson as he called 'Action' for the first time.

The film provided a multi-million-pound boost to the West Highland economy. Hotels and guest houses were taken over by cast and crew. Local tradesmen had been at work for weeks on the sets of Lanark village and the English stockade. Other locals were hired as drivers and extras. An agricultural supplier sold its entire stock of scythe shafts, horse and cattle feed and harness oil to the film, and the Islay Woollen Mill on the Hebridean island of Islay was commissioned to supply kilts. Costume designer Charles Knode was inspired by a sixteenth-century tartan, using dark, natural colours appropriate for camouflage and hunting – the brightly coloured clan tartans in common usage today are of a later design and their authenticity has been the subject of considerable controversy. Three thousand metres of plaid were woven in eight different colours on the mill's Victorian looms.

Nevis Bakery had a regular order for 'thirteenth-century loaves', dark flat loaves made without yeast, but it was not only the local people who benefited from *Braveheart* and got a flavour of film-making. Ewen Cameron's Highland cattle ate the thatch of the village roofs and were banished for the duration of filming. And the midges were having a rare old time. They were more difficult to banish. The only time they let up was when the heavens opened and the rain came hammering down, as it did almost every day of the six-week shoot in Glen Nevis, washing away the village that had been erected there and forcing the set builders to start again.

Catherine McCormack was on the film from the first day and did not realise the scale of it until she arrived in Glen Nevis. The company would swell to three thousand for battle scenes in Ireland, but the regular crew alone numbered around five hundred. As well as the main unit which was filming the actors and the dialogue scenes, a second unit had been recruited to provide additional footage. Its main job was going to be during the battles. Battle scenes are enormously complicated, expensive and time-consuming and it would be important to get as much quality footage as possible when action was called and the armies charged. However, Gibson decided to use the second unit to get shots of the Scottish landscape as well, which were used to open the film and at various other appropriate junctures to keep the film rooted in Scotland, even though much of the action would be shot in Ireland.

Almost all McCormack's scenes are with Gibson. 'He didn't direct me as such,' she says. 'It was very much more that we talked about what the action was about, and then we just did it and, if it worked, it worked, and we talked about why it worked. And if it didn't work, we swore and then did it again.'

McCormack's character, Murron, has a short, intense relationship with Wallace, squeezing courtship, romance, marriage and death into twenty-five minutes in the first quarter of the film. 'To actually be kissing Mr Gibby – as I don't call him – was good, really good . . . OK, he's a great snogger . . . He's a damn sexy man.' She admits to being nervous about a brief topless scene as the new Mr and Mrs Wallace are about to consummate their marriage, but not as nervous as she was cold, doing take after take. McCormack's scenes were not shot in sequence, some were done in Scotland and some later in Ireland, by which time her character had been executed in Glen Nevis.

Because Gibson was not in the execution scene he was able to concentrate entirely on McCormack's performance and that of Malcolm Tierney, the English magistrate, delivering Tierney's speech for him and showing him how to cut Murron's throat, with hardly a glance at the victim, and urging McCormack to play the scene entirely with her eyes. He showed her exactly what he wanted, going through the death scene as if he was playing it, draining himself of emotion and life. Gibson maintains, retrospectively, that being both actor and director sharpened his focus, that when he has the time he will dwell on something, but by doing both jobs he was sometimes forced to make hard choices immediately.

Murron's funeral, when she is buried in a shroud, was another intense scene. Instead of shouting 'Cut' when he had got what he wanted, Gibson broke the tension by spontaneously leaping into the grave with Murron with a lewd suggestion along the lines of 'one last time'. Gibson was still as keen on his practical jokes as ever. 'When people were going through serious scenes, he would look away from them,' says McCormack, 'and then turn back with this red nose on his face.' McCormack adds: 'Breaking wind was his biggest joke.'

Brian Cox, who played Wallace's uncle, Argyle, was involved in the early scenes. He says: 'The thing about Mel is that he's more serious than he gives himself credit for. He's got this kind of great jokey persona. There's that element to it. He loves to make it enjoyable.' But Cox recalls having a very serious conversation about the film's religious elements at their first meeting. Cox considers one of Gibson's strengths is his ability to delegate, but it was obvious within a few weeks that the long hours and the stress of directing such a huge film were beginning to take their toll. 'To be honest with you, I was a bit worried because he was really looking quite exhausted.'

Gibson had been plagued by light that was never the same from one take to the next, a flood that washed away the set, tabloid photographers looking for the first pictures of him in a kilt and low-flying RAF jets that were supposed to be observing a no-fly zone but continued to appear suddenly over the horizon and roar low over the set, ruining footage and ultimately resulting in a serious injury to one of the actors, whose horse bolted in alarm. Alan Tall, who plays the elder Stewart, broke his pelvis when he was thrown, spent several days in hospital and was out of work for months.

'I thought, Jesus, he's still got to go to Ireland,' says Cox. 'This is before he shot any of the big battle scenes.' In the middle of July the entire production moved to Ireland, with the exception of Brian Cox, who did not even have to change rooms in the Spean Bridge Hotel before beginning work on *Rob Roy*.

There were a few days' lull in filming, though preparations had been under way in Ireland since the decision to shoot there was made. Such was Gibson's determination to concentrate locations within as small an area as possible that he was going to use Trim Castle, the largest Anglo-Norman castle in Ireland, as both York and London. 'We just used two sides of the castle,' says production manager Mary Alleguen. 'We did York one side and London the other side.' Two months of building, painting and plastering had been necessary to turn Trim into twin towns. Dunsoghly Castle, a modest fifteenth-century tower, was to stand in for Edinburgh Castle, possibly the most famous ancient fortress in Britain, but it was reckoned international audiences would never know the difference. Battlements, a drawbridge and surrounding houses were added. The recreation of the Battle of Stirling Bridge was to be the most elaborate film sequence ever shot in Ireland and the Curragh Plains were already covered in tents and toilets, trailers and tractors. A tight security cordon had been thrown round the area and knights were going through their rehearsal for the big day, or rather days. The original battle was over by lunchtime, but the film version was to last a fortnight. Gibson wandered across his battleground, filming the action in his head. But there were other battlegrounds too.

Despite the stories in the press about Gibson going to Ireland because of tax incentives, the production was now running into financial difficulties. In order to qualify for those tax incentives, *Braveheart* had to employ a certain number of Irish crew, and they were more expensive than their British counterparts. Meanwhile, British technicians who expected to be working on *Braveheart* throughout the summer found their services were no longer required. To make matters worse, the dollar was falling against both the pound and the Irish punt. It lost three cents between July and October, two per cent of its value, which represented a sudden loss of more than $1 million even on the film's official budget figures.

The second unit, which had been called into action early, was now disbanded just when it would seem the need for it was greatest. Many of the personnel were absorbed into the main unit, but cameramen who had previously been directed by a specialist second unit director would now be directed by Mel Gibson's stunt double. 'The atmosphere was deathly after that,' says actor Peter Mullan. 'There was a very bad atmosphere amongst the crew members.' There were rumours of further redundancies, the studios were sending streams of faxes across the Atlantic on everything from costs to Gibson's hair and on one occasion four Hollywood executives arrived on the set wearing grey suits, black ties and shades, each carrying a briefcase. It seemed like a raid.

'Word was that they had another list of people who were going to get sacked, because they were running out of money basically,' says Mullan. 'One minute it just seems like money isn't an object and then suddenly everything was being thought about. Taxis for people, all these things became issues. Like, "Can that actor not wait until the other three actors are finished and then we'll drive them all back in a mini-bus?" which you'd normally expect in a low-budget production, but it seemed kind of strange in a Hollywood production. There was even nonsense about people counting toilet rolls and things like that. It was just getting really, really silly.'

Even before the exchange rate crisis, Bruce Davey had proved himself a tough nut in negotiations with various parties involved in the film. Randall Wallace was being paid much less than a writer would normally expect for such an epic film for such a major star, but he had no previous film credits on which to trade. When it came to shooting, Gibson said he wanted Wallace there, but Davey saw no reason to pay his expenses, with the result that Wallace missed the Scottish leg of filming. He was in Ireland several times, but on one occasion he paid his own way.

Ladd of course was the original producer, the man who did the traditional producer's job of putting together the package that would enable the film to be made. In Gibson's case the title of producer reflected the fact that he was more than a director for hire, that his company had taken on some of the packaging responsibilities and had been involved in the development, financing and production of the film. But, given that he was already directing and acting in the film, this was one area in which he certainly had to delegate. Bruce Davey was the man to whom Gibson delegated much of the production responsibility. If Ladd was the traditional creative producer and Gibson was the director-cum-producer then Davey was the man who earned the title of producer by dint of the fact that he held the purse strings. One individual, whose contribution to the film was such that his name is up there on the poster alongside Gibson's, describes Davey as one of their least favourite people in the world. Another says: 'He was a classic neurotic line producer. I never took to that guy at all.'

Difficult decisions had to be made. Gibson was making the difficult creative decisions. Davey was making the difficult financial decisions, necessary to enable Gibson to make his creative decisions. It was an arrangement that worked for Gibson. There were financial cuts and there were personality clashes on this film that went unremarked by the press at the time or afterwards. Arguably it was part of Davey's job to take the flak on set, and Gibson emerges unsullied from the various personality clashes and financial cuts.

He remained popular with cast and crew throughout. Unlike many Hollywood stars, Gibson did not hide himself away in his Winnebago at break times. He is not a Method actor who feels the need to remain in character even when not in front of the camera. Daniel Day-Lewis spent six weeks in a wheelchair and insisted on being spoon-fed when he played the handicapped artist Christy Brown in *My Left Foot*. Gibson stood in line for his food on *Braveheart* and ate with the rest of the cast and crew in the catering tents. His family were around him and his children played football with some of the actors. He often seemed to want to be one of the lads and would sit down with the cast and listen to the chat, though other actors were always aware that he was the boss and never sure whether he was coming for a blether or to tell them what to do, with the result that whenever he did join a group, whoever was speaking tended to abandon their story in mid-sentence, much to Gibson's annoyance.

'He does seem to like the banter,' says Mullan, 'but he's dead

shy. He never likes to be the centre of attention, he loves sitting
and listening to other guys' crack and then he chips in his story.
'He would be a very, very difficult man to dislike. And I say
this as a left-winger and I know how right-wing Mel is – he's
a serious frigging homophobe – but, when you're actually just
there on a purely human level, it would be almost impossible
to dislike him. But, politically, yeah, pretty abhorrent, to be
honest. His homophobia is just unbelievable. He's got a real
thing about it . . . *Braveheart* was the only set I've ever been on
in my life where there wasn't an openly gay person in Costume
or Make-up. And everybody noticed. There's always a queen.
I don't know why that is, but there's always one and they're
usually the lad that's most entertaining – they've come out
the closet big-time, they're queeny, they're very mincey, they're
screamers. Now I've never been on a set when there has not been
at least one, if not all of Make-up and Costume, who tend to be
openly gay.'

Make-up and costume was an enormous undertaking on
*Braveheart*. It needed not just flair but military discipline
to organise the extras for the big battle scenes. Gibson had
1,700 men from the Irish reserve army and hundreds of other
volunteers from all over Ireland. They were woken at 4 a.m. and
progressed through a series of tents in formation. They got their
costumes in the first, which would be either plaids if they were
playing Scotsmen or tabards, chain mail from Italy, and armour
if they were English. To maximise the numbers, Gibson used
the same men to play Scots and English at different times.

The second tent was make-up. Yet again Gibson appears to
have taken a lead from *Dances With Wolves*, for the Scots
are seen sporting war paint. Gibson's own design, which
involved covering one side of his face in blue paint, gave
the impression on first appearance in early publicity shots
that he was on his way to a football match to support
Sweden. Woad, a blue dye, was worn by ancient Britons as
body paint. Lois Burwell, Gibson's personal make-up artist,
says it developed into body art and tattooing. 'But for the
purposes of the film, because tattooing couldn't be done –
you would have had to wear it all the way through the film
– we changed it back to woad again.' Contemporary hygiene,

disease and lifestyle were considered in determining the look of the warriors.

The third tent was the hair department, where an entire team of hairdressers was standing by. Irish army rules forbidding beards had been relaxed for the film, but the chief hairdresser nevertheless had a thousand wigs and false beards. Finally, before reaching the set, the men were issued with swords, shields, hammers, picks, axes, lances, bows and arrows, spiked balls on chains and even antlers to use as weapons.

The battle scenes were complicated, time-consuming, expensive and potentially dangerous, with two thousand warriors in action at once, one hundred and fifty of them on horseback for the English charge at Stirling, forty-foot flames at Falkirk and mechanical horses that could accelerate from zero to thirty miles per hour on a twenty-foot track and finish off with a somersault. The one thing that Gibson's Battle of Stirling Bridge did not have was a bridge. The bridge had been the key to Scottish victory, with Wallace's troops attacking while the English army were still crossing the River Forth. 'To have a bridge, you've got to have something to put it over,' says Gibson. 'We went throughout Scotland looking for the right location but when we found a body of water it wasn't horse-friendly. Plus, I discovered that using a bridge on camera involves a lot of mechanics to explain strategies and this is not really very cinematic. To have these two massive forces clashing had much more visual impact.'

The action was planned in advance on storyboards, a series of pictures sketching out how it should look in the final film, and Gibson also used little plastic soldiers, arranged on a table. The battle scenes were inspired not only by the major epics, but also by Orson Welles's *Chimes at Midnight*. The viewer was to be pitched right into the midst of combat. But the Battle of Stirling would open with some great set-pieces, a deluge of English arrows, a show of rude Scottish defiance and then a massed cavalry charge on the Scots, who look as if they will be massacred but at the last minute pick up sharpened staves, twice as long as a man, that skewer the advancing cavalry like bloody great kebabs. There were rehearsals and when it came to the real thing, eight camera teams were at work at once, filming different parts of the battle from different angles.

Yet Peter Mullan was surprised at how disorganised every-thing seemed. He feels there were too many chiefs and not enough assistants to go round the extras telling each one what to do, saying who was going to be injured and who was about to die, and simply making sure they had water to drink when it was hot. 'It was in many ways one of the most disorganised sets I've ever been on . . . We'd do a scene and all these guys wouldn't know what they were doing. And obviously Gibson had to ask himself, "Well, what am I supposed to do here? Am I supposed to go round three thousand people and tell them all what they should be doing?"'

Because Gibson was in the battle scenes, much of the direction was left to the first assistant director David Tomblin, who worked extremely closely with Gibson, came up with ideas and created a very positive impression on those who worked with him. The actors and extras were assembled for one of the big battle scenes, in which the Scots charge the English, multiple camera teams were in position and Tomblin was obviously about to call 'Action' when one of the Scottish supporting actors worked up the courage to shout out: 'He's no' here, Mel's no' here.'

Peter Mullan recalls the incident: 'Nobody had thought to say to the great movie star, "Mel, you're on." He just didn't know and yet there were three and a half thousand of us all set to run two hundred yards in a shot that would probably cost at least a hundred thousand, just for the cameras and the time it would take for us all to go back to our first positions. It would have taken another two or three hours to do this damn thing again.'

The Irish soldiers were thrilled to be appearing in a film with Mel Gibson. He was a hero to them, but they were not overawed. His image was that of an action hero with a sense of humour, not a luvvy. They knew of his reputation as a practical joker and they thought they could enter into the spirit by cracking jokes, making smart remarks about his height and playing it cool every time they were asked to do something. When they were asked to yell, there was hardly any response. When they were asked to lift their kilts and flash their backsides at the English, it turned out most of them still had their underpants on. Gibson asked them to take them off, but they refused. Eventually he got them to agree to show him their bums if he showed them his first. The bum-flashing incident showed Gibson as a good sport, but as the star and director carrying the weight of a $70 million film on his shoulders, it had to be for him, rather than the extras, to dictate the jokes and the moments of light relief. And, as the pressure mounted, the jokes were becoming less frequent.

Seoras Wallace, the Wallace Clan chief executive who helped organise fight scenes, recalls charging into battle wearing a red nose and says that when Angus McFadyen, as Robert the Bruce, delivers the film's final, poignant call to arms, 'You have bled with Wallace; now bleed with me,' the response was that he should get lost, or words to that effect, that his men were away home. But there is disagreement over whether it ever happened.

'I was there for the Wallace stuff,' says Peter Mullan, who is in the middle of the front rank of soldiers at Bannockburn, 'and I don't remember that. It would have been a great gag. What would surprise me about that happening was it would have really been taking the piss out of Angus. Angus isn't like Mel, he doesn't take a joke. Angus is a very, very serious man and takes himself very seriously and that was his first day on set. Angus was pretty nervous and he was kind of bleeding that speech dry. Slow would be an understatement. He was really, really hogging his moment and Mel was getting slightly annoyed, so there was no frivolity.'

What Gibson did want his cast to do was to feel sufficiently comfortable in their parts to attempt to improvise their lines, but the practice of improvisation was foreign to many of them, and it was not made any easier by the fact that they had to improvise something that sounded reasonable in a thirteenth-century context. Most of the improvised moments remained on the cutting room floor, though McFadyen successfully argued to be allowed to walk up and down the table rather than the floor when waiting for Wallace, on the basis that it was his table and he was a noble and he was being kept waiting. McFayden says: 'A lot of directors, to something like that, would go, "Oh, no, no, no, you can't have that kind of stuff." They wouldn't understand how you can get to that place as an actor . . . He very much had faith in all of his actors.'

Peter Mullan has one of the best lines in the film when it is suggested the stranger arriving at the battlefield at Stirling is William Wallace and Mullan says he cannot be Wallace because he is not tall enough. Mullan says Gibson came up with the line at the time of filming, though there was certainly reference to Wallace/Gibson's lack of height in the original script. 'Lots of directors will basically only favour the star, and the rest will get wide shots, but you'll rarely get close-ups . . . You're made to feel like, just give the star his lines and then bugger off,' says Mullan. 'Gibson worked in almost exactly the opposite way. Gibson gave everybody, and I mean everybody, a close-up. He would encourage you to improvise and basically he was working as one actor to another, giving you the chance to build your part.'

Like most soldiers, the Irish enjoyed a few drinks at night, but the early start to the day meant that they were not getting a chance to sleep it off. Several were suffering the ill effects of the previous night's drinking in the next day's sunshine. One soldier decided the best remedy would be another can of beer. But before he finished it he passed out in the heat. As he keeled over, his can flew out of his hand and hit another soldier on the back of the head. The second soldier dropped, with blood spouting from his wound, at the sight of which a third soldier fainted. A tabloid newspaper reported multiple injuries had been sustained during one of the battle scenes.

'They were very rowdy,' says Gibson. 'The Irish by nature are really rowdy, but I like them for that and what worked for the battle scenes is that they were so into it. But they were also really safe. They had commanding officers and they were answerable to military law.' Gibson won considerable respect for the understanding way in which he dealt not only with the soldiers but with one of his principal supporting actors, who was drinking heavily at the time of the film.

Gibson had little time for socialising, though the Wallace Clan's tents offered a chance to get away from professional film people and rowdy Irish soldiers for a while and he did attend a surprise dinner party in a Dublin restaurant for Randall

Wallace's birthday and a ceilidh afterwards with the Wallace Clan. It was a brief escape from the twenty-hours-a-day, six-days-a-week schedule. 'He was really worn out,' says Seoras Wallace, 'but he just fought, fought, fought. We saw him on the set when he was really, really ill. The main thing that brought us all down was fatigue.'

Gibson himself felt he was close to breaking point at times. 'People were asking me questions and I was like "Uh-huh . . ." I couldn't really respond,' he says. 'It was neurological damage or something. I was really getting tongue-tied and frustrated by it. My brain shut down because I had overloaded it. It was saying, "OK, you bastard, see how you like this for a while."' It even seemed he was losing his hair, which he reckoned may have been due to stress and lack of sleep.

But he just had to keep going and it was beginning to get a little easier. His company shrank again in August when the battles of Stirling, Falkirk and Bannockburn had been respectively won, lost and initiated. And the studio work in September and October represented the final leg of a five-month journey. Everyone was encouraged by the quality of the rushes, the exposed film that was printed each day in London and sent back to Ireland for assessment. Gibson says: 'Sometimes you think it's a mire that you're in. Someone's dropped you off in the middle of the ocean and said, "Land is west, start swimming." So you just take it a stroke at a time. But to look back and see the distance you've covered, it's great to see it working.'

Gibson began supervising editing almost immediately after he finished shooting and was still editing in early 1995. He had sufficient footage of the Battle of Stirling to release a full-length feature film that consisted only of that single battle. He had an enormous amount of material and had to make some painful decisions about what to leave out. Despite his decision not to cast one of his sons as the young Wallace, he had given one boy the consolation of a brief appearance. 'That was one of the many scenes that ended up on the cutting room floor,' says Gibson. 'He'll get over it.' Braveheart was tested on preview audiences, the violence was toned down slightly and a marketing campaign devised using Sophie Marceau, who had proved extremely popular with the test audiences, up on the poster alongside Gibson to play up the romantic dimension of the film.

Gibson's old friend Jodie Foster led the star line-up at the world premiere in Los Angeles in May. It was well received, the word 'epic' was on everyone's lips, but Gibson was playing on home ground here to his home crowd. What would the public think? And what would the Scots think? Ros Davidson, filing from LA for *Scotland on Sunday*, wrote: 'The violence is brutal yet appropriate for the times, almost operatic in style as in Francis Ford Coppola's *Godfather* trilogy. Slow-motion, grisly fights unfold against a backdrop of Scottish-sounding flute music. Rain falls. Blood spurts. Mel wears a kilt and attempts a Scottish accent – and is eventually beheaded and disembowelled by Sassenachs.'

*Empire* film magazine's Ian Nathan gave it five stars and compared it to *Spartacus* and *El Cid*. He praised Gibson's majestic acting and passionate and controlled directing. His colleague Jeff Dawson said *Braveheart* would 'at the very least, go down as one of the best films of the decade'. It was the Scottish critics who seemed most divided. Bill Russell of the *Herald* called it a 'grandiose foolhardy epic', full of 'balderdash, bunkum, baloney, bad history and big battles'. In *Sight and Sound*, Colin McArthur accused the film of 'explicit unpleasantness' and 'cloying sentimentality', of pursuing 'regressive discourses' of tartanry and the Dark Ages and of a crude idealisation of Wallace and Bruce – despite the fact that Bruce is seen fighting for both sides turn about. But McArthur was famous, or infamous, for his single-minded advocacy of an indigenous low-budget Scottish film industry and there were criticisms that the review was a set-up by *Sight and Sound*, which prides itself on being the most intellectual of British film magazines and is hardly a barometer of popular taste or opinion.

At three hours, *Braveheart* is a very long film and it seems slow at times, particularly at the beginning where we cut between Wallace as a small boy, the English court and Robert the Bruce. Gibson is determined not to be hurried into the big battle sequences. Twenty minutes pass before Mel Gibson appears for the first time. We then have to sit through Wallace's entire, albeit unnaturally curtailed, relationship with Murron before we really get into the action.

Gibson's Wallace possesses the nobility of a humble peace-loving man, and a perfectly adequate lowland Scottish accent. Even though his father and brother have been killed by the English, all he wants to do is raise crops and children. It is Murron's brutal slaughter that prompts him to take up arms. At this point he is motivated by revenge, but, having killed the local magistrate, there is no turning back. Wallace can kill in cold blood, but he remains a deeply religious man, kneeling to receive the priest's blessing before the Battle of Stirling.

There is an uneven quality about the film. *Braveheart* is not a perfect film, but it is possibly as perfect as an uneven film can be. For its weaker moments come early on. It just keeps getting better and better, building up slowly through childhood, romance, the death of Wallace's wife, Wallace's revenge and the battles. The Battle of Stirling is a triumph for Gibson. The scene has a certain black humour in the exchanges between Wallace and Mullan's character, who is all for calling the whole thing off, followed by a speech from Wallace that would seem to echo the St Crispin's Day address in Shakespeare's *Henry V*. 'Aye, fight and you may die. Run and you'll live, at least a while. And dying in your beds many years from now, would you be willing to trade all the days from this day to that for one chance, just one chance, to come back here and tell our enemies that they may take our lives but they will never take our freedom?' And then there is probably the best cavalry charge ever recorded on film, with Gibson cranking up the tension as Wallace urges his men to 'hold . . . hold . . . hold . . .' before finally they produce their secret weapons – the long staves. Gibson does not just stand back and admire the hundreds of men he has assembled on the Curragh. He throws the viewer into the midst of the mayhem, as body parts are lopped off and blood splashes the camera.

And to top it all there is the incredible emotional impact of the final scenes. Wallace refuses to swear allegiance to Edward, even when Princess Isabelle tells him his refusal must surely cost him his life. 'Every man dies,' says Wallace. 'Not every man really lives.' He arrives at his place of execution with a demeanour that suggests Christ at Calvary, resigned to his fate, scared of physical pain but unbowed. He arrives on a cart, kneeling and at the same time tied to what looks like a cross – it is actually T-shaped. He is hanged, drawn and finally quartered on a table that is shaped liked a cross. The viewer sees him hanged and sees the various instruments the torturer will use to cut him open, though the camera focuses on his face rather than the final butchery. Gibson, as director, uses the way in which the hostile crowd softens and calls for mercy to heighten the horror of proceedings and the dignity of the victim. And as the ordeal comes to an end, he effectively cross-cuts between a whole series of different faces, all showing different emotions, not all of them present at the scene but all of them aware of it. There is King Edward on his deathbed, his son, his daughter-in-law Princess Isabelle with a tear falling from her eye, two of Wallace's men in the crowd, Bruce far away in Scotland, and even the ghost of Murron. And just when we think Wallace might beg for mercy he summons up a hidden reserve of courage and energy and yells out the single, final word 'Freedom'.

The film reopens at Bannockburn where it seems Bruce is about to pay homage to the English army. Angus McFadyen's Bruce has been a brilliant counterpoint to Gibson's Wallace throughout the film. Wallace starts off as a man of peace, events force him into violence and, having chosen that course, he pursues it single-mindedly unto death. Bruce is a weaker or perhaps simply a more complex man. He wrestles with his conscience and even when he changes sides he seems to be about to change back again. The English expect Bruce to pay homage to them at Bannockburn, the Scots expect it, perhaps even Bruce expects it. He addresses his troops dispassionately: 'You have bled with Wallace; now bleed with me.' The words are a variation on the Robert Burns song 'Scots wha hae wi Wallace bled'. And the film ends with the Scots charging the English and a broadsword sticking in the earth. In the shape of a crucifix. The voice-over tells us they fought like Scotsmen and won their freedom.

There was a strong religious element in Randall Wallace's script, but Gibson elaborated on it in his visual imagery. Other major stars may have wanted to tone it down, but it was part of the appeal to Gibson. 'That's what made the script so romantic,' he says. 'It's romanticism in the widest sense of the word. It's not just romantic love between two people, it's the yearning for something beyond earthbound. It's the reaching up, it's the spirit, it's the higher being. In all of it is romance . . . That came out of Randy's heart and soul, because he dwells on higher things sometimes and I kind of liked that aspect of it. And people in years past, I'm sure they were just different people. It's very easy to be cynical and material and earthbound in the nineties, it's so easy, and to perhaps scoff at the supernatural, or perhaps pass it by without good reflection, but I think in years gone by people paid more attention to that and indeed took better care of the spirit than they did of the body . . . They had a whole different value system.'

The film sparked fierce debate among politicians and historians. 'It got very little right,' says James Mackay, an award-winning biographer whose biography of Wallace appeared at the same time as the film. 'I went to it and totally suspended belief and sat back and enjoyed the spectacle of Mel Gibson with his face painted in woad, which was a thousand years late, wearing a kilt which was two or three hundred years early. I am sure it deserved all the awards that it got, it's magnificent, but it's not history. The core of the film is a love affair with the Princess of Wales . . . Because that's just totally untrue nothing else falls into place.'

Prince Edward is presented as a gay wimp, a characterisation that prompted protests from homosexuals in the United States. His wife Isabelle falls in love with Wallace. Her father-in-law Edward I orders Wallace's execution, but as he lies paralysed and speechless she whispers in his ear that she is pregnant with his enemy's son. So the House of Wallace may lose the battle, but it inherits the kingdom. Buckingham Palace declined to comment on whether the current queen may be descended, not from William the Conqueror, but from William Wallace, referring me to the history books, which appear to preclude the possibility, given that Wallace died in 1305 and Edward III was born in 1312. But then *Braveheart* did begin with the words: 'I shall tell you of William Wallace. Historians from England will say I'm a liar. But history is written by those who have hanged heroes.' Historians, professional and amateur, seemed to overlook the skill with which the film portrayed the duplicity of the nobles and the inspiration which Wallace provided to Bruce, and concentrated on the inaccuracy of period details and the romance with the Princess of Wales.

Randall Wallace stresses that he is not a historian, but a dramatist or 'sacred poet'. 'There is a quote from Horace and he said, "Many brave men lived before Agamemnon but all are overwhelmed in eternal night and left unknown because they lack the sacred poet." And when I read that quote I felt that's what I do. I'm trying to be the sacred poet of William Wallace.

'In every substantive way my picture is historically accurate . . . There are certain facts about William Wallace that aren't in dispute: that he was a commoner, that he led the Scottish at Stirling and that he was executed in the most horrible fashion. It seems to me that his execution, far from suppressing Scottish nationalism, lit the fire of passion that culminated in Bannockburn. I told that story and tried to use history as an inspiration and draw from legends that may or may not be historically correct.'

A feature film is not a history lesson; it needs a more formal narrative structure, it needs focus in terms of character and motivation and it does not normally allow for discussion of three or four different theories. Given the criticism of films dealing with much more recent history, such as *JFK*, *Panther* and *In the Name of the Father*, *Braveheart* is remarkable not for how much it gets wrong, but how much it gets right.

The idea of a romance between Wallace and the Princess of Wales may seem like nonsense inspired by the carryings-on of the current royal bunch, but in fact it is nonsense inspired by Blind Harry's poem *The Wallace*. Harry wrote his epic poem in the fifteenth century, more than one hundred and fifty years after Wallace's death, though Harry claimed to have had access to a Latin manuscript, long since lost, compiled by Wallace's chaplain John Blair.

Harry's poem, which takes enormous relish in long descriptions of the killing of Englishmen, was enormously popular in its time and shaped perceptions of Wallace as national hero as surely as *Braveheart* has done. For a while the details in the poem were accepted as history, subsequently they were dismissed as worthless. More recently James Mackay has been arguing for a reassessment of the historical content, while acknowledging some episodes are sheer invention. In Harry's heavy-going old Scots there is a definite suggestion of a relationship between Wallace and Edward I's young French queen Marguerite. It may be rubbish, but at least it is indigenous Scottish rubbish, and not simply Hollywood invention, as has been suggested.

Even before the film was shot, Randall Wallace had admitted it was nationalist 'in a way'. It was obvious when I saw it for the first time three months before its European premiere that the film was political dynamite. The English are the villains and the film clearly equates freedom with independence, albeit in a thirteenth-century context. It would have been surprising if the Scottish National Party, which promotes independence from England, had ignored a marketing tool that looked as useful to it as to the Scottish Tourist Board. The party immediately produced a leaflet bearing the title 'Braveheart' and a picture of Gibson as William Wallace.

Gibson had not seen it until I showed him it on the day of the European premiere in Stirling. 'I find this a little scary actually.' He takes time to read it. The leaflet concludes: 'Today it's not just bravehearts who choose independence, it's also wise heads – and they use the ballot box.' He asks: 'They're a peaceful party, right?' Not only are they a peaceful democratic party, but they have the support of Gibson's fellow superstar Sean Connery. 'Well, that's fine,' he says. 'I didn't make the film for any kind of political use like that. I wanted to make a really good yarn, a good story.'

But if Gibson were Scottish would he follow Big Tam's lead and vote SNP? 'I may,' he says, 'but I'm not Scottish.' Most Americans may regard Scotland as a region of England, but Gibson is well aware of the differences between Scots and English, from the obvious to the more profound. 'They speak different and I think what they want from life is different . . . It's just a different attitude.' The month after the film's release, the SNP rose to its highest position in opinion polls for seven years and political commentators started talking about 'the *Braveheart* factor'. By the end of the year SNP support had fallen back to previous levels, though the film was still playing in Scottish cinemas.

The Scottish film industry was encouraged to see Michael Forsyth, the country's right-wing Secretary of State, taking a belated interest in film. He invited Gibson to dinner at Edinburgh Castle to ask his advice, but the advice Gibson gave may have surprised some, given that he had just benefited from the Irish tax regime. He was now curiously ambivalent about tax incentives. 'Perhaps something like an incentive would be helpful,' he told me afterwards. 'That's not always the best answer though, because they've tried that before in places like Australia and Canada and it has worked for a while, but then all of a sudden, you know, a lot of people take advantage of these things and destroy the industry. This was the case in Australia. They had a thing down there called 10BA, huge tax incentives on film-making and every miserable script in the universe came out of someone's bottom drawer and there was so much garbage done. And it wasn't about the integrity of the work, it was all about making money in tax kickbacks and things. So you have to be very careful with that stuff and make sure that it's got to be ordered very specifically, I think, otherwise it can become used in the wrong way.

'I think, with any film industry, it doesn't matter about all that stuff like tax incentives in the end if you don't have an organic base to the whole thing – and that means a reserve and a talent pool of people who are on fire. And I know that they exist here, and they're probably living hand to mouth someplace in a flat in Glasgow or maybe they're here in Edinburgh and, you know, they've got this yearning and desire, and perhaps they haven't got a mechanism that allows them an outlet. But it doesn't matter, you know. Sometimes the harder you have to fight for something, the better it is. In Australia, for instance, the film industry, before they had tax incentives, was a kind of filter. The people with the real passion and the real drive and the good stories and the belief in them would get through no matter what obstacles.'

Forsyth reckoned the premiere alone would inject £5 million into the Stirling area, quite apart from tourist spin-off for the whole of Scotland. Admissions to the Wallace Monument at

Stirling trebled in the four months after the premiere. Forsyth announced extra cash for the tourist board and ordered a review of the Scottish film industry. It is curious to reflect that the visit of an American tourist called Randall Wallace to a slightly underwhelmed Scottish Screen Locations in Edinburgh in 1993 would within three years result in their relocation to Glasgow as part of a much larger Scottish Screen agency.

*Braveheart* grossed $200 million at cinemas worldwide and topped the video charts on both sides of the Atlantic. Hollywood has a habit, of course, of resurrecting characters who seem to have breathed their last, but, given the nature of Wallace's final scene, *Braveheart II: Brave Hearter* seems unlikely. 'No, no,' says Gibson. 'You could have a story that sort of focuses on his entrails being thrown into the rosebush and then the rose would grow up, right, and then a young woman would come and pick it and you'd follow her into a whole other story.' *Braveheart* has proved beyond all doubt that Gibson has great creative flair and vision, but it is perhaps no surprise that he has never written a script himself.

# 13

# FAMILY MAN,
# BUSINESSMAN; JOKER, GRUMP

Even during the production of *Braveheart* Gibson was dogged by speculation over a fourth *Lethal Weapon* film. He insisted he simply was not interested. When it was raised at a press conference in Scotland, he told reporters: 'I'd have to have my children held at knifepoint, some location I didn't know about.' Which, as it turned out, was pretty much the plot of the film he eventually chose to do next. He did not make *Lethal Weapon 4*; he did make a film in which his son is held at knifepoint in a secret location. *Ransom* was not mooted until a year after the *Braveheart* press conference. Spooky.

*Ransom* opens with Mel Gibson's character Tom Mullen, a self-made multi-millionaire, talking about his background, his achievements and what he values in life. 'I came from fairly humble beginnings, from upstate New York,' he says. Gibson could be introducing the audience to his own life story rather than that of his character. Mullen is an entrepreneur rather than a showbiz celebrity, who has seen his airline grow from nothing to become the fourth largest in the United States. 'The most important thing to me these days?' he asks himself in a new television commercial. 'Family.' And again Gibson could be talking about himself.

Mullen's only son is kidnapped, and held to ransom for $2 million, which is small change to Mullen and just one-tenth of what Gibson got for doing the movie. His $20 million fee accounted for a third of the budget. But the producers reckoned he was worth it and were proved right when *Ransom* took $34 million in its opening weekend in North America, ending up grossing more than $130 million there, more than any of Gibson's previous films, except the *Lethal Weapon* sequels. But *Ransom* was a much more cerebral thriller than *Lethal Weapon*. Gibson was looking older, with heavy lines across his brow and around his eyes, playing a captain of industry in dark suit and tie rather than a lethal cop. *Ransom* was proof Gibson could play mature character roles, the sort of parts that might, a few years earlier, have gone to Paul Newman.

Gibson did not need to become the character, he already was the character – not just a self-made multi-millionaire, but a devoted family man. He saw the kidnapping of a child as his worst nightmare come true. 'The character I play seems to have it all – money, a loving family, a great business – and then this incident brings him back to what he is: a squirming mass of tingling nerves,' he says. 'He's horrified, terrified and he's made to suffer.'

Mullen could easily pay the ransom and that is his original intention. He goes to deliver the money, but the handover is botched. The contact attempts to make off without giving him the address where he can find his son, and then the FBI appear and shoot the kidnapper. The rest of the gang renew their demands and Mullen sets out once again with the money. But he becomes convinced that, if he pays, they will kill his son. To the horror of the police and his wife, he goes on live television and announces he is turning the ransom into a bounty on the kidnappers; their only escape clause is to return the boy alive.

The script is credited to Richard Price and Alexander Ignon and the original story to Cyril Hume and Richard Maibaum. Maibaum wrote or co-wrote most of the James Bond films. But there is no indication on the *Ransom* credits that Hume and Maibaum's story was actually filmed forty years earlier. Even director Ron Howard did not realise there had been a previous version until shortly before shooting began, and he made a point of not seeing the 1956 film. It may be fairly obscure now, but the cast list boasted Glenn Ford, star of *The Big Heat*, *The Blackboard Jungle* and *3.10 to Yuma*, as the industrialist who turns the tables on the kidnappers, Donna Reed as his wife and, as a crime reporter, Leslie Nielsen, who became a major comedy star in the eighties with spoofs like *Airplane!* and *The Naked Gun.*

But that was not the original either. The project began as a television play called *Fearful Decision.* Hume and Maibaum doubled it in length for the movie version and Price and Ignon have added another twenty minutes for the remake. The ransom has quadrupled since 1956, but the central narrative remains the same – the kidnapping of a rich man's son, the protagonist's doubts that payment will ensure his son's return, the television transformation of ransom into bounty and a great deal of worry and soul-searching.

Gibson had not been in front of a camera for more than a year when he began shooting *Ransom* in New York in January 1996. It shot at the Kaufman Astoria and Silvercup Studios in Queens and on location in Queens and elsewhere in the city. The abduction was shot in Central Park and the climactic confrontation between Mullen and the leader of the kidnappers was filmed on Manhattan's Upper East Side. New Yorkers have become blasé about filming, but this was the first opportunity they had ever had to see Gibson at work on their streets, and hundreds of onlookers turned out to watch.

The shoot was hampered by heavy snow, the annual awards season – in which the film's star and director emerged as rivals – and Gibson's emergency appendectomy. He developed acute stomach pains 33,000 feet over Montana and by the time he reached his New York hotel he was grey-green, shivering and burning with fever. It was a Saturday night and the international superstar sat in the hotel lobby while vain efforts were made to get a taxi to take him to hospital. Passers-by enjoyed the chance to have a good look at a film star, even if he did seem rather washed out in real life. The hospital diagnosed acute appendicitis, when it eventually got the chance. Gibson was in and out in twenty-four hours, minus the offending organ, plus a unique Mel Gibson film, of his insides.

Within days Gibson was back at work, the sort of strength of personality possessed by his character as well. Observant viewers might spot, in the opening scenes, a framed cover from *Business Week* magazine showing Mullen with the headline 'Mr Risk'. Which is really the key to the whole film as a drama and as a character study. Mullen is prepared to take risks when he believes it is the right thing to do, even when his son's life is on the line. The opening sequence, in which Mullen is screening his new commercial at a cocktail party in his Manhattan apartment, very neatly provides the audience not only with a portrait of the character's lifestyle but also with a brief history of his life. Some critics compared Mullen to Richard Branson, but the commercial tells us Mullen started off not in the record business but as a combat pilot, a fairly significant difference.

Director Ron Howard had progressed from playing juvenile lead Richie Cunningham in the seventies television sitcom *Happy Days* to making comedies, such as *Splash* and *Parenthood*, and celebrations of the human spirit, most notably *Apollo 13*. But from the outset he seems comfortable with the much darker subject matter of *Ransom*, intercutting the Mullens' chic Manhattan party with shots of some low-life characters furnishing a room with a bed, mattress and handcuffs and soundproofing the walls with foam. We know they are low-life because the ashtray is overflowing and they look as if they got a group discount on tattoos. Worryingly, a tattoo is just visible above the collar of the uniform worn by a waitress at the Mullen party (Lili Taylor).

A reporter's attempts to quiz Mullen, at the party, on allegations that he bribed a union official to avoid a strike is an early indication that Mullen did not build his empire without bending a few rules here and there, though he has been the subject of intensive investigation without any charges being made. All this information is delivered before the opening credits conclude.

The film is built on a number of plot twists, all rooted within the characters of the principal players. Jimmy Shaker (Gary Sinise from *Forrest Gump* and *Apollo 13*) is a cop who follows one of the kidnappers back to their lair, and then turns out to be the leader of the gang. He appears to have drawn his philosophy from H. G. Wells's *The Time Machine*, with its two social classes of the pampered Eloi and the subterranean Morlocks. The Morlocks maintain the Eloi in comfort, but occasionally they will come and take one to eat. Shaker targets Mullen in the belief that he did bribe the union official and will pay up again, though once Shaker gets his money he intends to kill the boy, played by Brawley Nolte, son of actor Nick Nolte, star of *The Prince of Tides*.

Mullen admits to FBI agent Lonnie Hawkins (Delroy Lindo) that he did indeed bribe the union man, though even his wife knew nothing of it. The moral ambiguity was developed after Howard and Gibson committed to the film. Gibson felt Mullen, as originally drawn, came over like Captain America. He participated in lengthy script conferences to discuss the character. The idea that Mullen may have contributed to his own misfortune made for better drama and would seem to increase the pressure on him to take personal responsibility for getting his son back. Gibson looks like a man who is being tortured physically, mentally and spiritually as his past catches up with him and his present falls apart, a man who is indeed a squirming mass of tingling nerves.

Sinise's character gets his big dramatic moment when he decides the time has come to revert to being a policeman, kill everyone else in the gang, including girlfriend Taylor, and claim the reward.

The film did very good business and got some extremely impressive reviews, with critics generally impressed with Gibson's performance. Even *Sight and Sound* enthused. John Wrathall put it rather nicely when he wrote: 'The intricacies of poker have seldom made for satisfying cinema, but the principles of the game – of bluff, raise and counter raise – have rarely been more grippingly deployed.' Wrathall reckoned Gibson's 'mercurial, slightly haunted quality' was perfect for the role and Todd McCarthy in *Variety* considered the mix of introversion and occasional volatility made for one of Gibson's best performances. Several critics complained Rene Russo had little to do as his wife – Gibson and Russo seem less intimate here than they did in *Lethal Weapon 3* when they were playing characters who had just met.

But *Ransom* pivots between Mullen and Shaker, two very extreme men, both dedicated to the pursuit of money. The difference between the two men is that Shaker will kill his 'family' for money whereas Mullen will spend money and kill to keep his family together. But when it comes to decision-making he is a loner, the head of the family, Mr Risk. 'Mel has a philosophy that's really right for this role,' says Howard. 'He has a lot of integrity, but he's not a consensus-taker. He's not a consensus guy at all. If conventional wisdom dictates one thing, he believes you ought to think very seriously about doing the other.' There are similarities between Gibson and the character, but it would be wrong simply to see them as one and the same, and attribute the nuances of the Mullen family relationships to the actor, for Gibson himself believes he was playing Everyman.

'It's any parent's nightmare,' he says. 'It's beyond someone stealing something valuable from you. It's not about something that can be replaced. It would be worse than taking your heart out . . . How do you have that end happily? How do you get your child back? Have you got any power to do anything about it? It's an interesting dilemma, for the character and for the audience.' Once again Gibson is playing a character motivated by loss, although on this occasion he does have the power to do more than simply exact revenge.

It ended happily for Mullen and for Gibson, with the box-office returns justifying his $20 million fee and setting a benchmark for future projects. Although it was hardly the sort of worthy film that usually figures in awards, Gibson landed an unexpected Golden Globe nomination as best dramatic actor, although he lost out to Geoffrey Rush who had played opposite him in *Waiting For Godot* back in 1979 in Sydney's little Jane Street Theatre, and who belatedly rose to international prominence with *Shine*.

Gibson still seemed uncomfortable at times with the press. The distributors hoped he would visit Britain to promote *Ransom*, but he decided it did not need such assistance. Interviewing him for *Empire* in New York, John Naughton found him monosyllabic and reported that the only time he showed any enthusiasm for proceedings was when recounting details of his practical jokes. One concerned a woman on the gate at Shepperton Studios. Her name was Denise and Gibson convinced a third party that she had no legs. When he and his associate reached the gate, Gibson said: 'It's funny you being called Denise when you were cut off at de knees.' Denise was in on the joke and the other person was suitably shocked. Gibson then asked if he could look at her stumps for a fiver. 'I'd left a plastic prosthetic leg in there for her, so I'd pretend to rip it off and I'd put it up there on the shelf and I'd go "Wow" and he'd be out there in the car going "Oh my God, oh my God". He couldn't believe it.'

It is one of Gibson's more sophisticated and more amusing jokes, but Naughton pointed out that Gibson finds it less amusing when the joke is on him, recalling how he stormed out of the MTV movie awards ceremony in June 1996 when co-presenter Janeane Garofalo attempted to send him up. At the time an MTV spokeswoman said there had been a 'mix-up'. Gibson's spokesman said: 'They fucked up.' Gibson told Naughton: 'I got sick and tired of being there and so I just walked away . . . It was better than being in a shitty mood and staying there.'

During the interview with Naughton, Gibson also railed against the 'angst crap' that co-star Rene Russo put herself through for her characterisation, all American politicians, *Entertainment Weekly*, and Wensley Clarkson who wrote a previous Gibson biography. Rather than focusing his complaints on its factual inaccuracies and muck-raking approach, Gibson claimed the book had nothing to do with him and was really a self-portrait of the author. He suggested he should have hired 'some Yugoslav cab drivers' to deal with the situation.

Some stars have suffered appallingly at the hands of journalists, but Gibson has had a largely positive press, with *Empire* particularly supportive. Nevertheless, Naughton was moved to suggest that 'somewhere in the insanely cosseted court of the movie star, with its myriad demands and endless sycophancy, Mel appears to have lost a bit of perspective'. The press themselves have more often been sycophantic than hostile to Gibson, and over the years Gibson has probably treated the press worse than they have treated him. He may have matured, but what he has not lost is the anger of his youth. It is that anger, that edge, which, when channelled into his acting, produces such mesmerising cinema. And we saw that once again in *Ransom*.

Even before *Ransom* came out and *Braveheart* won its Oscars, Gibson was being offered an incredible $30 million to make a fourth *Lethal Weapon* film. But he did not need the money.

He now had several large properties in the United States and Australia, though Malibu had become his main residence. He could command $20 million-plus for any mainstream film in which he deigned to appear, and his company, Icon Productions, had just signed a deal with not one but two Hollywood studios, which was reckoned to be worth at least $100 million over three years. Under the terms of the deal eight pictures would be split evenly between Warner and Paramount for American distribution. It was anticipated Gibson would direct or star in some of them, but his involvement in others would be in a producer or executive capacity.

It has attracted little publicity outside the trade press, but the rise of Gibson's company has been phenomenal. Prior to the deal with Warner and Paramount, Icon had made eight films, only three of which did not have Gibson as their star – the 1993 rollerblading film *Airborne*, the 1994 Beethoven biopic *Immortal Beloved*, starring Gary Oldman and directed by Bernard Rose, and *Dad and Dave: On Our Selection*, directed by Gibson's old drama school tutor George Whaley. All three disappeared more or less without trace. But they were cheap, and constituted a valuable learning process. By early 1997 Icon's logo was appearing in Warner's British preview catalogue, alongside those of the powerful Morgan Creek and Regency production companies and that of Warner Brothers themselves.

Icon had three feature films in the catalogue: *Anna Karenina*, an epic shot on location in Moscow and St Petersburg at a cost of just $20 million, Gibson's fee for *Ransom*; *Fairytale: A True Story*, an English children's film with Peter O'Toole and Harvey Keitel; and *187*, in which *Pulp Fiction*'s Samuel L. Jackson plays a teacher returning to work in Los Angeles after being attacked by a pupil. Paramount had US rights to *Fairytale*. It was not only the distribution arrangements that were confusing on this film, for by the time it appeared in the Warner catalogue it was on to its third title, having shot under the name *One Golden Afternoon* and spent time in post-production as *Illumination*.

Although Gibson was not in any of these films, he was continuing his policy of hiring familiar faces. *Anna Karenina* stars his *Braveheart* co-star Sophie Marceau and his adversary from *Maverick*, Alfred Molina, and it was written and directed by Bernard Rose, who made *Immortal Beloved*. Bruce Davey, Gibson's old accountant buddy from Sydney and Icon president, was producer of all three.

Several months after the announcement of the link-up with Warner and Paramount, Icon secured a deal with a third major Hollywood studio. Icon and Fox agreed to work together to develop and produce films and television projects in Australia. Icon now had deals with Warner, the studio with whom Gibson had traditionally had the closest ties, and with Paramount and Fox, the two companies that backed *Braveheart*. Even at this level Gibson was cementing relationships with those with whom he had previously worked successfully.

Gibson and Davey also set up a London operation, Icon Entertainment International, to sell international rights to Icon films and buy a stake in various European projects. While Mel Gibson is the big star name, Bruce Davey is the man who was driving forward their business strategy, and it was clear virtually from the outset that they were placing a much greater emphasis on Europe, east and west, than other American production companies. In late 1996 Icon Entertainment International took over Majestic, the London company that had helped finance and sell Icon films before pulling out of *Braveheart*.

Gibson had personally been linked with several projects that Icon had been developing, most notably *Fahrenheit 451*, an adaptation of Ray Bradbury's sci-fi novel, previously filmed by François Truffaut, with Julie Christie and Oskar Werner, in the mid-sixties, and *Thank You For Smoking*, adapted from Christopher Buckley's comic novel about a tobacco lobbyist, a project which particularly appealed to Gibson because of his own continued smoking and his revulsion at political correctness. But, having deprived his old friend Richard Donner of the opportunity to make *Lethal Weapon 4*, and the large pay cheque that would have accompanied it, Gibson opted to follow up *Ransom* with another thriller, directed by Donner and produced by *Lethal Weapon*'s Joel Silver, for Warner Brothers.

*Conspiracy Theory* gave Gibson the chance to work with Julia Roberts, with whom he almost made the Western *Renegades* five years earlier. Gibson plays Jerry Fletcher, a New York cab driver who finds a conspiracy around every corner, and Roberts is Alice Sutton, a sceptical Justice Department official. 'He's a weird character,' says Gibson. 'She is kind of repulsed and attracted to him at the same time. It's an interesting movie.' One of Fletcher's wildest theories just happens to be true, and they find themselves pursued by the mysterious Dr Jonas, played by Patrick Stewart, Captain Picard from *Star Trek: The Next Generation*.

They began filming in October 1996 and production ran through until the following February. Stewart managed to combine shooting with appearing on stage in Los Angeles in *A Christmas Carol* and even fitted in a trip to London for the premiere of *Star Trek: First Contact* in December. He enthused about working with Gibson and Roberts, though their approaches to movie-making could not be more different: Gibson with his practical jokes, funny voices and red noses, and Roberts with her Method approach to her craft. I have seen her escorted to a set surrounded by minders and shielded from public view by umbrellas, so that nothing might break her concentration. The crew on Steven Spielberg's *Hook* nicknamed her 'Tinkerhell', but *Conspiracy Theory* seems to have gone rather more smoothly. Stewart described Roberts as 'a real movie performer, an extraordinarily charismatic and intense person'.

Stewart was delighting in the speculation over whether his character was a goodie or a baddie. 'The audience, if the film is working, should be in considerable doubt as to who the good guys and who the bad guys really are, even to the last climactic moments of the movie . . . I'm the other protagonist, along with Mel, in a sense duelling for the soul of the character that Julia plays. It's wonderful roles for both of them.' The day after the *Star Trek* screening, Stewart was returning to LA for an evening performance of *A Christmas Carol*, followed by night shooting on *Conspiracy Theory*.

There were reports that Gibson was seen in various celebrity watering holes during the New York leg of production, though no suggestion of any repeat of the alcoholic binges and con- frontations of the eighties. He was still teetotal. 'I've hung out a few nights with the guys when we weren't working,' he told a reporter. 'We've been to shows, the opera, the circus and then maybe hit a late nightclub and maybe smoked a stogie. It was like Mars to me.' He seemed more relaxed with life than he had been earlier in his career, more at ease with his celebrity status.

He has become a hero for men around the world and a sex symbol for women. 'Hey, if you say so,' he tells me. 'I don't necessarily perceive myself in that way . . . I think that's the kind of thing people might discuss, you know, away from me. It's not apparent or evident.' On fame, he says: 'It's much more easy to deal with. It's, you know, not something that you go to school for, no one does. There's no School for Celebrities Incorporated . . . You have to find your own way around that and adapt accordingly and take the good with the bad, because it's got as much upside as it has downside.'

Sometimes he wants to retreat from the public gaze. 'And other times I just refuse to do anything but behave in a normal fashion in a normal society, just go out, take a walk, go shopping and not be special . . . because I think that's very important to remain part of society and not become some sort of recluse.' Often he and his family will be followed by a minder, though he enjoyed working on *Ransom* and *Conspiracy Theory* in New York, where he found the vast majority of people walk straight by without giving him a second look.

The society of which he has become increasingly a part is the United States of America, even though he maintained for a long time that he would never leave Australia. Pictures appear in papers and celebrity magazines of Gibson trying to lead a regular life. *Hello!* magazine published shots of the Gibson family in a Malibu park, where the children were playing soccer, near one of their several homes. The report noted Gibson was rigged up with a special hand-controlled device to alleviate continuing back pain, and that he and Robyn seemed happy and relaxed, despite rumours of marital problems, rumours that seemed to stem largely from a previous report in *Hello!*

'I also have an eight-hundred-acre cattle ranch in Australia,' says Gibson, 'but I have no plans to go back and live there.' So California is now his main home? 'The planet is my main home,' he tells me, hinting perhaps that there may be a villa on Jupiter or Venus of which *Hello!* is as yet unaware. 'I've lived so many places in the past five years, there is no main home. It's the whole planet. I'm moving around all the time.'

Mel Gibson has become an international star and an international business. He has achieved popular and critical success as an actor, won Oscars as director and producer and need never work again. He reckons his fortieth birthday in 1996 marked the halfway point in his life, but he is not the sort of man to take it easy just because he is ahead at half-time. He recognises his achievements and limitations as an actor and plans to develop his career as a director and producer. 'I'm not Laurence Olivier,' he says. Maybe not. But Olivier never managed to transcend his reputation as, first and foremost, a classically-trained, English stage actor. Gibson has played comedy, drama, action and Shakespeare and he has undoubtedly transcended his reputation as the sexiest man alive. A Harris poll found that, in his forties, Gibson had taken over from John Wayne as the most popular movie star in the world, alive or dead.

# FILMOGRAPHY

Ratings:
★ Bad,  ★★ OK,  ★★★ Good,
★★★★ Very good,  ★★★★★ Outstanding

This filmography follows standard practice in using the year of release rather than production. Films normally take several months to edit and complete other post-production procedures, which may or may not happen in the year filming took place. The exception to the rule is *Attack Force Z*, which filmed in 1979 but was not released in Australian cinemas until 1982. It was shown at the Cannes Film Festival in May 1981. However, it was copyrighted and certificated, and therefore complete, in 1980.

SUMMER CITY ★★
Australia, 1977, 83 minutes
Phil Avalon (Robbie Woods), Steve Bisley (Boo), John Jarratt (Sandy Harrison), Mel Gibson (Scollop), Debbie Foreman (Caroline), James Elliott (Mathews), Abigail (woman in bar), Ward 'Pally' Austin (himself)
Director: Christopher Fraser; Script: Phil Avalon; Photography: Jerry Marek; Music: Phil Butkis; Producer: Phil Avalon; Production Company: Avalon Films

MAD MAX ★★★★
Australia, 1979, 91 minutes
Mel Gibson (Max Roçkatansky), Joanne Samuel (Jessie), Roger Ward (Fifi Macaffee), Steve Bisley (Jim Goose), Tim Burns (Johnny the Boy), Hugh Keays-Byrne (The Toecutter), Vince Gil (Nightrider), Geoff Parry (Bubba Zanetti), David Bracks (Mudguts), Paul Johnstone (Cundalini)

Director: George Miller; Script: James McCausland and George Miller; Story: George Miller and Byron Kennedy; Photography: David Eggby; Music: Brian May; Producer: Byron Kennedy; Production Company: Kennedy Miller

## TIM ★★★
Australia, 1979, 109 minutes
Piper Laurie (Mary Horton), Mel Gibson (Tim Melville), Alwyn Kurts (Ron Melville), Pat Evison (Em Melville), Peter Gwynne (Tom Ainsley), Deborah Kennedy (Dawnie Melville), David Foster (Mick Harrington), Michael Caulfield (John Harrington), Margo Lee (Mrs Harrington), James Condon (Mr Harrington)
Director: Michael Pate; Script: Michael Pate, based on the novel by Colleen McCullough; Photography: Paul Onorato; Music: Eric Jupp; Producer: Michael Pate; Production Company: Pisces Productions

## ATTACK FORCE Z ★★★
Australia/Taiwan, 1980, 93 minutes
John Phillip Law (Jan Veitch), Mel Gibson (Paul Kelly), Sam Neill (Danny Costello), Koo Chuan-Hsiung (Lin Chan-Lang), Chris Haywood (Bird), John Waters (King), Sylvia Chang (Chien Hua), O Ti (Shaw Hu), Lung Shuan (Watanabe), Yi Yuan (Captain Imanaka)
Director: Tim Burstall; Script: Roger Marshall; Photography: Lin Hun-Chung; Music: Eric Jupp; Producer: Lee Robinson; Production Companies: John McCallum Productions and Central Motion Picture Corporation of Taiwan

## GALLIPOLI ★★★★★
Australia, 1981, 111 minutes
Mark Lee (Archy Hamilton), Mel Gibson (Frank Dunne), Bill Hunter (Major Barton), Robert Grubb (Billy Lewis), Tim McKenzie (Barney Wilson), David Argue (Snowy), Bill Kerr (Uncle Jack), Ron Graham (Wallace Hamilton), Harold Hopkins (Les McCann), Charles Yunupingu (Zac)
Director: Peter Weir; Script: David Williamson; Story: Peter Weir, inspired by *The Broken Years* by Bill Gammage and war histories by C. E. W. Bean; Photography: Russell Boyd; Producers: Robert Stigwood and Patricia Lovell; Production Company: Associated R & R Films

## MAD MAX 2 (US title: THE ROAD WARRIOR) ★★★
Australia, 1981, 96 minutes
Mel Gibson (Max Rockatansky), Bruce Spence (Gyro Captain), Vernon Wells (Wez), Emil Minty (Feral Kid), Mike Preston (Pappagallo), Kjell Nilsson (Humungus), Virginia Hey (Warrior Woman), Syd Heylen (Curmudgeon)
Director: George Miller; Script: Terry Hayes, George Miller and Brian Hannant; Photography: Dean Semler; Music: Brian May; Producer: Byron Kennedy; Production Company: Kennedy Miller

## THE YEAR OF LIVING DANGEROUSLY ★★★
Australia, 1982, 115 minutes
Mel Gibson (Guy Hamilton), Sigourney Weaver (Jill Bryant), Linda Hunt (Billy Kwan), Bembol Roco (Kumar), Michael Murphy (Pete Curtis), Noel Ferrier (Wally O'Sullivan), Paul Sonkkila (Kevin Condon), Mike Emperio (Sukarno), Bill Kerr (Colonel Henderson), Cecily Polson (Moira)
Director: Peter Weir; Script: David Williamson, Peter Weir and C. J. Koch, based on the novel by C. J. Koch; Photography: Russell Boyd; Music: Maurice Jarre; Producer: James McElroy; Production Company: McElroy & McElroy Productions for MGM/United Artists

## THE BOUNTY ★★
Great Britain, 1984, 133 minutes
Mel Gibson (Fletcher Christian), Anthony Hopkins (Lieutenant William Bligh), Laurence Olivier (Admiral Hood), Edward Fox (Captain Greetham), Daniel Day-Lewis (John Fryer), Bernard Hill (Cole), Philip Davis (Young), Liam Neeson (Churchill), Wi Kuki Kaa (King Tynah), Tevaite Vernette (Mauatua)
Director: Roger Donaldson; Script: Robert Bolt, based on the book *Captain Bligh and Mr Christian* by Richard Hough; Photography: Arthur Ibbetson; Music: Vangelis; Producer: Bernard Williams; Production Company: Dino de Laurentiis Corporation

## THE RIVER ★★★★
USA, 1984, 124 minutes
Mel Gibson (Tom Garvey), Sissy Spacek (Mae Garvey), Scott Glenn (Joe Wade), Shane Bailey (Lewis Garvey), Becky Jo Lynch (Beth Garvey), Don Hood (Senator Neiswinder), Billy Green Bush (Harve Stanley), James Tolkan (Howard Simpson), Bob W. Douglas (Hal Richardson), Andy Stahl (Dave Birkin)
Director: Mark Rydell; Script: Robert Dillon and Julian Barry; Photography: Vilmos Zsigmond; Music: John Williams; Producers: Edward Lewis and Robert Cortez; Production Company: Universal

## MRS SOFFEL ★★★
USA, 1984, 111 minutes
Diane Keaton (Kate Soffel), Mel Gibson (Ed Biddle), Matthew Modine (Jack Biddle), Edward Herrmann (Peter Soffel), Trini Alvarado (Irene Soffel), Jennie Dundas (Margaret Soffel), Danny Corkill (Eddie Soffel), Harley Cross (Clarence Soffel), Terry O'Quinn (Buck McGovern), Pippa Pearthree (Maggie)
Director: Gillian Armstrong; Script: Ron Nyswaner; Photography: Russell Boyd; Music: Mark Isham; Producers: Edgard J. Scherick, Scott Rudin and David A. Nicksay; Production Company: MGM/UA

## MAD MAX BEYOND THUNDERDOME ★★★
Australia, 1985, 107 minutes
Mel Gibson (Mad Max), Tina Turner (Aunty Entity), Bruce Spence (Jedediah), Adam Cockburn (Jedediah Jnr), Frank Thring (The Collector),

Angelo Rossitto (Master), Paul Larsson (Blaster), Helen Buday (Savannah Nix), Mark Spain (Mr Skyfish), Tom Jennings (Slake)
Directors: George Miller and George Ogilvie; Script: Terry Hayes and George Miller; Photography: Dean Semler; Music: Maurice Jarre; Producer: George Miller; Production Company: Kennedy Miller

## LETHAL WEAPON ★★★★
USA, 1987, 109 minutes
Mel Gibson (Martin Riggs), Danny Glover (Roger Murtaugh), Gary Busey (Joshua), Mitchell Ryan (General McAllister), Tom Atkins (Michael Hunsaker), Darlene Love (Trish Murtaugh), Traci Wolfe (Rianne Murtaugh), Jackie Swanson (Amanda Hunsaker), Damon Hines (Nick Murtaugh), Ebonie Smith (Carrie Murtaugh)
Director: Richard Donner; Script: Shane Black; Photography: Stephen Goldblatt; Music: Michael Kamen, Eric Clapton; Producers: Richard Donner and Joel Silver; Production Company: Silver Pictures for Warner Brothers

## TEQUILA SUNRISE ★★★
USA, 1988, 115 minutes
Mel Gibson (Dale McKussic), Michelle Pfeiffer (Jo Ann Vallenari), Kurt Russell (Nick Frescia), Raul Julia (Carlos/Commandante Escalante), J. T. Walsh (Maguire), Arliss Howard (Lindroff), Ayre Gross (Andy Leonard), Gabriel Damon (Cody McKussic), Garret Pearson (Arturo), Budd Boetticher (Judge Nizetitch)
Director: Robert Towne; Script: Robert Towne; Photography: Conrad L. Hall; Music: Dave Grusin; Producer: Thom Mount; Production Company: Warner Brothers

## LETHAL WEAPON 2 ★★★★
USA, 1989, 114 minutes
Mel Gibson (Martin Riggs), Danny Glover (Roger Murtaugh), Joe Pesci (Leo Getz), Joss Ackland (Arjen Rudd), Derrick O'Connor (Pieter Vorstedt), Patsy Kensit (Rika Van Den Haas), Darlene Love (Trish Murtaugh), Traci Wolfe (Rianne Murtaugh), Steve Kahan (Captain Murphy), Mark Rolston (Hans)
Director: Richard Donner; Script: Jeffrey Boam; Story: Shane Black and Warren Murphy; Photography: Stephen Goldblatt; Music: Michael Kamen, Eric Clapton and David Sanborn; Producers: Richard Donner and Joel Silver; Production Company: Silver Pictures for Warner Brothers

## BIRD ON A WIRE ★★
USA, 1990, 111 minutes
Mel Gibson (Rick Jarmin), Goldie Hawn (Marianne Graves), David Carradine (Eugene Sorenson), Bill Duke (Albert Diggs), Stephen Tobolowsky (Joe Weyburn), Joan Severance (Rachel Varney), Harry Caesar (Marvin), Jeff Corey (Lou Baird), Alex Bruhanski (Raun), John Pyper-Ferguson (Jamie)

Director: John Badham; Script: David Seltzer, Louis Venosta and Eric Lerner; Photography: Robert Primes; Music: Hans Zimmer; Producer: Rob Cohen; Production Company: Universal

## AIR AMERICA ★★★
USA, 1990, 118 minutes
Mel Gibson (Gene Ryack), Robert Downey Jnr (Billy Covington), Nancy Travis (Corinne Landreaux), Ken Jenkins (Major Donald Lemond), David Marshall Grant (Rob Diehl), Lane Smith (Senator Davenport), Art La Fleur (Jack Neely), Ned Eisenberg (Pirelli), Marshall Bell (OV), David Bowe (Saunders)
Director: Roger Spottiswoode; Script: John Eskow and Richard Rush, based on the book by Christopher Robbins; Photography: Roger Deakins; Music: Charles Gross; Producer: Daniel Melnick; Production Company: Carolco

## HAMLET ★★★★
USA, 1990, 134 minutes
Mel Gibson (Hamlet), Glenn Close (Gertrude), Alan Bates (Claudius), Paul Scofield (Ghost), Ian Holm (Polonius), Helena Bonham Carter (Ophelia), Stephen Dillane (Horatio), Nathaniel Parker (Laertes), Sean Murray (Guildenstern), Michael Maloney (Rosencrantz)
Director: Franco Zeffirelli; Screenplay: Christopher De Vore and Franco Zeffirelli, based on the play by William Shakespeare; Photography: David Watkin; Music: Ennio Morricone; Producer: Dyson Lovell; Production Company: Icon Productions for Carolco

## LETHAL WEAPON 3 ★★★
USA, 1992, 118 minutes
Mel Gibson (Martin Riggs), Danny Glover (Roger Murtaugh), Joe Pesci (Leo Getz), Rene Russo (Lorna Cole), Stuart Wilson (Jack Travis), Steve Kahan (Captain Murphy), Darlene Love (Trish Murtaugh), Traci Wolfe (Rianne Murtaugh), Damon Hines (Nick Murtaugh), Ebonie Smith (Carrie Murtaugh)
Director: Richard Donner; Screenplay: Jeffrey Boam and Robert Mark Kamen; Photography: Jan De Bont; Music: Michael Kamen, Eric Clapton and David Sanborn; Producers: Richard Donner and Joel Silver; Production Company: Silver Pictures for Warner Brothers

## FOREVER YOUNG ★★
USA, 1992, 101 minutes
Mel Gibson (Daniel McCormick), Jamie Lee Curtis (Claire), Elijah Wood (Nat), Isabel Glasser (Helen), George Wendt (Harry), Joe Morton (Cameron), Nicolas Surovy (John), David Marshall Grant (Wilcox), Robert Hy Gorman (Felix), Millie Slavin (Susan Finley)
Director: Steve Miner; Screenplay: Jeffrey Abrams; Photography: Russell Boyd; Music: Jerry Goldsmith; Producer: Bruce Davey; Production Company: Icon Productions for Warner Brothers

## THE MAN WITHOUT A FACE ★★★
USA, 1993, 115 minutes
Mel Gibson (Justin McLeod), Nick Stahl (Chuck Norstadt), Margaret Whitton (Catherine), Fay Masterson (Gloria), Gaby Hoffman (Megan), Geoffrey Lewis (Chief Stark), Richard Masur (Carl), Michael Deluise (Douglas Hall), Ethan Phillips (Mr Lansing), Jean De Baer (Mrs Lansing)
Director: Mel Gibson; Screenplay: Malcolm MacRury, based on the novel by Isabelle Holland; Photography: Donald M. McAlpine; Music: James Horner; Producer: Bruce Davey; Production Company: Icon Productions

## MAVERICK ★★★★
USA, 1994, 127 minutes
Mel Gibson (Bret Maverick), Jodie Foster (Annabelle Bransford), James Garner (Zane Cooper), Graham Greene (Joseph), Alfred Molina (Angel), James Coburn (Commodore Duval), Geoffrey Lewis (Matthew Wicker), Paul L. Smith (Archduke), Max Perlich (Johnny Hardin)
Director: Richard Donner; Screenplay: William Goldman, based on the TV series *Maverick* created by Roy Huggins; Photography: Vilmos Zsigmond; Music: Randy Newman; Producers: Bruce Davey and Richard Donner; Production Company: Icon Productions for Warner Brothers

## BRAVEHEART ★★★★★
USA, 1995, 177 minutes
Mel Gibson (William Wallace), Sophie Marceau (Princess Isabelle), Patrick McGoohan (King Edward I), Catherine McCormack (Murron), Brendan Gleeson (Hamish), James Cosmo (Campbell), David O'Hara (Stephen), Alun Armstrong (Mornay), Angus McFadyen (Robert the Bruce), Ian Bannen (Bruce's father)
Director: Mel Gibson; Screenplay: Randall Wallace; Photography: John Toll; Music: James Horner; Producers: Mel Gibson, Alan Ladd Jnr and Bruce Davey; Production Companies: Icon Productions and the Ladd Company

## POCAHONTAS ★★★
USA, 1995, 81 minutes
Voices of: Irene Bedard (Pocahontas), Judy Kuhn (Pocahontas's singing voice), Mel Gibson (John Smith), David Ogden Stiers (Governor Ratcliffe/Wiggins), Russell Means (Powhatan), Christian Bale (Thomas), Linda Hunt (Grandmother Willow), Billy Connolly (Ben)
Directors: Mike Gabriel and Eric Goldberg; Script: Carl Binder, Susannah Grant and Philip Lazebnik; Music: Alan Menken; Lyrics: Stephen Schwartz; Producer: James Pentecost; Production Company: Walt Disney Pictures

## RANSOM ★★★★
USA, 1996, 121 minutes
Mel Gibson (Tom Mullen), Rene Russo (Kate Mullen), Brawley Nolte (Sean Mullen), Gary Sinise (Jimmy Shaker), Delroy Lindo (Lonnie

Hawkins), Lili Taylor (Maris Connor), Liev Schreiber (Clark Barnes), Donnie Wahlberg (Cubby Barnes), Evan Handler (Miles Roberts), Nancy Ticotin (Kimba Welch)
Director: Ron Howard; Screenplay: Richard Price and Alexander Ignon; Story: Cyril Hume and Richard Maibaum; Photography: Piotr Sobocinski; Music: James Horner; Producers: Scott Rudin, Brian Grazer and B. Kipling Hagopian; Production Company: Touchstone Pictures

Gibson also made fleeting appearances in *The Chain Reaction* (Australia, 1980) and *Casper* (USA, 1995).

# SELECT BIBLIOGRAPHY

Ashworth, Juliet: 'Mel Gibson's Private Diaries, Day by Day: How I Made *Hamlet*' (*Today*, 17 April 1990)

Bart, Peter: *Fade Out: The Calamitous Final Days of MGM* (Simon and Schuster, 1990)

Buscombe, Edward: *The BFI Companion to the Western* (André Deutsch, 1988)

Carnes, Mark C. (editor): *Past Imperfect: History According to the Movies* (Cassell, 1996).

Clarkson, Wensley: *Mel Gibson: The Inside Story* (Blake, 1993)

Duncan, Susan: 'Home, Church and Family ... The Forces that Shaped Mel Gibson' (*Australian Women's Weekly*, February 1987)

Film Index International CD (British Film Institute, 1993–1995)

Finler, Joel W.: *The Hollywood Story* (Mandarin, 1992)

Fraser, George MacDonald: *The Hollywood History of the World* (Harvill, 1996)

Gibson, Hutton: *Paul VI's Legacy: Catholicism?* (Leo Panakal Publishers, Australia, 1979)

Hanrahan, John: *Mel Gibson* (Little Hills Press, Sydney, 1986)

Holden, Anthony: *The Oscars* (Little, Brown, 1993)

Kasper, Roger: 'Mel Gibson Fury Over Sex Blackmail' (*News of the World*, 31 January 1993)

Mackay, James: *William Wallace, Brave Heart* (Mainstream, 1995)

McWilliam, H. R.: 'The Career of Eva Mylott' (a short series of articles in the *Moruya Examiner*, New South Wales, 1950)

Melbourne *Herald*: 'Meet the Gibsons – 12 of Them' (4 November 1968)

Murray, Scott (editor): *Australian Film 1978–1994* (Oxford University Press, Australia, 1995)

NIDA Annual Report 1977 (National Institute of Dramatic Art, Sydney, 1977)

Ragan, David: *Mel Gibson* (W. H. Allen, 1985)

Robertson, Patrick: *The Guinness Book of Movie Facts and Feats* (Guinness, 1988)

Smith, Margaret: 'Mel Gibson' (*Cinema Papers*, Australia, March 1983)

*Variety, Screen International, Hollywood Reporter, Sight and Sound, Monthly Film Bulletin, Empire, Premiere,* 1979–1997

# INDEX